THE NEW LIBERALISM

An Ideology of Social Reform

BY

MICHAEL FREEDEN

CLARENDON PRESS · OXFORD

Oxford University Press, Walton Street, Oxford OX2 6DP

Oxford New York Toronto
Delhi Bombay Calcutta Madras Karachi
Kuala Lumpur Singapore Hong Kong Tokyo
Nairobi Dar es Salaam Cape Town
Melbourne Auckland

and associated companies in
Beirut Berlin Ibadan Nicosia

Oxford is a trade mark of Oxford University Press

Published in the United States
by Oxford University Press, New York

© Michael Freeden, 1978

First published 1978
Reprinted with corrections 1986

British Library Cataloguing in Publication Data
Freeden, Michael
The new liberalism.
1. Liberalism—Great Britain
I. Title
320.5'1'0941   JN216   77-30169
ISBN 0-19-822961-5

Printed in Great Britain by
J. W. Arrowsmith Ltd,
Bristol

£9.95

to
My Parents

Preface

THE acquaintance of the world of scholarship with the term 'new liberalism' is of recent standing and as yet little research has been devoted to a movement of ideas which is now part and parcel of modern British political thought. For those interested in the development of turn-of-the-century liberal theory, in the ideological background to the social legislation of the Liberal Governments before the First World War, and, more generally, in the mental climate in which political activity occurs, there is still a wealth of information awaiting release from obscurity. Several studies have recently appeared about various aspects of the Liberal party and its social policy in the generation prior to the war, but we are not very much wiser than before about the political theory of the new liberalism. In that sense this book departs from the traditional concerns of British scholarship. The era dealt with is not scrutinized through the eyes of the historian, in particular the political historian, who has virtually monopolized the study of nineteenth- and early twentieth-century British politics. This is the work of a political scientist (no pretensions should be read into the *terminus technicus*) who specializes in political thought. Consequently the New Liberalism of the party must not be confused with the ideas originating with the liberal thinkers and ideologists of the period, as will be clarified in the pages to come.

To a certain extent the methods of the historian are adopted, in particular detailed analyses of primary sources, though by primary is meant first-hand rather than unpublished material. The socio-political books and periodicals of the period are rich and intellectually stimulating treasures, vast and still largely untapped receptacles of the thought of the times. Especial credit is due to the weeklies *Speaker* and *Nation* which reflected developments and changes amongst the liberal intelligentsia in a manner invaluable to the student of liberalism. On the other hand, private papers have had little to offer, displaying in the main a paucity of comment or reflection relevant to this study, or merely repeating what the printed sources have presented in greater detail and depth. The emphasis of this book is however on the nature, patterns, development, and continuity of political ideas through whose examination, it is hoped, some light may be cast both on problems concerning the study of ideology and on a period of interest to the historian of modern England.

A wide spectrum of thinkers is reviewed in this book, many of whom are virtually unknown, some of whom do not directly consider conventional liberal issues. This approach has proved useful in probing the liberal mind and in adumbrating the diffusion of the new liberal ideology. Though a few central theorists emerge, it is often the odd article which best vents a particular issue. The focus remains directed at the development of patterns of thought rather than at the isolated individual thinker. Nor do the questions posed concern the influence of this or that thinker on events or legislation. The theorists are analysed as contributing to or symptomatic of the course liberalism was taking. Though the analysis proceeds structurally from the general to the particular, from an examination of the root forces at work in the transformation of liberal thought, through the crystallization of an ideology of social reform, and to an illustration of some of those themes in recommended social policy, it will be seen that the very nature of new liberal thought cannot always support this delimitation. The interplay between social philosophy and specific measures is one of the characteristics of the new liberalism. Limitations of space have precluded detailed analysis of all fields of social reform. Thus issues such as land and temperance, though constantly on the agenda of the Liberal party, were not among the central concerns of new liberal thought or were subsumed within a more general set of principles.

My special thanks are due to Mr. Maurice Shock who, as my Oxford supervisor, provided the counsel, encouragement, and stimulation which rendered my original labours a rewarding intellectual experience. Professor Bernard Crick and Mr. J. F. Lively offered invaluable criticism and advice which I have tried to follow to the best of my ability. Dr. H. C. G. Matthew commented helpfully on early versions of the text and served as a sharp foil for many arguments. Mr. A. F. Thompson gave generously of his time and energy to see the manuscript through its final stages. A shortened version of Chapter Three previously appeared in *Political Theory*.

I would like to acknowledge the kind permission of the Clerk of the Records, House of Lords; Sir John Colville; and the Beaverbrook Foundation and Mr. A. J. P. Taylor to quote from private papers. I would also like gratefully to record assistance received from the staff of the following libraries: the Bodleian library; St. Antony's College library; Nuffield College library; the British Library; the British Library of Political and Economic Science; the Cambridge University library; the House of Lords Record Office; the Beaverbrook library. Thanks are due also to the University of Haifa for awarding me a grant towards the costs of preparing the manuscript.

My wife Irene and children Jonathan and Daniella provided—to borrow terms familiar to the new liberals—the environment without which neither character nor heredity would have sufficed to complete this work.

Michael Freeden

Contents

List of Abbreviations

CR   *Contemporary Review*
ER   *Economic Review*
EW   *Ethical World*
FR   *Fortnightly Review*
IR   *Independent Review*
MG   *Manchester Guardian*
NC   *Nineteenth Century*
NR   *New Review*
PR   *Progressive Review*
SPM   *South Place Magazine*
SR   *Sociological Review*
WG   *Westminster Gazette*
WR   *Westminster Review*

Hansard's Parliamentary Debates have been abbreviated as follows: *Hansard*, 4th Ser. LI 1304 for *Hansard*, 4th Series, vol. LI, col. 1304.

The following usage of capital letters has been adopted:

'Liberal' pertains to the institutional and official aspects of the Liberal party; 'liberal' denotes the body of thought. The same applies to 'Conservative' and 'conservative'.

'Socialism' refers to dogmatic, orthodox, and institutionalized manifestations of the term; 'socialism' denotes the general sense of the term as explained in Chapter Two.

'Individualism' pertains to the specific doctrine of self-support and independence of individuals, sometimes called the 'atomistic' concept of society; 'individualism' refers in general to a belief in the importance of individual self-expression and development.

'Idealism' denotes the philosophical school of that name.

In quoting, however, the original spelling is retained, even when differing from this usage.

Unless otherwise stated, the place of publication of books cited is London.

I

Introductory

ENGLISH liberal thought after John Stuart Mill has not received the treatment it merits. Whereas volumes have been written on what is known as 'classical liberalism' and the chief political thinkers voicing it have been thoroughly examined, indeed dissected, very little has been done to illuminate the paths by which liberalism came to grips with the problems and issues of modern, highly industrialized society. In most textbooks and general surveys English liberalism ends with T. H. Green and occasionally a passing reference to L. T. Hobhouse. Separate studies of Herbert Spencer, while important for a variety of reasons, some of which will be touched on in this study, cannot by the very nature of his writings have anything new to contribute directly to an analysis of the body of liberal thought of the times. In fact, students of political thought, even more than historians—who have also been very late on the trail—have been guilty of a sin of omission in all that concerns what is commonly termed the 'new liberalism'.

Modern liberalism has suffered mainly through sheer ignorance of its nature. Even now, many of its modern opponents assail with venom a set of principles that liberalism itself discarded almost a century ago. In the generation preceding the First World War the basic tenets of liberalism were fundamentally reformulated in a crucial and decisive manner. A band of eager and dedicated men of ideas, immersed in the pressing social issues of the day, transformed liberalism quietly from within, and retrieved for it the qualities of immediacy and relevance without which every ideology must ossify. The causes of the demise of Liberalism as a political movement cannot be attributed to the intellectual failure of its theorists. Indeed, from the vantage point of the modern British welfare state it is the new liberalism of the turn of the century which appears to have gained the upper hand over its rival ideologies, conservatism and socialism.

This study was prompted by a number of complex and diverse questions to which no satisfactory answer had been given. First of all, there is a striking historical phenomenon which calls for investigation: what happened in the minds of liberals to account for the drastic change of temper in Liberal political activity between 1886 (and even 1893) and the deluge of social legislation of the 1905–14 Governments? It must, however, be made clear at the outset that, this not being an historical study, no attempt will be made to supply either a chronological survey of facts or a general description and interpretation of a period. Furthermore, though the period under consideration has been delimited within the span of two points in time, the opening date of 1886 is no more than a rough demarcation point of the advent of the new trends in liberal thought. This analysis has been written from the perspective of one interested in the formation, meaning, and interaction of political ideas, and this will be further elucidated in the epilogue. The historian of political ideas will also, no doubt, find common ground with another question posed here, namely, what developments did liberalism undergo after Mill and Green? What happened between the landmarks of 'On Liberty' and the 'Beveridge Report'? But primarily this work concerns itself with the transformation of an ideology and with—a variation upon the 'intellectual in politics' theme—the ideological contribution of a group of individuals towards solving some of the burning social and political problems of their times. The lack of a figure of the stature of Mill is at first sight obvious, but as the richness of new liberal thought emerged, it became clear that in this case at least, the undue obsession with 'Great Men' in political thought might obscure the possibility of tracing ideological developments within a group of opinion-forming intellectuals who collectively combined to rethink mundane and concrete, rather than abstract philosophical issues, apparently independent of time and space. The group of liberal theorists and intellectuals discussed here, who are responsible for the reformulation of liberalism, played a role *vis-à-vis* political thought no less profound and pervasive than did many of the better-known theorists which scholarship tends to single out. Being social reformers in the concrete sense, they were practically oriented towards current social ills, to which they applied their mental energies and general principles. To focus on their achievements in interpreting liberal theory and in adumbrating guidelines to public policy, is to attempt to illuminate a political process, as well as to probe the intellectual complexity of the late-liberal ideology. This work should therefore be regarded both as a case-study in ideological adaptation and as an analysis of the coherent and viable body of thought which was the result of this adaptation.

Here a few words on the new liberal thinkers are in order, in relation to Victorian types of ideologues. The free professions, attached in life-style even if not always in sympathy to the middle class, were in this case, as in others, the principal suppliers of the ideological fodder which sustained many of the most significant social and political trends in Britain. It has been said about the role of the professional (middle-class) thinkers that their lack of distinct class roots enabled them to produce 'disinterested', objectivized, theories of society for all three traditional classes.[1] In particular, the 'man of letters' had, when devoting his energies to political argument, the dual advantage of independent means, which rendered him relatively immune to the vicissitudes of politics and free to indulge in unremunerative theorizing,[2] and of the key position of influence which the periodicals and important weeklies of his day afforded him. The liberals we deal with, however, had less of the separatist and elitist characteristics which some historians have found in the mid-nineteenth-century groups they investigated, such as professional norms and administrative expertise, or pure and detached theorizing that denied them a political role or even an audience.[3] The new liberals did not have a sub-culture, as did the Philosophical Radicals, the Positivists, and the Fabians; they did not see themselves consciously and emphatically as the leaders of the future, the ideological wielders of power, neither did they try as a group to enter the first ranks of politics. But they were a definite group of like-minded individuals who moved in similar circles and were

[1] H. Perkin, *The Origins of Modern English Society 1780–1880* (1972), pp. 252–70. This would have made their theorizing particularly amenable to the classless, universalistic tendencies in liberalism (see below, Chapter Four).

[2] Cf. J. A. Hobson, *Confessions of an Economic Heretic* (1938), pp. 72–4.

[3] J. Hamburger, *Intellectuals in Politics: John Stuart Mill and the Philosophical Radicals* (Yale U.P., 1965), p. 280.

nourished by common ideas they then proceeded eloquently to develop. The Press was their chief instrument of power, of influencing men's minds, and also their prime means of mutual communication, though there existed withal semi-institutionalized foci of their activities: the 'Nation' lunches, the Rainbow Circle, the Ethical Societies, and small groups operating on the periphery of the Liberal party, such as the Young Liberals, regular gatherings within the framework of the National Liberal Club, or even the Settlement Movement. Unlike most other ideological groupings in nineteenth-century England, with the notable exception of the Fabians, they did not theorize in a vacuum.[4] They dealt with acute problems such as dire poverty, unemployment, and disease, which constituted the immediate challenge to the policy-makers of the period. Their achievement lies in the quiet yet impressive way in which they combined the major intellectual tendencies of the time, to form a powerful framework within which to tackle those concrete issues. In an era which witnessed the emergence of new demands upon the political system due to the increased awareness of social issues and to the widening circle of politically active, or activated people consequent to the extension of the franchise in 1884, they went a long way towards providing the necessary solutions. This they did while preserving the essential continuity of the liberal tradition. The preoccupation with the 'social problem' served as a catalyst for a remarkable synthesis of political ideas which ensured the survival of the liberal tradition at a time when its eclipse was heralded by many. We shall not be concerned with what the new liberals thought about constitutional or political reform, for to concentrate on liberal attitudes towards social reform is to penetrate into the essence of the new liberalism.

During a period of socio-political change an ideology should be judged by its transformative capacities. On the dawn of the twentieth century, the relics of nineteenth-century liberalism were about to be stranded on the shores of conservatism, as the progressive tide shifted the centre of ideological gravity towards

---

[4] Cf. e.g. R. Harrison, *Before the Socialists* (1965), p. 262, who notes that Comte warned his philosophers to avoid parliamentarianism and journalistic activity that involved preoccupation with day-to-day events and with the management of periodicals. The young Positivists resisted, therefore, these temptations.

the 'left'. This is why, for students of liberal thought, it seems justified to consider the utterances of an *avant-garde* minority of liberals as descriptive of the new channels into which the liberal mainstream as a whole was flowing. At the same time, the 'old' or 'moderate' liberalism has obviously to be taken into account in order to understand the 'new'.

In any work on liberal thought the question of definition must arise. It would be unwise to attempt to specify this undogmatic and loose set of ideas, often described as a 'spirit' rather than a creed. Still, the problem cannot be circumvented in this fashion. It is the conviction of this writer that a core of beliefs which gives liberalism its separate identity can be delimited without too much difficulty, but any attempt to enumerate them *a priori* would be to impose a false order and precision upon a dynamic and flexible subject-matter. An ideology like liberalism is rather the outcome of a constant interplay between thinker and idea. A liberal would be one who defined himself as such, or who was considered as such by his contemporaries, but also one whose political and social thought revolved round issues that had always concerned liberals. Like the organic analogy that figures so prominently in these pages, the liberal mainstream differs from the sum of its parts (or contributors). It is the intellectual product that remains after fringe variations have been discounted. It then reacts on individual liberals by creating for them a frame of reference. And like the organism, it too evolves and develops new forms which grow out of the old. The successful combination of continuity with sensitivity to the political, social, philosophical, and scientific stimuli of its environment is what made English liberal thought at the turn of the century not only politically but intellectually satisfying. This is precisely what adaptation is all about.

The concern of liberals with problems of social reform was of course part of a general movement of progressive thought that had existed as an undercurrent in the first half of the nineteenth century and gradually swelled to become a dominant factor in social thought towards the end of the Victorian era. To understand the nature of the developments within liberalism, it has to be placed firmly and squarely in the context of the major patterns of thought that captured the intellects and the imaginations of serious thinkers. There is always a sense in which a political ideology reflects the intellectual fashions of its time and the new liberalism was no exception. But the issue runs deeper. Firstly, philosophy, religion, science, social and political thought were all beginning to concentrate on the issues relevant to the 'social problem' and often arrived via their respective paths at similar conclusions regarding possible solutions. This obviously could hardly have been sheer coincidence, and explanations must be sought both in the particular moral and mental make-up of cultural leaders and innovators, and in the growing consciousness of social facts that was so crucial to the working out of solutions. It also highlights the interdependence of the fields of human knowledge, a fact which is vital to understanding nineteenth-century English thought and which itself produced a binding image for the intellectual activities of many important contemporary thinkers.

Secondly, the new liberals played a key role in moulding this very drive for a synthesis, for a general view of the human condition nourished by the united effort of the best that the various intellectual traditions could offer. Bearing in mind that progressive and reformist tendencies extended beyond the merely political, and noting further that not all their political manifestations adopted the form and the spirit of liberalism, the question that will constantly be posed throughout this study is, how did liberals reconcile the general flow of ideas with their principles, what was their part in it, and how did they adjust their faith to the moral and scientific 'truths' then gaining acceptance? This will appear to have been a much more complex issue than simply moving from a negative to a positive concept of liberty; it was one involving new conceptions of human nature concurrently with new theories of society. But the challenge of continuity had to be, and was indeed, met. Otherwise, there might have been no point in talking about a new *liberalism*—a danger made all the more acute by its ideological rivals hovering in the background, trumpeting all the while its impending bankruptcy or supersession.

When sifting through the various elements of which advanced liberalism was constituted, one characteristic is immediately salient. This is the mutual reinforcement of dominant ethical and scientific trends, constituting twin cornerstones of the comprehensive liberal approach to social reform. The mutual links between the moral and the empirical traditions, between values and facts, are themselves a central factor in the Victorian mind. It has frequently been pointed out in recent years that British sociology flowered in the soil prepared by Comte and Spencer—that of positivism. But those studies, while recognizing the interdisciplinary and unitary tendencies in what would now be called the social sciences, were not written from the perspective of political thought, but solely with the development of sociology or anthropology in mind. It remains, however, a fact that social and political thought were indistinguishable as separate specialisms before the First World War and perhaps even well into the 1930s. If Annan therefore claims dominance for the positivist tradition in English intellectual life,[5] in which sense is this true in relation to the political ideology here under consideration?

Positivism, not to be confused with the secular religion of the Positivists, is widely recognized to be a general and variegated term.[6] Yet beyond its basic characterization as the application of scientific methods to social questions, further definitions of positivism as a whole *are* attempted. Annan, for example, regards positivism as a disturbing influence on English political thought because of its undue concern with values rather than empirical methods of analysis. For him, positivism signifies an individualistic, rationalistic, moralizing approach to human behaviour in society.[7] Burrow, too, sees positivism as 'rooted in the nominalist and individualist traditions', and as eschewing moral relativism.[8] Peel defines positivism 'more clearly' as 'materialism, mechanism, behaviourism, or determinism'[9] but this hardly links up with Annan's mention of rational choice. What is one to make of this confusion, short of disregarding the

[5] N. Annan, *The Curious Strength of Positivism in English Political Thought* (L. T. Hobhouse Memorial Trust Lecture No. 28, 1959). Cf. also J. W. Burrow, *Evolution and Society* (Cambridge U.P., 1966), p. 1.

[6] P. Abrams, *The Origins of British Sociology 1834–1914* (University of Chicago Press, 1968), p. 7; Burrow, op. cit.; J. D. Y. Peel, *Herbert Spencer: The Evolution of a Sociologist* (New York, 1971), p. 238.

[7] Annan, op. cit., pp. 6–8, 15–18.

[8] Burrow, op. cit., pp. 102–3, 226–7.

[9] Peel, op. cit., p. 238. See also H. Stuart Hughes, *Consciousness and Society: The Reorientation of European Social Thought 1890–1930* (Paladin Books, 1974), p. 29.

concept altogether? How does all this square with the common denominator, the positivist search for a science of society?

Part of the answer lies in the imprecision of the concept of 'science', which was often used in a purely deductive rather than an inductive sense, as in the false empiricism of the Utilitarians. Beyond this, however, the above delineations of positivism fail to apply to the peculiar brand taken up by new liberals. It would be incorrect to include them in what Hughes has called the 'revolt against positivism' characteristic of the Continent at the turn of the century.[10] It would be justified, though, to regard them as continuing in a modified form some central motifs of the positivist heritage, compatible with elements of belief apparently ruled out by other definitions of positivism. The new liberal position was not atomistically Individualist, nor hostile to Idealism. It combined empiricism both with a distaste for the quantification of human behaviour—because quantification excluded the thinking of ideas and the expression of preferences—and with a rejection of a value-free approach to the study of man. This was something entirely different from merely confusing the 'is' with the 'ought'. It embodied a deliberate recognition that the two were linked, that—in J. A. Hobson's words—'moral import is part of the nature of the fact'.[11] Above all, it was positivist in its evolutionary or developmental outlook, in its emphasis on the social system as a whole as the subject of interest, in its espousal of a unified social science, and in its belief that man could rationally control his environment and himself.[12] The central bequest of positivism—a conviction that ethics can be put on a scientific basis—was, however, transformed by the new liberals into a more complex *Weltanschauung*. They too were motivated by the assumption that moral truths were there to be discovered. Indeed, they felt assured not only of the righteousness, but of the irrefutable reality of their principles. But they did not aspire to 'create a science of morals and legislation'.[13] Or rather, science had for them a general and a narrow sense: on

[10] Hughes, op. cit., pp. 29–30.

[11] J. A. Hobson, *The Social Problem* (1901), p. 67.

[12] Cf. R. Fletcher, *Auguste Comte and the Making of Sociology* (Auguste Comte Memorial Trust Lecture 7, 1966), pp. 9–12; Abrams, op. cit., p. 57.

[13] Which Burrow has described as 'the central ambition of social thinking of a positivist complexion since the seventeenth century...', op. cit., p. 21.

the one hand, the empirical verifiability of an assertion; on the other, the commitment to a certain method, or technique, the essence of which was quantification.[14] In the general sense, it rejected in the grand positivist manner abstract and self-evident statements, requiring instead some kind of empirical proof for social theories. This in itself constituted a reversal of liberal modes of thinking, previously linked to pseudo-historical and pseudo-natural interpretations of human behaviour. One cannot, however, claim that the late-liberals revolutionized the approach to political theorizing. They were perhaps more rigorous in their adhesion to empirical facts than the previous positivist generations, but basically this can be attributed to their conformity to scientific fashion, rather than to a radical change in orientation. What had shifted was the attractiveness and popularity of certain trends in scientific thinking. Associationist psychology, Benthamite utilitarianism, the axioms of political economy, were making way for evolution, Darwinism, biological inquiry, and field research. New laws of social progress together with new explanations of human nature were being established through historical and comparative observations, as well as through detailed studies of contemporary British society. Extreme deduction was abandoned but this was not exchanged for the mere accumulation of facts. The two most profound of the liberal thinkers of the period, J. A. Hobson and L. T. Hobhouse, had much to say on the subject. As Hobhouse saw it: 'The social ideal is not to be reached by logical processes alone, but must stand in close relation to human experience.'[15] But social ideals, or ethical ends, were deduced from philosophical first principles[16] and were as such abstract.[17] Similarly Hobson argued that 'the first and simplest step in every "inductive science" is directed *a priori*'—the ordering of facts had to take place with some principles or ends in mind. He emphatically held that 'not merely is purely inductive science impossible, but close scrutiny of scientific method assigns the actual sovereignty and directing force to an idea which is

[14] Cf. K. Mannheim, *Ideology and Utopia* (Harvest Books, New York, n.d.), p. 165.
[15] L. T. Hobhouse, *Sociology and Philosophy. A Centenary Collection of Essays and Articles* (1966), p. 8.
[16] L. T. Hobhouse, *Social Evolution and Political Theory* (New York, 1911), p. 83.
[17] L. T. Hobhouse, 'The Ethical Basis of Collectivism', *International Journal of Ethics*, vol. 8 (1898), 137.

outside the range of knowledge except in the shadowy form of an ideal.' Only thus could a scientific basis of social reform be furnished.[18]

A mutual buttressing of science and ethics was emerging among the leading liberal thinkers. They outgrew the mechanical obsession with creating a science of society or of morals and sought instead to reach similar conclusions by the separate but parallel paths of science and ethics. Indeed, they were more concerned with the primacy of the ethical system in that they believed it was up to human choice and values to realize the ethical potentiality of the scientific-historical process. They would not contemplate a political ethics subservient to—that is, dependent on—science, as happened in the last analysis with Bentham, Malthus, Spencer, and others. This connects up with their consequent eschewal of science in the narrow sense, a question treated within the framework of the science-versus-art issue. Following J. S. Mill, art was to define the end which science should study. [19] For Hobson, the study of human life in society—which he termed sociology and which was to provide the basis for radical social reform—was both a science and an art. It was based on physiology and psychology and supplied answers to the question: 'What are the probable net social results over different periods of time of particular changes in social institutions achieved by such and such methods, and at such and such a pace?'[20] Building on this edifice, sociology could furnish a true art of social progress. Science was for Hobson the field of facts, of mechanism, of routine, and of quantification. But explanation had to take account of qualitative or creative action, of 'art-values'.[21] These standards were 'extra-scientific'. Hence, the social sciences were 'servants rather than directors of social progress'.[22] This, far from being an unscientific approach, could better be described as 'super-scientific'. It was a false over-specialist type of science to which Hobson and Hobhouse objected. The unity of social science was not only a question of drawing together the different disciplines devoted to observable human behaviour, but a synthesis of

[18] Hobson, *The Social Problem*, pp. 65–6.
[19] J. S. Mill, *A System of Logic* (1911), pp. 616–17.
[20] Hobson, *The Social Problem*, p. 262.
[21] J. A. Hobson, *Work and Wealth* (New York, 1914), pp. 330–2.
[22] Ibid., p. 359.

external facts with the product of the human mind. Hence Hobhouse's concern with a social philosophy and Hobson's notion of humanism, themes which pervade their writings. As has already been mentioned, the chief scientific influence on late-Victorian social thought was that of biology. Pursuant to the above discussion, one of the important conclusions of this study is that Social Darwinism was not the only, or even the most significant, manifestation of this influence. Once again a textbook version has to be called into question. Biology has been presented as supplying an amoral, perhaps immoral, tone to the social theories of the times[23] and this, of course, cannot be denied. The survival (or selection) of the fittest argument in its various forms had strength, persuasiveness, even flair. But two questions must be asked: was Social Darwinism generally adopted, and is it justified to regard it as the representative link between biological and social theory? An emphatic negative reply must be given to both questions. Social Darwinism never captured the central bastions of English social thought. At its worst it was allied with a reactionary anti-humanist cause that never became assimilated into the English bent of mind. At its best it was a misconceived and misapplied theory that promised progress at a price civilization would not tolerate. Its appeal was restricted to hard-core conservatives who, try as they might, could not mask their alienation from the liberal-progressive cause. Instead, as I shall try to show, other variants, different interpretations, of biological ideas were gaining a pervasive influence. Darwinism and evolutionary theory were of far greater consequence both in the philosophical and historical assumptions that underlay them and in the opposing implications of the empirical evidence to which biological research pointed. It was this particular incarnation of the positivist spirit that was the inspiration of new liberal theory and profoundly influenced English social reform thought.

In turning to an examination of the nature of advanced liberal ethics, Herbert Samuel's dictum must be uppermost in the mind: 'The trunk of the tree of Liberalism is rooted in the

[23] See, e.g., S. Low, 'Darwinism and Politics', *FR*, vol. 86 (1909), 519–33; B. Semmel, *Imperialism and Social Reform* (1960), pp. 29–52; R. J. Halliday, 'Social Darwinism: A Definition', *Victorian Studies*, vol. 14 (1971), 389–405; R. Hofstadter, *Social Darwinism in American Thought* (Beacon Press, Boston, 1955).

soil of ethics'.[24] The essence of the search for truth, for directives
for political action, had always been an ethical concern with a
rational, responsible, and just society. Liberalism shares this
central preoccupation with moral precepts with other ideological systems, and a prime objective of this study is to elucidate the
detailed interpretations and modifications of liberal principles
in the light of the issues which served as their testing ground. But
at its simplest, the gradual liberal shift of focus to the 'condition
of the people' question intensified and recast in a new light the
ethical foundations of liberalism, though continuity of terminology and concepts was preserved.

To ascertain the ethical elements acting on the advanced
liberal mind is a complex operation, perhaps because so many
of the components of nineteenth-century English thought seem
to be relevant. We claim, after all, to be dealing with a
mainstream. The task at hand is to attempt to analyse the
nature of the materials culled from the major idea-movements
of the century, and their reaction upon each other, which
produced the liberal alchemy. Needless to say, one is not
dealing in exact science when tracing the origins and estimating
the relative weight of an idea. But the territory can be mapped.

The origins of advanced liberalism are situated at a number
of crossroads: Utilitarianism—in itself a system of thought no
less influential in the Western world than Marxism—was
undergoing refinement; the evangelical spirit which pervaded
the English religious scene was becoming secularized and
generalized; the peculiar characteristics of British Idealism
ensured compatibility with a range of ideas seemingly remote
from its basic maxims; political economy was climbing down
from a world of abstractions and grappling with the economic
disorder it had previously relegated to individual moral
deficiency. In relation to all this, liberalism was no passive
bystander merely absorbing the impact of changing philosophies and theories. It was an important, sometimes crucial
agent of their transformation, as shall repeatedly be
demonstrated in these pages. Moreover, it had its own specific
contribution to make to the new edifice of social thought now
beginning to rise: it evolved from within itself a concept of

[24] H. Samuel, *Liberalism. An Attempt to State the Principles and Proposals of Contemporary Liberalism in England* (1902), p. 6.

community as a meaningful entity and thus conferred fresh relevance and significance on classical liberal tenets.

Utilitarianism—to be distinguished from Benthamism proper—paved the way for the emergence of three major components of advanced liberalism. Firstly, in conjunction with evangelicalism it supplied the motivation and orientation towards social reform—conceived as the rational and planned remedying of social ills. Though much of the written work of important social reformers is devoted to concrete analyses of specific measures, or to detailed administrative and legislative programmes, it would be entirely erroneous to conclude that no principles or aims are discernible behind the minutiae—as do those who still commit themselves to the notion of an administrative state, developing out of its own pragmatic momentum as a mechanical response to random stimuli.[25] The practical nature of utilitarian reform—political, legal and social—left an indelible mark upon the ideological development of English social thought.

This brings us to the second contribution of utilitarianism— in its later modifications—to liberalism. Utilitarianism had originally been linked with a number of central concepts, apparently indispensable: the individual as the unit under discussion, the greatest happiness of the greatest number principle, and the felicific calculus which lent it the aura of an exact science, rooted in associationist psychology.[26] The amazing thing about utilitarianism is that it outgrew all these three original components, a fact which attests to the force of the concept of utility as such. Whereas classical liberalism fell neatly into line with Benthamite premises regarding the isolated and autonomous individual, social activity being the sum of free choices of rational individuals, new liberal thought operated under a clearly different set of assumptions. The salient issue in the liberal transformation was the awareness of the 'social' in addition to, and qualitatively different from, the 'individual' and hence the coining of the phrase 'social utility'.

[25] Cf. O. MacDonagh, 'The Nineteenth-Century Revolution in Government: A Reappraisal', *Historical Journal*, I (1958), 52–67; D. Roberts, *Victorian Origins of the British Welfare State* (New Haven, 1968). See Chapter Seven, pp. 247–8.

[26] Cf. R. Anschutz, *The Philosophy of J. S. Mill* (Oxford, 1953), pp. 13–14; Burrow, op. cit., pp. 24–42.

It can, of course, be claimed that, as Annan paraphrases Leslie Stephen,[27] 'what is social welfare but another name for utility?' Nevertheless, the aggregative definition of society was definitely dropped by advanced liberalism, even if there was no unanimity about the concept of society. As Hobhouse explained: 'The interests of every man are no doubt in the end bound up with the welfare of the whole community, but the relation is infinitely subtle and indirect ... the direct and calculable benefit of the majority may by no means coincide with the ultimate good of society as a whole.'[28] Moreover, for original utilitarianism, as Stokes has observed,[29] happiness, not liberty, was the end of government. This is important to the comprehension of the new liberalism, because it reflected the utilitarian emphasis on welfare no less than the obvious liberal emphasis on liberty. Liberty and welfare became twin goals, each in a way defining and explaining the other.

The third contribution of utilitarianism was the overcoming of the nineteenth-century liberal hostility to the state. Such hostility was by no means deducible from utilitarian principles, despite the practical support of many Philosophical Radicals for laissez-faire. Hobhouse stated the extreme implications of Benthamism when he wrote that a community following its principles 'may do with the individual what it pleases provided that it has the good of the whole in view ... It contemplates, at least as a possibility, the complete subordination of individual to social claims.'[30] Stokes, too, has analysed the authoritarian aspects of utilitarianism, which required positive intervention of government to enforce its basic premisses. Embodied in this ambiguity characteristic of utilitarianism were two traditions, elaborated on by Halévy[31]—the one insisting on the natural identity of human interests, the other demanding the coercion and manipulation of human beings to achieve an artificial identity of interests. This conceptual polarization could of course call into question the very need for social reform—

[27] N. G. Annan, Leslie Stephen: His Thought and Character in Relation to his Time (Harvard U.P., 1952), p. 213.
[28] L. T. Hobhouse, Liberalism (New York, 1964; 1st ed. 1911), p. 41.
[29] E. Stokes, The English Utilitarians and India (Oxford, 1959), p. 63.
[30] Hobhouse, Liberalism, p. 38.
[31] E. Halévy, The Growth of Philosophic Radicalism (1972; 1st ed. 1928), pp. 15–17, 370–2, and passim.

assuming that a state of natural identity was attainable. In the case of this not being the best of all possible worlds, social reform—according to which tradition was adopted—signified either the 'removal of hindrances' to natural harmony, or the establishment of new patterns of social behaviour, in which case education was at least as important as legislation. The fall from favour of the first tradition ensured a more positive role for social reformers, though not quite as manipulative and coercive as utilitarian notions would permit.[32]

State intervention in the service of social utility was divested of its arbitrary character by the abandonment of the numerical approach to happiness. What had disturbed liberals was the possibility of sacrificing the happiness of the few in order to score higher on the total sum of individual 'happinesses'. The issue of the equal claim of each to the realization of his individuality was here at stake. New liberals would have agreed with D. G. Ritchie: 'We have come again to recognise, with Aristotle, the moral function of the State.'[33] The re-establishment of the connection between ethics and politics strikes one of the key notes of the new liberalism. Moreover, the utilitarian shift from quantity to quality is itself deeply symptomatic of the changes the Victorian mind was undergoing. It was reflected both in the Ruskinian rebellion against the production of wealth as the goal of human activity and in the eugenic interest in the improvement of human matter. Social reform was after all an attempt to reassert the quality of human life in the face of industrialism.

Two major aspects of utilitarianism were discarded by the new liberals: its ahistorical approach and its exaggerated faith in the power of the expert. Nevertheless, utilitarianism bequeathed to the new liberalism important modes of thinking about society even after it had ceased to exist as a definite philosophical movement. In this it followed a pattern similar to evangelicalism, whose influence survived its organized religious existence. Indeed, the two movements are jointly responsible for the moral fervour of English social reform, although progressive liberalism was not nourished by religious movements as such. This is certainly the case with Nonconformism, which served as a powerful ally of middle-class liberalism

[32] See below, Chapter Three, p. 91.
[33] D. G. Ritchie, *The Principles of State Interference* (1891), p. 169.

throughout the nineteenth century. But the battles it fought—
over temperance, education and disestablishment—were not
those of the new liberalism. They were the tail-end of the
struggle of the middle class to free itself from the control of
privileged and entrenched social groups, rather than being of
relevance to the new social conceptions and policies which
emerged later. The decline of Nonconformism is corroborated
by Halévy,[34] who originally formulated the thesis about the
influence of evangelicalism on the peculiar nature of reform in
England. As a source of ideas and a motivating force for the
intellectuals we are concerned with, it does not seem very
profitable to speak in terms of the inspiration of evangelicalism.
The original impetus of the mission to evangelize emerged as
secularized and quasi-scientific. It is probably correct that
evangelicalism can account for the ethical overtones of reform
and, in Stokes's words, for the 'belief that human character
could be suddenly and totally transformed by a direct assault on
the mind.'[35] But the new liberalism, while absorbing the
significance of education, never underestimated the importance
of material environment for the formation of character, and
pursuant to this the ability of concerted social action to control
environment. In sum, it seems of greater benefit to drop the
question whether or not the evangelized ethos underlies the
'isms' of the later nineteenth century[36] and to inquire instead
into the development of the sense of social service, by then so far
removed from the original as to acquire a significance of its own.
The picture emerging here is, as so often in the period, one of
various semi-independent movements of ideas supporting each
other in many fields and frequently converging upon a single
point. This is true not only of evangelicalism and utilitarianism
but of Idealism as well.

   This study will challenge the textbook version that credits
British Idealism, and T. H. Green in particular, with prime, if
not sole, responsibility for the transformation of liberal ideas.[37]

---

[34] E. Halévy, *A History of the English People in the Nineteenth Century*, Vol. 5: *Imperialism and the Rise of Labour* (1961; 1st ed. 1929), pp. ix, 176–9.

[35] Stokes, op. cit., p. 30.

[36] Cf. M. J. Wiener, *Between Two Worlds, The Political Thought of Graham Wallas* (Oxford, 1971), pp. 1–2; G. Himmelfarb, *Victorian Minds* (New York, 1970), p. 291.

[37] See, e.g., A. D. Lindsay, Introduction to T. H. Green, *Lectures on the Principles of Political Obligation* (1941), p. vii: 'Green and his fellow-idealists represent the renewed

Ritchie, in discussing Green *vis-à-vis* the evolutionists, had already occasion to remark : 'This "convergence of results", on the part of those who have approached the subject [concerning the relation between individual and society] from different sides, is one of the most hopeful signs in the present revived interest in Ethics.'[38] At the very most, Idealism must be regarded as one element amidst a general progressive movement in ideology, philosophy, economics, science, and practical politics. Had Green not existed, liberalism would still have become collectivist and favourably oriented to progressive social reform. More influence on, and responsibility for, events and trends has been ascribed to him than he actually exercised. This not infrequent phenomenon can be partly explained in this case. Owing to the historically 'accidental' fact that Idealism dominated for a while the training ground of England's intellectual and political élite—Oxford—it came to assume an importance disproportionate to what it would normally have received in the English climate of ideas. There is evidence that Idealism was never properly digested by liberal Oxford students, products of the 1880s and 1890s, who notwithstanding were under the spell of Green and what he symbolized. But rather than symbolizing an intellectual philosophical movement, Green and Arnold Toynbee were paragons of a social crusading spirit hardly connected by their followers with theoretical conceptualization, as for example an analysis of the Settlement Movement would demonstrate. This was, after all, a prime characteristic of evangelicalism.[39] Oxford provided the *emotional* atmosphere and motivation to study social problems and undertake social work rather than the intellectual justification and framework for social reform. Hobson, too, referred to 'dispositions' and 'valuations' antagonistic to materialism and to narrow utilitarianism received from the 'atmosphere of an Oxford in which Jowett, T. H. Green, and Mark Pattison

liberalism of the last quarter of the nineteenth century.' Cf. also H. Laski, 'Leaders of Collectivist Thought', in *Ideas and Beliefs of the Victorians* (1949), pp. 418–19; G. de Ruggiero, *The History of European Liberalism* (Boston, 1959), pp. 146–9; G. H. Sabine, *A History of Political Theory* (1951), pp. 607 ff.; E. Barker, *Political Thought in England 1848 to 1914* (1963), p. 4.

[38] Ritchie, op. cit., p. 168. Cf. also p. 138.

[39] As Richter has argued, Green's teachings epitomized the evangelical impulse (M. Richter, *The Politics of Conscience: T. H. Green and his Age* (1964), pp. 134–5).

were leading figures . . .' [40] Yet as far as the nature of Hobson's thought is concerned, H. N. Brailsford was substantially correct in asserting: 'I doubt whether T. H. Green or any of the Neo-Kantians influenced him greatly: the cast of his mind was traditionally English.' [41]

In short, Idealism gained in retrospect an impoi tance for liberalism it would not otherwise have had as a school of political thought, and this process was facilitated by the happy convergence of Idealism and the direction liberalism had been taking since J. S. Mill. Rather than Idealism giving birth to a new version of liberalism, it was liberalism that was able to assimilate certain aspects of Idealism into its mainstream and thus bestow new meaning upon Idealist tenets. This applies primarily to Green's concept of the common good which blended perfectly with the 'classlessness' of the liberal approach; to the non-materialism of Idealist thought with which liberalism was in sympathy (often against certain marked socialist tendencies); and to the early notion of social reform as the removal of hindrances to the exercise of man's positive powers, which characterized mid- and late-century liberal political action. Moreover, Green himself absorbed the elements of the utilitarian outlook in his attempt to adumbrate conduct and describe institutions whose end is to supply permanent contributions to the social good. [42] The efforts of liberalism to revitalize itself activated a spectacular process of intellectual synthesis.

The contention of this study is that biological and evolutionary theories, grafted on to the liberal tradition itself, were an independent source of liberal philosophy—more sophisticated, more immediately concerned with the issues of the times, and almost certainly more widespread as well. It is, of course, undeniable that many people, among them liberals, considered

[40] Hobson, *Confessions of an Economic Heretic*, p. 26.
[41] H. N. Brailsford, *The Life-Work of J. A. Hobson* (L. T. Hobhouse Memorial Trust Lecture No. 17, 1948), p. 6. Asquith too, though his Balliol background was thought by Laski to have been a direct cause of his responsibility for Liberal collectivist legislation (Laski, op. cit., p. 420), expressed politely his complete ignorance of Idealism: 'For myself, though I owe more than I can say to Green's gymnastics, both intellectual and moral, I never "worshipped at the Temple's inner shrine". My own opinions on these high matters have never been more than those of an interested amateur, and are of no importance to anyone but myself.' (*Memories and Reflections*, vol. I (1928), p. 19.)
[42] Ritchie, op. cit., pp. 143-4.

themselves heirs to Green's ideas. But of that number, the two
most interesting for our purposes—Hobhouse and Ritchie—not
only differed essentially from Green on seminal points but
derived their conclusions about the nature of society from
biological and evolutionary data.

Any discussion of social reform must touch upon the developments in economic thought, for one of the main instruments of
reform hinged upon financial measures aimed at improving the
material condition of the underprivileged. Many new liberals,
Hobson and J. M. Robertson in particular, had important
contributions to make to the redefinition of political economy
and they often pushed the discipline in directions the academic
economic world was not yet ready to accept—although it too
had modified its views in significant ways. Most crucial of all
was the ending of the theoretical and practical isolation of
economics from other fields of human conduct, politics and
ethics in particular. The sharp criticism of political economy
had finally borne fruit. It was exposed as irrelevant to the
comprehension and control of the results of the industrial
revolution. Ruskin's famous dictum, 'there is no wealth but
life', became the motto of the transformation. The preoccupation of economics with production made way for an
interest in the individual as consumer and for concentration on
the centrality and problems of distribution. Economics de-
scended from the realm of a master-science to that of an
instrument for realizing human values and social ends. A total,
unified, view of the individual in society was embraced by
liberal social reformers as part of their qualitative and integrated approach to man. They regarded various economic
measures, such as redistribution of wealth and the placing of
resources at the disposal of the community, as steps on the way
to the realization of their ethico-scientific concept of society.
The development of a liberal notion of community was also
abetted by the decline of competition both as a theoretical
economic maxim and as a moral dogma. The idea of a free, self-
regulating market, reflecting natural law and epitomizing
social justice, collapsed in the face of the facts uncovered by the
increased awareness of socio-economic ills. Moreover, the
recurring capitalist crises with their mass unemployment
indicated some inherent defect in the system, which had to be

remedied from without, i.e. by political means. This was notably the case in the reaction to 'Say's law', which stated that production created its own demand, a reaction that gave rise to the 'underconsumptionist' theories that challenged the whole nineteenth-century economic edifice.

In the realm of detailed economic theories a constant process of erosion supported the changing attitude to the discipline as a whole. J. S. Mill had dealt the old theory of distribution a severe blow by withdrawing his support from the wage-fund theory towards the end of his life. This now meant that wage earners could press, in organized form, for a larger income. Although in practice there were clear limits imposed upon wage increases, the denunciation of the theory as such shook the image of political economy as an exact science. The notions underlying current interpretations of the minimum wage were also being questioned because of the growing interest in biology (and to a much lesser extent, psychology, mainly through an airing of incentives and motivation in industry) which shed new light on the subsistence level.

All this was of course connected with the Malthusian doctrine of population. The population question in one form or another overshadowed the nineteenth century, which witnessed its transformation from a bogey threatening human existence to a controllable phenomenon that could, in the opinion of many scholars, be set to beneficial social use. Malthus's pessimism dressed in scientific language had a considerable influence on the growth of political economy. His writings lent support to those who objected to helping the poor (raising their standard of living would cause it to crash down again because of subsequent multiplication—hence a further law which set wages at subsistence level). Only the few who cared to read his later work thoroughly could appreciate that Malthus's belief in the ability of the masses to exercise self-control or 'moral restraint' modified the original incompatibility of social welfare and natural laws. Beyond this, however, Malthus's very theory of rent opened up the way to a principle of taxation that came to have immense influence on the development of liberal thought. This was the taxation of the unearned increment which, after having been adopted by Mill, was extended by later liberals and used to locate distinct forms of social property that supported their concept of community. Similarly, the existence of large monopolies was not only a living contradiction of a free market, but inevitably raised questions of control and restriction that assumed some public good that had to be protected and some collective action to do so.

One last remark on political economy concerns its status as a science. Beginning with Malthus's arithmetical and geometrical ratios, through the abstract laws of the political economy model and the empirical and atomistic fact-finding of the Statistical Society,[43] the quantitative, exact, and ostensibly value-free approach to science had had the upper hand. Later, as we have mentioned, other ideas concerning science came to the fore with biological positivism. But economics remained, in the hands of new liberals as well, a scientific proving-ground of their ethical outlook, precisely because no contradiction was seen to exist between an economic science and humanism, and precisely because economic theories were now dedicated to the examination of remediable distress rather than a perfectly functioning society.

A cardinal issue in this book is the metamorphosis of liberal ideology from a decaying creed under attack from all sides to an aggressive, modernized set of ideas serving as a springboard for political action. A question still very much in the forefront of scholarly discussion is—who gave liberalism that push? Until recently, the credit has gone to the Socialist movements culminating in the Labour party which, it was maintained, forced liberalism leftwards by political competition and supplied its advanced wing with a ready-made ideology until then just out of the reach of liberals intellectually limited by their own dogmas. In the past few years, much evidence has been offered to demonstrate that the Liberal party was a going concern before the First World War, not at all at the mercy of its rivals on the left.[44] The theme of this study is to demonstrate that intellectually and ideologically, liberalism itself was fully responsible for, and capable of, transforming its political doctrines (though naturally, one cannot ignore the simple fact that there always is an interflow and exchange of ideas in an

---

[43] Abrams, op. cit., pp. 13–30.
[44] H. V. Emy, *Liberals, Radicals and Social Politics 1892–1914* (Cambridge U.P., 1973); P. F. Clarke, *Lancashire and the New Liberalism* (Cambridge U.P., 1971).

open society). If the question is posed as one of liberal continuity versus a break in the liberal tradition, the reply must decidedly be in favour of continuity.

Though it might indeed be unwise to attempt a precise definition of liberalism, the components of liberalism can nevertheless be reduced to two groups—the essential and the incidental, the unchanging fundamentals and the garb they don in response to fashions and pressures of the times. In the opinion of the leading liberal intellectuals here analysed, the new liberalism was a necessary and logical link in the chain to which they were heirs. The English liberal tradition developed over a period of centuries and cannot be regarded as a given and static doctrine. However, during the time-span stretching roughly from Locke to the early J. S. Mill, it had incorporated a number of postulates: a fundamental belief in the rationality of man as an individual, which could be expressed in social organization; a faith in the perfectibility of man which lent itself to conceptions of progress and development and hence to gradualist reform; the notion of empirical freedom both as condition for and as expression of rationality and justice; a concern with the interests of society as a whole rather than with advantages for particular individuals or groups, based on reasons irrelevant to the general interest; constitutional and institutional arrangements to ensure unfettered functioning of individuals within the framework of the law, with the concomitant of limited, responsible, and representative political power. To the above one might add a description which was widespread among the liberals of our period. They conceived of liberalism as a 'faith', 'attitude of the mind', 'affair of spirit', 'intellectual attitude', and 'moral temperament',[45] rather than a creed, doctrine, or definite and prescribed programme. New wine was constantly flowing into the old bottles because by nature liberalism was dynamic, flexible, and progressive.

On the other hand, until the nineteenth century, liberalism had been associated with a number of apparently inseparable elements which turned out to be dispensable. First and foremost among them was the doctrine of natural rights which had

---

[45] See, e.g., Anon., 'Liberalism Philosophically Considered', *WR*, vol. 132 (1889), p. 340; R. B. Haldane, 'The New Liberalism', *PR*, vol. 1 (1896), p. 141; J. M. Robertson, *The Meaning of Liberalism* (1912), pp. 25, 40.

already been dealt fatal blows by Burke and Bentham. This had far-reaching consequences for liberal theory. The notion of man existing independently of society, his innate and absolute inviolability and autonomy in matters concerning his life, liberty, and property, the notion of society and its political institutions as an artifact, the contractual relations between humans—all these were swept away. The idea of private property as the concrete embodiment and expression of man's worth was a second concept that underwent important modifications. Rooted as it was in a specific socio-political culture, it mellowed under a combination of economic changes and a socially-oriented definition of human nature. Thirdly, the predominant nineteenth-century association of liberalism with economic freedom and unrestrained competition, and with atomistic Individualism was proved to be transient. Fear and distrust of the state and insistence on weak government, it transpired, had not been a true characteristic of liberals.[46] The *laissez-faire* of the Manchester School was also no more than the application of liberal principles to the particular constellation set up by the laws of political economy and early utilitarianism. When they collapsed, liberalism managed to scramble out of the falling debris—bruised, shaken perhaps, but alive.

Mill, the dominant figure of English liberalism, had himself an important role to play in the forming of the liberal tradition. He clarified and crystallized a tendency which was to become as central to liberalism as liberty itself, namely, the concept of individuality. The Philosophical Radicals had already focused on the individual as the unit of social analysis; Mill developed the qualitative aspects of character and personality into a supreme value, a theme which was taken up and expanded by his successors. Individuality thus replaced Individualism, and by regarding a socially rooted individuality as the main attribute of human welfare, social reformers crucially complemented the previous liberal stress on liberty. The later Mill, furthermore, through his conversion to a mild form of socialism,

---

[46] Cf. M. Seliger, *The Liberal Politics of John Locke* (1968), pp. 18–21; G. Watson, *The English Ideology: Studies in the Language of Victorian Politics* (1973), p. 75; Stokes, op. cit., pp. 63, 290–3 (quoting J. F. Stephen). Stokes sees the appeal to law and government as opposed to the popular liberalism of the early nineteenth century but recognizes that the utilitarian legacy changed the existing conception of liberalism.

personified the continuity between the 'new' liberalism and the 'old', thus smoothing the transition towards a socially concerned ideology.

The body of this study, then, is devoted to the adaptation of the liberal *Weltanschauung* to the intellectual and material environment of the Victorian *fin-de-siècle*. It was perhaps the last attempt to treat a rational world rationally, and as such it is a success story. The challenge of social reform was met in theory and in practice. In doing so, liberal essentials acquired new significance. Human rational development became empirically and scientifically demonstrable. The appreciation of freedom was deepened because the interaction between man and man, and man and environment, was elucidated. Instead of rationality being perceived by contract theory to lie in man overcoming the state of nature, the historical concept of the state transformed rationality into the effort necessary to overcome the latent determinism in man's social and evolutionary existence. Above all, a new understanding of the social nature of man revitalized basic political symbols and issues such as rights, property, equality of opportunity, the individual in relation to the state, citizenship, communal responsibility, and social welfare. The new liberals constructed a powerful, coherent and relevant edifice without compromising on what was inherently liberal in their outlook. It is hoped that the following pages will give some due to this achievement.

II
Socialism in Liberalism—Towards the Realization of a Social Ethics

I. CONTENTIONS OVER CONCEPTS

A. 'We Are All Socialists Now'

ANY appreciation of late-Victorian liberalism has to proceed from an examination of the English idea of socialism, to the extent it differed from the continental varieties. If by socialism is meant the body of doctrine which, in institutional form, pitted itself against the Liberal party at the turn of the century, the transformation of liberal theory was not caused by Socialist influences. Socialism emerged rather as one of the most elusive, vague, and diverse concepts of English social and political thought, and, by its very ubiquity, constituted as great a challenge to liberalism on the intellectual level as conservatism did on the party political and Parliamentary levels.[1] Sir William Harcourt's endlessly re-echoed phrase 'we are all socialists now' epitomized the new preoccupation of liberals at the end of the 1880s. A complicated love–hate relationship with socialism, certainly more a question of ideology than of political action, forced a clarification of basic problems on liberal thinkers and did much to bring liberalism to a fresh awareness of its powers and potentials.

Leading social theorists of the period, unlike many present-day commentators,[2] were aware of the varieties of socialism. They realized that both academic and popular innovative nuances had to be analysed to comprehend changes in social

---

[1] On many ideological questions, such as those concerning individual liberty and property, conservatism followed liberalism with a time-span of a few decades. This opinion was already held at the time. See Anon., 'The Future of the Radical Party', *FR*, vol. 34 (1883), 4.

[2] A notable exception is T. H. Marshall, who distinguishes between Socialism A (bent on abolishing capitalism) and Socialism B (humanitarian). However, new liberals would not, as shall be seen, have described their socialism as purely 'humanitarian' or have considered it 'vague'. *Class, Citizenship and Social Development* (New York, 1965), pp. 284–7.

practice and opinion.[3] In the main, an analytical examination
of the predominant meanings of socialism has to operate on two
planes: did socialism necessarily entail fundamental ideological
changes or could it refer to practical adjustments as well; and
was it primarily an economic or an ethical term?

The *Speaker*, the leading liberal weekly, wrote in 1893: 'If it
be Socialism to have generous and hopeful sentiments with
regard to the lot of those who work...we are all Socialists in
that sense.'[4] This statement, appearing on the pages of an organ
undisguisedly antagonistic to organized Socialism, may serve as
typical of one of the main uses of the term. From the 1880s
onwards any adequate treatment of English domestic issues was
bound to consider the social question. And on the simplest level,
any public awareness of and desire to confront the social
question was socialism. As John Rae remarked, those who
demanded some immediate reforms were called socialists
'merely because they make it part of the State's business to deal
with social questions, or perhaps more particularly because
they make it the State's business to deal with social questions in
the interest of the working class'.[5]

This approach to socialism implied its integration into
certain established aspects of the British political process. L. A.
Atherley-Jones, the son of the Chartist leader and in his own
right a respected Liberal M.P. for almost thirty years, saw the
extending of legislative and administrative aid by the state to
permanently disadvantaged individuals as 'English Socialism,
or—as it may more properly be termed—Social Reform', this
being 'merely an expansion of the application of a principle
fully established and by statesmen of both political parties
recognised and accepted'.[6] Far from being an alien or new
force, socialism was here equated with what came to be the rival
to official Socialism. Liberals of course realized that opposing

---

[3] See J. Rae, *Contemporary Socialism* (1884), pp. 10–11, and T. Kirkup, *A History of Socialism*, 3rd ed. (1906), pp. 4–5. Both writers were well-known observers of socialism; the former a critical, though not unduly hostile, outsider; the latter a moderate sympathizer on lines very close to advanced liberal thought.

[4] 'Are We All Socialists Now?', *Speaker*, 13.5.1893. See also J. Morley, 'Liberalism and Social Reforms', *The Eighty Club Yearbook* (1889).

[5] Rae, *Contemporary Socialism*, p. 11. For the significance of the second half of the quotation see Chapter Four, section 1.

[6] L. A. Atherley-Jones, 'Liberalism and Social Reform: A Warning', *NR*, vol. 9 (1893), 631.

political groups claimed the term 'socialism' for their own,[7] yet it is significant that liberals such as Atherley-Jones—a man closely connected with labour questions—insisted on regarding socialism not as a definite theory but as being outside the range of party terminology and as synonymous with the British way of tackling the social problem. But then Joseph Chamberlain himself, the doyen of practical social reform, had declared with gusto of governmental attempts to fight social inequality: 'Of course it is Socialism . . . every kindly act of legislation by which the community has sought to discharge its responsibilities and its obligations to the poor is Socialism, but it is none the worse for that.'[8]

Beyond this 'popular' way of adopting socialism—which was at the same time intended to prove natural liberal sympathy with social problems, and, intellectually, to take the wind out of Socialist sails, the whole issue received a more theoretically sophisticated treatment. The major premises of liberal social reform thought developed in an atmosphere of interminable discussions on individualism versus socialism, on socialism and collectivism, on municipal and state socialism. These discussions were linked to various assumptions about human and social nature that directed liberals to seek certain sets of solutions to the social problem. As a theory socialism signified for advanced liberals an ethical, humanistic conception of man in society as opposed to the diverse shades of doctrinaire, deterministic, Utopian and Marxist creeds. That approach was common to a wide spectrum of progressive thinkers—Christian Socialists, Positivists, Idealists, and Fabians—and was basically no more than stating the obvious: the truth of socialism was in the perception that man was a social being. There had always been some socialism since society came into being.[9] As the liberal editor of the Christian Social monthly *The Commonwealth* wrote in the opening number, by talking about socialism people were not advocating a scheme but recognizing a fact: 'We mean that there is no private action that has not a social value, a social significance.'[10] It was in this form that socialism penetrated the

[7] R. B. Haldane, 'The Liberal Creed', *CR*, vol. 54 (1888), 467–8.
[8] J. Chamberlain, *The Radical Platform* (Edinburgh, 1885), p. 23.
[9] J. M. Robertson, *The Future of Liberalism* (1895), p. 24.
[10] H. Scott Holland, 'Introductory', *Commonwealth*, vol. 1 (Jan. 1896), 4.

consciousness of the British liberal intelligentsia. It appealed to liberals and to progressives in general because it underlined the cardinal belief of a pre-sociological age in the inseparability of ethics and politics. As far as liberals were concerned this was an essential part of the liberal heritage, in the grand tradition of Mill and Gladstone. The alarming discoveries about the 'condition of the people' necessitated a reaffirmation of the liberal faith precisely in the field where public morality seemed blatantly wanting.

For liberals, unlike for some of their progressive colleagues, socialism pertained first to the ethical and only then to the economic sphere. Kirkup thought of socialism fundamentally as a theory of social and moral evolution: 'Progress chiefly and supremely consists in the growing control of ethical principle over all the forms of selfishness . . . The ethical progress of man is largely a development of the principle of sociality, community, or association.'[11] Society was becoming a moral entity and the adhesion to socialism was perceived as due to the growing influence of altruistic feelings. The agitation in connection with social reform pointed 'to the increasing desire for improvement in the social condition of life; and offer[ed] eloquent proof that Socialism is accepted more on account of its humanitarian ideals than through the influence of its economic doctrines.'[12] As a rule, new liberals would have accepted the position of Henry Dyer—a Glaswegian educationalist—that socialism had moral *and* economic importance, but that an intellectual and moral revolution had to precede a social and industrial one. Social reform was attainable only via moral reform—a clear echo of evangelicalism. True socialism was much more a question of spirit than of organizational form.[13]

Moderate liberals did not, however, wax enthusiastic over the use of 'socialism' to describe liberal ethics, for the emergence of Socialist movements on the political scene had bestowed upon the word a very definite connotation. Some liberals insisted that their brand of progressiveness was identical to socialism in ends,

[11] Kirkup, op. cit., pp. 303, 305, 281.
[12] R. G. Davis, 'The Evolutionary Trend of British Political Parties', *WR*, vol. 157 (1902), 516.
[13] H. Dyer, *The Evolution of Industry* (1895), p. 55; 'The Future of Politics', *WR*, vol. 145 (1896), 5.

but different in methods.[14] It was only 'by a curious freak in the
misuse of words', complained the *Speaker*, that socialism was
being applied to an agreement on ends as well.[15] Theorists to
the left of liberalism, such as Sidney Ball, the Fabian and
Oxford don, reinforced this position for reasons of their own. He
claimed that socialism accepted the classical liberal ends but
was opposed to its economic tradition.[16] By seeing the uniqueness of socialism in its economic critique, Ball implied both that
liberalism had failed to offer such a critique and, conversely,
that the traditional liberal concern with individuality and
freedom was no longer central to the condition of modern
society. These fallacies concerning end-of-the-century liberalism were common. However, not a few liberals perceived
the existence of a fundamental difference in outlook between
liberalism and socialism as to ends and as to what constituted a
good personal and social life.[17] Hobhouse made this abun-
dantly clear in his now classic exposé of liberalism. He described
in a nutshell the two types of Socialism which liberals rejected:
mechanical (or economic) and official (or political). The former
constructed a system on a single factor and substituted artificial
ideas for living principles. The latter was bureaucratic and
elitist in aspiring to dictate to each individual the organization
of his life. Socialism conceived of in these terms had 'in essentials
nothing to do with democracy or with liberty.'[18] These were
the two necessary components of a liberal socialism or, to use
perhaps a more accurate phrase, a social liberalism.

The Liberal interpretation of socialism had concurrently to
clarify the relationship between socialism and individualism.
The literature of the period is stock-full with attempts to place
the two concepts in either an antagonistic or complementary
position. Here again a good deal of confusion reigns owing to
the dual sense in which individualism was used at the time, and
is in fact still being used today. On the one hand it referred to

[14] H. Samuel, *Liberalism*, pp. 4–6; Robertson, op. cit., p. 16.
[15] 'Are We All Socialists Now?', *Speaker*, 13.5.1893.
[16] S. Ball, 'Individualism and Socialism', *ER*, vol. 8 (1898), 229.
[17] After all, as J. A. Hobson reflected: 'Sir William Harcourt's famous saying . . . does
not seem to throw much light upon the question, or to carry us much farther than the
still more famous saying of Aristotle, that "Man is by nature made for society".' ('What
is a Socialist?', *EW*, 12.3.1898, p. 162.)
[18] Hobhouse, *Liberalism*, pp. 88–90.

the development and self-expression of the individual; on the other, to a specific socio-economic doctrine concerning self-support and independence of social actors, sometimes called an 'atomistic' concept of society. In its first usage individualism, more correctly referred to as individuality, had been glorified by mid-nineteenth-century liberalism, especially by Mill. But his liberal arch-principle, adopted from W. von Humboldt, concerning the highest and most harmonious development of man's powers[19] had, as many liberals recognized, been distorted by the Benthamite heritage, political economy and *laissez-faire*. As Dyer pointed out, 'our individualism has lost us individuality'.[20]

To talk, therefore, of a transformation from individualism *per se* to collectivism or socialism, as did many eminent scholars,[21] thereby setting a contagious intellectual fashion, does not do justice to a configuration of ideas from which both sides emerged richer and more refined. A great amount has been written about the change from an atomistic to an organic conception of society as laying the foundation for modern social politics, and the use of dichotomous concepts as Weberian 'ideal types' has no doubt great explanatory-didactic value. But it is all too common for them to serve in accounts of the period as substitutes for descriptions and analyses of processes whose essential complexity does not lend itself to such treatment. This not only evades the subtleties of individualism but ignores the fact that it was considered an indispensable part of the more socially oriented theories. It is to the merit of a few theorists of the time that they realized that liberal individualism had more to it than appeared on the surface. Hobhouse, for example, denied that a consistent theory of liberty could rest satisfied with a socio-economic system which interpreted individualism as linked to property rights.[22] This was true neither of land nor of monopolies in general. Hence the conclusion that 'a thoroughly consistent individualism can work in harmony with socialism,

---

[19] J. S. Mill, *On Liberty*, (Everyman's Library 1910; 1st edn. 1859), p. 115.

[20] Dyer, *The Evolution of Industry*, p. 262.

[21] See H. Laski, 'Leaders of Collectivist Thought', in *Ideas and Beliefs of the Victorians* (1949), p. 418; H. M. Lynd, *England in the Eighteen-Eighties* (New York, 1945), pp. 16–17, 175, 427–8; A. V. Dicey, *Lectures on the Relation Between Law and Public Opinion in England* (1905), lectures vii–ix.

[22] Hobhouse, *Liberalism*, p. 51.

and it is this partial alliance which has, in fact, laid down the lines of later Liberal finance'. And if 'individualism, when it grapples with the facts, is driven no small distance along Socialist lines',[23] then obviously talk of a dichotomy glosses over the possibility that the two can co-exist.

Similarly, the Individualist Grant Allen, Spencer's disciple, warned against opposing individualism and socialism: '... Individualism, in any true sense of the word, is only possible where all start fair.'[24] This entailed free and equal access to the common gifts and energies of nature and the common stock of raw material, which in itself was an important step in the direction of a wider comprehension of individual needs. What was common to both socialist and individualist ideals, alleged Allen, was a strong sense of the injustice and wickedness of the existing system, a hatred of inequality and a desire for a more equitable distribution of the goods of life. Even an old-fashioned liberal like J. G. Rogers, the Nonconformist, agreed that the function of the Liberal party was 'to safeguard the rights of the individual while at the same time it harmonises with them such action of a true collectivism as shall do something to mitigate evils which are the scandal of our boasted modern civilisation'.[25] And from the Idealist side came a reinforcement from Henry Jones, who held that the nature of the individual is essentially social, just as the nature of society is essentially individual. Indeed, the ultimate identity of the private and public wills to do good—a concomitant of their rationality—inevitably led to the conclusion that individualism and socialism were two aspects of the same fact.[26]

As to the distinction between collectivism and socialism, it should be useful to regard the former as a method of social organization, of concerted social action, whereas socialism denotes an ideological system—a comprehensive set of beliefs which interprets and induces political action. This would warrant the combination 'liberal collectivism' when referring to the political methods which new liberals were increasingly

[23] Ibid., p. 54.
[24] G. Allen, 'Individualism and Socialism', *CR*, vol. 55 (1889), 730, 731–2, 738.
[25] J. G. Rogers, 'Is the Liberal Party in Collapse?', *NC*, vol. 43 (1898), 151.
[26] H. Jones, *The Working Faith of the Social Reformer and Other Essays* (1910), pp. 233–4, 255.

advocating,[27] bearing in mind that in the period under discussion this distinction was in no way generally accepted and no consistency was evident in the use of the terms. Collectivism and socialism were often confused or considered identical. Even Hobhouse was not wholly alive to the distinction and saw collectivism merely as a vaguer term for socialism.[28] However, many liberals were aware of the difference. This was perhaps best put as follows, referring to Progressive achievements on the L.C.C.: 'The British workman dislikes the term Socialism owing to its past associations, but to the thing—to Collectivism in its modern form—he is far more favourably disposed than is sometimes imagined.'[29] It was S. Webb who may have set the pattern for this use of collectivism among advanced liberals, for Fabianism had anyhow divorced the term socialism from much of its ideological content. As Webb remarked: '. . . the elector or statesman, whilst strongly objecting to being called a Socialist . . . demands the addition of collectivist items to the party programme.'[30] But on this line of investigation, too, no regular pattern can be discerned. In sum, no meaningful contrast is evident between individualism and socialism or individualism and collectivism. Both sets of pseudo-antonyms were used by liberals and it is quite obvious that individualism could be compatible with certain connotations of the two other terms.

B. The Liberal Dissociation from Laissez-Faire

The contention that the end-product of the ideological development of liberalism did not do away with individualism must further be reinforced by the fact that from the very outset

[27] Cf. also Laski, op. cit., p. 419. Two points must be made here: (1) Collectivism, by implying common or concerted social action, was of course not compatible with any ideology whatsoever. There was a range of ideologies which could, or had to be, realized in conjunction with collectivist methods. This study will hope to have demonstrated that liberalism could figure on such a range as much as socialism. (2) Collectivism, too, could be an ideologically meaningful term, though not a complete system incorporating human ends.

[28] L. T. Hobhouse, *Democracy and Reaction* (1904), p. 226. Cf. also H. Sidgwick, *The Elements of Politics* (1891), p. 158, and R. Wallace, 'The Decadence of the House of Commons', *PR*, vol. 2 (1897), 425.

[29] R. Dell, 'Cleaning the Slate', *Monthly Review*, vol. 7 (1902), 62.

[30] S. Webb, 'Lord Rosebery's Escape from Houndsditch', *NC*, vol. 50 (1901), 374. This is not to claim that Fabianism also established the liberal tendency to collectivism. See below, Chapter Four, pp. 145–8.

liberals did not identify the liberal concept of individualism with *laissez-faire*.[31] To label liberalism as *laissez-faire* and thus to deem it incapable of thinking out schemes of *social* reform was mistaken or unjust. Actually, by the end of the 1880s, the *laissez-faire* credo was much more likely to be heard from Conservatives of the type of Lord Wemyss.[32] Otherwise it was mainly official Socialists who raised the image when anachronistically taunting the Liberal party. As to the political views of Herbert Spencer, they were primarily limited to the small band of people who called themselves 'The Liberty and Property Defence League',[33] and who at best were benevolently smiled upon by new liberals. Believing as they did in 'the harmonising power of a free society', this group dismissed all schemes of social reform by legislation as ignoring the natural processes of social growth.[34] It was not in their stress on personal responsibility as such, as in their denial of any other method of human improvement, that these 'administrative nihilists'[35] or 'philosophical anarchists'[36] were hopelessly out of step with the times.

The effort to dissociate liberalism and the liberal brand of individualism from *laissez-faire*[37] was attempted in a number of ways: by claiming that the latter was a general rule intended to encourage voluntarism in preference to state action under circumscribed conditions only; by insisting on its never having existed at all; or by showing that liberal principles existed independently of it. The first approach was adopted by R. B. Haldane, who interpreted the issue in the light of Jevons's utilitarian guidelines. *Laissez-faire* was to be rejected when it injured health and no other remedy was available. The term

---

[31] See A. Bullock and M. Shock (eds.), *The Liberal Tradition* (Oxford, 1956), p. xxvii.

[32] *Hansard*, 3rd Ser. CCCXLIV 1215–8, 1231–9 (19.5.1890). See also E. Dicey, 'The Plea of a Mal-Content Liberal', *FR*, vol. 38 (1885), 463–77, for the voice of the right of the Liberal party which was shortly to break with liberalism.

[33] See T. Mackay (ed.), *A Plea for Liberty* (1891).

[34] Cf. H. Spencer, *The Man Versus the State* (ed. D. MacRae, Penguin Books, 1969), pp. 134–5, 147; T. Mackay, *Methods of Social Reform* (1896), pp. 12, 311.

[35] T. H. Huxley, 'Administrative Nihilism', *FR*, vol. 10 (1871), 525–43.

[36] Anon., 'Liberalism Philosophically Considered', *WR*, vol. 132 (1889), 343.

[37] This is not the by now familiar argument that *laissez-faire* never actually existed, and that collectivist measures were already part of the British legislative and administrative tradition in the first half of the nineteenth century. Rather this is a denial that *laissez-faire* as a theory was ever part of the liberal ideology at the time.

should never have been expanded as a competitive principle concerning men as well as merchandise.[38] Elsewhere Haldane was even more explicit:

The great error which has been made, and which has led to much of the popularity of what is currently called Socialism... has been its identification with the bare fact of a departure from the principle of *laissez-faire*... The truth is, that it is not a mere departure from the principle of *laissez-faire* which sensible people mean when they object to propositions as Socialistic or economically unsound! Such departures are even recognized as essential for the promotion of real freedom between contracting parties.[39]

Departures from *laissez-faire* were especially necessary in the field of securing conditions favourable to individual morality.[40] The position was summed up in J. M. Robertson's main book on liberalism: '"Laissez-faire"... is not done with as a principle of rational limitation of State interference, but it is quite done with as a pretext for leaving uncured deadly social evils which admit of curative treatment by State action.'[41]

The second liberal approach to *laissez-faire* was the obvious concomitant to the assertions of men like Rae and Atherley-Jones about the historical nature of the English legislative process. Rae alleged that the English economists had never held the theory of *laissez-faire* because they too had supported the broader doctrine of the state's functions which 'might very properly be called the English doctrine of social politics'. Government action that increased the productive capacity of the community was 'quite consistent with the principles of men like W. von Humboldt, who contend that the best means of national prosperity is the cultivation to the utmost of the individual energy of the people...'[42] Havelock Ellis, too, took a similar stand years later when he remarked that 'the phrase *laissez-faire* is sometimes used as though it were the watchword of a party which graciously accorded a free hand to the Devil to

---

[38] R. B. Haldane, 'The Eight Hours Question', *CR*, vol. 57 (1890), 242–3. See W. S. Jevons, *The State in Relation to Labour* (1882), *passim*.

[39] R. B. Haldane, 'The Liberal Party and its Prospects', *CR*, vol. 53 (1888), 154.

[40] Ibid. Here Haldane was following Green, *Lectures on the Principles of Political Obligation*, pp. 39–40.

[41] Robertson, *The Meaning of Liberalism*, p. 64.

[42] J. Rae, 'State Socialism and Social Reform', *CR*, vol. 58 (1890), 435, 437.

do his worst'. But 'no one nowadays wants the hungry to hunger or the suffering to suffer. Indeed, in that sense there never has been any *laissez-faire* school.'[43]

The third approach took exception to the charge that *laissez-faire*, though historically existent, was an integral part of liberal theory. Not only was this untrue of the present, as Samuel retorted to Keir Hardie's accusations,[44] but—and it is reassuring to hear this from the mouth of Sidney Webb: 'The Liberal Party is in no way pledged, if indeed it ever was, to a blind adhesion to *laisser-faire*.'[45] Hobhouse, too, questioned whether the rise of practical collective measures had any direct bearing on the nature of the old liberalism and whether it occasioned the latter's demise. As he pointed out, the cleavage of opinion in the *laissez-faire*–interventionist issue cut across the ordinary divisions of party.[46] On the other hand, Hobhouse did not consider the Manchester School, and Cobden in particular, as having solely recommended *laissez-faire*. If indeed there had been an association between liberalism and *laissez-faire* at any time, it had had regrettable consequences for liberalism, because the reaction to *laissez-faire* had caused other, unrelated, virtues of liberalism to go by the board as well.[47] Cobden's principles were 'precisely the principles on which the advocates of much of what is called 'socialistic' legislation habitually rely'.[48] This denial of the existence of *laissez-faire* especially in the sphere of social legislation had also been made by Chamberlain in reference to John Bright.[49] Here were the rudiments of the continuity claim liberals were seeking to apply to their theories.

C. Practice in Theory

By the 1880s *laissez-faire* had been definitely abandoned by the liberal mainstream and socialism in its general ethical sense had

[43] H. Ellis, 'Individualism and Socialism', *CR*, vol. 101 (1912), 527.

[44] H. Samuel, 'The Independent Labour Party', *PR*, vol. 1 (1896), 258.

[45] S. Webb, 'Lord Dunraven and the Eight Hours Bill', *Speaker*, 11.1.1890. Cf. also Davis, 'The Evolutionary Trend of British Political Parties', 517–18; Anon., 'Liberalism Philosophically Considered', 343.

[46] Hobhouse, *Liberalism*, p. 49.

[47] Hobhouse, *Democracy and Reaction*, pp. 10–12.

[48] Ibid., p. 214. Cf. Rae, 'State Socialism and Social Reform', op. cit., 435.

[49] J. Chamberlain, 'The Labour Question', *NC*, vol. 32 (1892), 679.

become part of the liberal terminology as the consequence of a process by which former ideological distinctions were blunted. Reflection on the part of thoughtful and socially aware liberals had led to a breaking down of conceptual barriers. This ideological realignment did not occur, however, only on a theoretical, conceptual level. A practical development of immense importance came to the aid of progressive theorists— the growth of municipal socialism. In itself, it is difficult to attribute this growth to any of the official political ideologies. It is perhaps symbolic that Joseph Chamberlain, the great municipal reformer, bridged the political spectrum on many issues of social reform. Chamberlain claimed that he had achieved a peaceful revolution in Birmingham by legislative means, thus discounting both the doctrinaire Socialist disbelief in ameliorative legislation, and the anti-interventionists' horror of 'grandmotherly' restriction. Birmingham had set the pattern for British municipalization by acquiring control over the private monopolies of gas, water, and sewage, by providing hospitals, baths, parks, free libraries, and museums, and by enforcing standards of health and education. Chamberlain saw this municipal socialism as

the result of a wise cooperation by which the community as a whole, working through its representatives for the benefit of all its members, and recognizing the solidarity of interest which makes the welfare of the poorest a matter of importance to the richest, has faced its obligations and done much to lessen the sum of human misery, and to make the lives of all its citizens somewhat better, somewhat nobler, and somewhat happier.[50]

With his stress on popular representative local government and his acceptance of a utilitarian doctrine of state interference Chamberlain was at one with some aspects of nineteenth-century liberalism. Although those principles alone did not suffice to make him a liberal in his own time, they appealed greatly to the progressive imagination, which in this case included many Tories as well. H. W. Massingham, the renowned liberal journalist, when drawing up in 1891 a

[50] J. Chamberlain, 'Favourable Aspects of State Socialism', *North American Review*, vol. 152 (1891), 536–8.

programme of municipal services which added to the points made by Chamberlain, communal trams and trains, and the municipalization of land values, freely admitted that 'neither party could or would do such a consummately foolish thing as to turn its back on fifty years of municipal Socialism'.[51] But while many Tories might have welcomed the encouragement of local action and control, most would have been startled by the opinion that 'municipal gas and water, municipal trams, art-galleries and museums, free libraries and reading-rooms ... are important steps in the direction of Socialism'.[52] Yet this realization was slowly dawning upon liberal and Radical thinkers. Even Charles Dilke, perhaps the most radical of the Liberal front rank but one too concerned with the small details of legislation and administration to give vent to theoretical philosophical utterances, was led to a few general remarks when reflecting on the advance of municipalization. While reiterating the conviction that 'in many matters municipalities may be expected to go right even where States go wrong, because in the smaller area there is direct and immediate responsibility to a ratepaying electorate', he went on to predict that 'the Radical ideal will be the municipally-socialist State in which each community will manage its own concerns'.[53]

One aspect of the contribution of municipalization to British political thought was in paving the way for a corporate conception of a community that co-operated in public action for its own good. As Lord Rosebery expressed it: 'The age seems to be tottering now between two powers, neither of which I altogether follow, but each of which has its seductive sirens wooing the spirit of the age. The one is Socialism, and the other is Individualism...' He advocated borrowing 'from Socialism its large conception of municipal life, and from Individualism ... its spirit of self-reliance and self-respect in all practical affairs.'[54]

[51] H. W. Massingham, 'Wanted, A New Charter', *NR*, vol. 4 (1891), 255, 261, 264.
[52] W. B. Columbine, 'Social Problems', *WR*, vol. 151 (1899), 376. He saw the present achievements in municipalization and nationalization as the outposts of socialism for fifty years to come.
[53] C. W. Dilke, 'A Radical Programme', *NR*, vol. 3 (1890), Pt. II, 166–7; Pt. V, 412.
[54] Quoted in H. Dyer, 'The Future of Politics', *WR*, vol. 145 (1896), 5. See also Rosebery, 'Municipal and Social Reform', speech in London, 21.3.1894, for an adumbration 'of that new spirit which is passing from municipal into Imperial Politics'.

Or, in the words of a contributor to the *Westminster Review*: '... Socialism in its practical evolution has taken a different form altogether from that which its advocates, a quarter of a century ago, expected it to take. Municipalism is likely to be the platform around which Socialism will play its most important part in the future.'[55]

A second aspect was, according to the *Speaker*, 'that Municipal Socialism offers so valuable a mediation between the still dominant Individualism of England and the State as Universal Providence in Germany'. It was centralization, by supplanting individual energy, that constituted the real danger. 'Whatever farther steps are made towards Socialism must be taken along the road of Local Option.'[56]

Though municipalism was a move in the direction of socialism, it had also tamed socialism. It was the concrete embodiment of the socialism that most liberals condoned, and above all it was practical socialism. Practical socialism was related in liberal usage with two, not always differentiated, elements. On the one hand it was substantially distinguished from theoretical socialism through denoting what was actually attainable in view of human nature and social conditions. In Robertson's words: '"Wherever feasible", remember—the whole secret of practical Liberalism is in that modifying clause. The broad, practical differentiation between Liberalism in this sense and Socialism in anything like a precise sense lies in that principle of feasibility.'[57] On the other hand it was linked with the time-honoured method of English social reform, namely gradualism. A typical exponent of the gradualist approach was S. A. Barnett, the founder of the first University settlement in London, Toynbee Hall, who was eulogized on his death by the *Nation* as perhaps 'the most representative Liberal of his day'.[58] In a collection of essays entitled *Practicable Socialism* Barnett had written:

All real progress must be by growth; the new must be a development of the old, and not a branch added on from another root. A change which does not fit into and grow out of things that already exist is not a

---

[55] J. Armsden, 'First Principles of Social Reform', *WR*, vol. 169 (1908), 642.
[56] 'A Test for Socialism', *Speaker*, 1.4.1893.
[57] J. M. Robertson, *The Mission of Liberalism* (1908), pp. 10–11.
[58] *Nation*, 21.6.1913, p. 448.

practicable change, and such are some of the changes now advocated by socialists upon platforms.[59]

An attempt at drawing a sharp line between gradualist and non-gradualist reform was a recurring theme among liberals. The middle class in particular associated the unqualified term 'Socialist' with 'sudden and violent change, involving confiscation, disturbance of the social order, perhaps revolution'.[60] But as Robertson wrote:

...anything in the nature of revolutionary legislation...is not rationally to be apprehended. All that is conceivably workable in the proposals of British Socialists, while society remains broadly what it is, is only a further development of plans already laid down by Liberalism...The notion that any legislation going much further than this will be carried in our generation can be harboured only by those heads which cannot distinguish between ideals and programmes, between absolute conceptions and living adjustments.[61]

It must be emphatically stated that to claim that advanced liberalism eschewed 'utopian' ideals by dint of its adherence to the politically possible must not lead to the conclusion that comprehensive principles played no part in liberal thought. Here we arrive at an issue crucial to the development of the new liberalism and liberal social reform thought in particular.

2. EMERGENCE OF A LIBERAL NOTION OF COMMUNITY

A. Towards a Theory of Society

If something more than a palliative was aspired to, the practical 'socialism' adopted by liberals had not only to entail immediate state-initiated reforms but to involve a new fundamental ethical principle or viewpoint. The ethical perspective developed by advanced liberals was the guiding force and the final end of social life, essential to lasting social improvement. Underlying any concrete changes that had to be made was a need for a moral and spiritual transformation. The quest for an ethical

---

[59] S. A. Barnett, *Practicable Socialism* (1888), p. 194; also Barnett, 'The Unemployed', *FR*, vol. 54 (1893), 749.

[60] C. F. G. Masterman, 'Liberalism and Labour', *NC*, vol. 60 (1906), 709.

[61] Robertson, *The Meaning of Liberalism*, p. 140. Cf. also H. J. Darnton-Fraser, 'A Programme of Real Social Reform', *WR*, vol. 177 (1912), 118.

political system was an inseparable part of the liberal tradition without which the liberal social thought of the period is incomprehensible.[62] Socialism was but another word for that ethical viewpoint, for the idea of a just society. The new liberal aim was to establish an ethical framework to prescribe and evaluate human behaviour and, where necessary, to re-create social institutions.

The search for a general ethical conception of society was dictated to liberalism by the enormity of the social problems facing English society at the time and by the inadequate utilization of existing liberal principles; but, as we shall see, it was not forced on liberalism from the outside by rival progressive ideologies. However, on the issue of general ethical conceptions, the lines between progressive ideologies were often blurred, even though the development of such conceptions and their assimilation into the respective political theories followed different paths. Thus the new liberals would certainly have endorsed Ramsay MacDonald's description of socialism not as 'a state but a tendency, a mode of thought, a guiding idea'.[63]

It is true, of course, that most liberals interested in the 'condition of the people' were, before the turn of the century, satisfied with the achievements of municipalism, without the 'socialist point of view'. But liberal social thinkers, on the other hand, had been trying to give some kind of definite substance to Arnold Toynbee's ambitious desire 'to embrace in one grand view the human world'.[64] There began to take root within liberalism a holistic approach to the study of society at variance with the more accepted piecemeal approach which seemed to typify practical socialism. Such was also MacDonald's standpoint: 'Point of view counts for everything in politics that are constructive; programmes and labels for next to nothing'[65]—

---

[62] A major breeding ground of progressive liberalism were the Ethical Societies. They served as a fusion point of liberal, Idealist, evolutionary, and moderate socialist thought, and redirected the traditional liberal concern with morals and justice. Their membership rolls included personalities such as J. M. Robertson, J. A. Hobson, J. R. MacDonald, J. H. Muirhead, and D. G. Ritchie, to name but a few of the influential thinkers of the time. See G. Spiller, *The Ethical Movement in Great Britain* (1934), and S. K. Ratcliffe, *The Story of South Place* (1955).

[63] J. R. MacDonald, 'The Labour Party and its Policy', *IR*, vol. 8 (1906), 264.

[64] A. Toynbee, *Lectures on the Industrial Revolution of the Eighteenth Century in England* (1884), reprinted 1969, p. 255.

[65] MacDonald, 'The Labour Party and its Policy', op. cit., 265.

although new liberals would have regarded the distinction as spurious.[66] Perhaps S. Ball was more succinct when he wrote: '... a Socialist is tested by the general ideas or criteria he applies to particular reforms'.[67] But there was nothing specifically Socialistic in these formulations. Hobson, though no formal Socialist,[68] had preceded MacDonald and Ball on this question. On the one hand he expressed concern over the lack of ideals, considerations of justice or social expediency to guide politicians, now propelled mainly by public opinion based on 'small local concrete grievances' in conjunction with a growing sentiment in favour of improving the conditions of the poor. Yet this process was deceptive:

> Underneath these detailed actions, which seem in large measure the product of chance, or of the selfish or sentimental effort of some individual or party, the historian is able to trace the under-working of some large principle which furnishes the key to the real logic of events.[69]

This work of detection was the essential preliminary to the task of the social reformer.

Indeed, the great achievement of liberals such as Hobson was to supply what Barnett had termed 'a conception of society as it might be' which was 'necessary to social reform'.[70] This was in direct contrast to the old liberal attitude which was unwilling to regard human welfare as a legitimate field of concern for the community, precisely for lack of a concept of society which could link the various aspects of human existence and underscore the idea of mutual responsibility for the 'condition of the people' issue. Such liberals—as typified by J. Annand, journalist and politician—could therefore regard reforms which improved the condition of the working class as an attempt on the part of the latter to force class legislation via Parliament on the country at large. State interference in human livelihood and

[66] See below, Chapter Seven.
[67] S. Ball, 'Socialism and Individualism; A Challenge and an Eirenicon', *ER*, vol. 7 (1897), 497.
[68] Hobson, *Confessions of an Economic Heretic*, p. 29.
[69] J. A. Hobson, *Problems of Poverty* (1891), pp. 195–6.
[70] S. A. Barnett, 'Social Reform', *IR*, vol. 1 (1903), 32. See also Barnett, 'Distress in East London', *NC*, vol. 20 (1886), 678–9, where he echoed Arnold Toynbee in demanding a 'body of doctrine' to deal with the poor.

industry was pernicious because it united two fields that ought
to remain separate—the political and the economic.[71] Hobson,
however, believed that there already existed within society an
unconscious recognition of the principles justifying and directing practical socialism.[72] What was now necessary was a
transition from unconscious to conscious socialism. As L. G.
Chiozza Money, Liberal M.P. and economist, wrote:

If the Liberal Party is to live, it can only do so by consciously
continuing the collective efforts which have been increasingly exerted,
and not by one party alone, in the past forty years. The period 1865–
1900, which Professor Dicey has called the period of Collectivism, may
be termed the period of Unconscious Socialism. With the twentieth
century begins a period of Conscious Socialism.[73]

B. Ideological Continuities

In its search for guidelines, advanced liberalism moved towards
a comprehensive and conscious theory of social life which could
yet retain its specific liberal characteristics. The culmination of
this theory was in the postulation of a distinct social sphere,
analytically and empirically identifiable. Its roots could be
traced back to the instinctive gropings of progressives, which
Hobson described as follows:

When it is said that 'we are all socialists to-day', what is meant is, that
we are all engaged in the active promotion or approval of legislation
which can only be explained as a gradual unconscious recognition of
the existence of a social property in capital which it is held politic to
secure for the public use.[74]

The rudiments of the theory were common to most radicals of
the time and involved, as we shall see, an extension of the
concept of unearned increment. Liberals, however, saw this
principle as an indigenous part of the liberal tradition and
attempted consequently to demonstrate the inherent liberalism
of the social tenets deduced from it. The special place of the

[71] J. Annand, 'Liberalism, Old and New. I. The Old', *Daily News*, 11.1.1899.
[72] Hobson, *Problems of Poverty*, p. 199.
[73] L. G. Chiozza Money, 'Liberalism, Socialism, and the Master of Elibank', *IR*, vol.
11 (1906), 13.
[74] Hobson, *Problems of Poverty*, p. 199.

unearned increment in liberal thought was due to its having been adopted and expanded by J. S. Mill. It achieved vital significance as a link between liberal and socialist precepts or, rather, as a proof that socialism was an element of liberal thought.[75] Mill had analysed the taxation of the unearned increment in relation to rent and had stated: 'it would merely be applying an accession of wealth, created by circumstances, to the benefit of society'.[76]

For a long time the land question was seen to be the main, if not the only, arena of social reform. It was only slowly realized that the elimination of the land problem would neither dispense with other iniquities nor provide enough funds for further social reforms. As Hobson explained, the insistence on free and equal access to the land as a 'natural right' was an Individualist doctrine and, moreover, one that did not appreciate the social origins of the value of capital as well as land. But once the idea of rent as a social product—as popularized by Henry George— was substituted for Mill's vaguer 'general circumstances of society', such an appreciation was an inevitable and logical outcome.[77] The concept of unearned increment thus became a major mechanism in the development of a new concept of society and of social relations. The leading liberal thinkers coped with the new pressures on their existing terminology by extending the range of unearned increment to apply to a refined concept of wealth and property in general. Robertson had already made a move in that direction when he called for discrimination between all earned and unearned incomes. He then added: 'Merely to tax objects of property, however, would be to miss entirely the just principles of taxation. The measure must be, not the nature of the objects individually possessed, but

[75] As the *Speaker* observed about unearned increments: 'The doctrine was preached with great vigour by Mr. Chamberlain in 1885, and was defended at that time by Mr. Morley, who showed, in some telling letters to the *Times*, that it had the authoritative sanction of John Stuart Mill ... Upon this question the disciples of Henry George make common cause with the disciples of Richard Cobden; at this point the Liberal tradition and the Socialist movement converge.' ('Towards a Social Policy, VII', 3.12.1904.) See also C. W. Dilke, 'John Stuart Mill 1869–1873', *Cosmopolis*, vol. 5 (1897), 630.

[76] J. S. Mill, *Principles of Political Economy*, ed. by D. Winch (Penguin Books, 1970), p. 169.

[77] J. A. Hobson, 'The Influence of Henry George in England', *FR*, vol. 62 (1897), 842.

individual *command of wealth*...'[78] And Hobson grasped the essence of the matter: '... the community refuses to sanction any absolute property on the part of any of its members, recognizing that a large portion of the value of each individual's work is due, not to his solitary efforts, but to the assistance lent by the community.' The community, by educating the individual in the skill which he puts in his work, by allowing him to use parts of the material universe, by protecting him, and by providing a market of exchange,

has given a social value to his product which cannot be attributed to his individual efforts. In recognition of the co-operation of society in all production of wealth, the community claims the right to impose such conditions upon the individual as may secure for it a share in that social value it has by its presence and activity assisted to create.[79]

Liberal thought was thus taking a new direction on the issue of the public and the private spheres. The traditional liberal struggle against monopoly and privilege was harnessed to a new social purpose. This general process of investing traditional liberal concepts with new meaning ensured a smooth transition from the 'old' to the 'new' liberalism. It significantly enhanced the power of liberal ideas to apply to current social problems while retaining their original ideological impact. The first step in this process was when, as Hobhouse demonstrated, people began to read the genesis of socialist principles into the well-established tenet of free trade. Rae, indeed, had already noted a 'germ of socialism' in *laissez-faire*, hinging upon what he regarded as the false assumption of the natural equality of the competitors.[80] Reversing Rae's values, Hobhouse came to the conclusion that such equality, though not natural, was an important ethical goal. Monopolies had been attacked for hindering free competition and for distorting the haloed freedom of contract.[81] They restricted freedom of action by

---

[78] J. M. Robertson, *Modern Humanists* (1891), pp. 267–8.
[79] Hobson, *Problems of Poverty*, p. 198. Cf. Hobhouse, *Democracy and Reaction*, pp. 230–1.
[80] Rae, *Contemporary Socialism*, p. 391.
[81] This point had already been made by T. H. Green in relation to the land question. He asked for legal sanction to be withheld from settlements which interfered with the distribution and improvement of land, because this would 'render English land on the whole a much more marketable commodity than it is at present... It would, therefore, have the support of those Liberals who are most jealous of any interference with freedom

imposing inequalities detrimental to such freedom. From this point it required no great intellectual effort to advance to an attack on the whole myth of freedom of contract itself. Legislation to counter the power of monopolies, maintained Hobhouse, was socialistic legislation of the same type as the factory laws, being 'directed to the redressing of inequality in bargaining'. And he elaborated: 'Rightly understood... this kind of socialistic legislation appears not as an infringement of the two distinctive ideals of the older Liberalism, "Liberty and Equality". It appears rather as a necessary means to their fulfilment'.[82] Another major step in this process of ideological adaptation was to show that society had a right and a duty to administer or alternatively to tax heavily monopolies in general, because, due to the help and acquiescence of society: 'Whenever monopoly or restriction of markets enables a trade or profession, or any of its members, to secure a rate of profit or other income beyond what would prevail under free competition, an income exists which is rightly regarded as belonging to society...'[83] The advocacy of taxation instead of nationalization of monopolies was in itself an endorsement of a society based on private property, though one in which individuals relinquished all claims to income unnecessary to their effective functioning as members of society, such surplus income being regarded as social property. And here came a further consolidation of the idea of community, for was not property an attribute of personality? An interesting extension of current notions of property was effected by Hobson in justifying this line of thought. Existing theories, such as those of Hegel and of Green, had been grounded on the assumption that individual property was required for self-realization, for externalization and objectivization of self.[84] Hobson used the same argument with respect to the community—conceived of as an 'individual' with moral ends of its own:

of contract'. (*Liberal Legislation and Freedom of Contract* (Oxford, 1881), p. 16.) See also A. Hoare, 'Liberalism in the Twentieth Century', *World's Work*, vol. 1 (1902), 85; J. Rae, 'State Socialism and Popular Right', *CR*, vol. 58 (1890), 883.

[82] Hobhouse, *Democracy and Reaction*, pp. 214, 217; *Liberalism*, p. 54.

[83] J. A. Hobson, 'The Taxation of Monopolies', *IR*, vol. 9 (1906), 25. Cf. Hobson, 'Is Socialism Plunder?', *Nation*, 19.10.1907.

[84] *Hegel's Philosophy of Right*, translated with notes by T. M. Knox (Oxford, 1962), paras. 41–51; Green, *Lectures on the Principles of Political Obligation*, paras. 213–14, 217.

Just as it is essential to the progress of the moral life of the individual that he shall have some 'property', some material embodiment of his individual activity which he may use for the realisation of his rational ends in life, so the moral life of the community requires public property and public industry for its self-realisation, and the fuller the life the larger the sphere of these external activities.[85]

Because, as Hobson was aware, 'every defence of the principle of individual property is likewise a plea for social property',[86] it was part of the inner logic of an individualist, capitalist society to arrive at this radical 'progressive-socialist' conclusion. The significance of this perception was considerable, inasmuch as it postulated a separate social entity or personality whose existence was externally and concretely embodied in tangible goods of its own.[87] It was this ethical argument, in conjunction with the biological theories surveyed in the next chapter, that facilitated the incorporation of a definite and comprehensible concept of community into liberal thought.

It is, however, important to note that unlike some socialist notions of property, liberals were at pains to emphasize that not all value is social. As Hobhouse remarked:

The ground problem in economics is not to destroy property, but to restore the social conception of property to its right place under conditions suitable to modern needs. This is not to be done by crude measures of redistribution, such as those of which we hear in ancient history. It is to be done by distinguishing the social from the individual factors in wealth...[88]

This distinction was of great moment, for it defined the watershed between social-liberalism and, say, continental evolutionary Socialism. Here lay the substantial difference between practicable and theoretical socialism, as Hobson saw it:

---

[85] J. A. Hobson, 'The Ethics of Industrialism', in S. Coit (ed.), *Ethical Democracy: Essays in Social Dynamics* (1900), p. 104. Cf. also L. T. Hobhouse, 'The Historical Evolution of Property, in Fact and in Idea', in C. Gore (ed.), *Property, Its Duties and Rights* (1913), p. 31: '... if private property is of value ... to the fulfilment of personality, common property is equally of value for the expression and the development of social life.'

[86] Hobson, *The Social Problem*, p. 150.

[87] See Chapter Three, pp. 105–8 on the general will.

[88] Hobhouse, *Liberalism*, p. 98.

[Practicable Socialism] aims primarily not to abolish the competitive system, to socialise all instruments of production, distribution, and exchange, and to convert all workers into public employees—but rather to supply all workers at cost price with all the economic conditions requisite to the education and employment of their personal powers for their personal advantage and enjoyment.[89]

This proposed course was probably as radical as one could get within the limits of the existing system. Here again, a very generous—indeed maximalist—definition of equality of opportunity was a mechanism by which an accepted term was infused with new substance. As Hobson observed,[90] there was a continual shifting of the area and nature of the opportunities which had to be equalized as advanced liberals acquired a deeper understanding of human needs.

Apart from the convergence between liberalism and socialism by means of the unearned increment and monopoly issues, a more general link was perceived between the two. Hobhouse expressed this well when he declared: 'The ideas of Socialism, when translated into practical terms, coincide with the ideas to which Liberals are led when they seek to apply their principles of Liberty, Equality and the Common Good to the industrial life of our time.'[91] After all, 'Amid all differences and conflicts one idea is common to the modern democratic movement, whether it takes the shape of revolution or reform, of Liberalism or Socialism. The political order must conform to the ethical ideal of what is just.'[92] In effect, Hobhouse was maintaining that one could not demand of liberal thought more than to uphold the morality of the age.[93] Mid-nineteenth-century liberalism might have seemed to be indifferent to questions of social justice, but those had not been the questions of the day. The moment the social problem came to the fore, liberal principles moved by their own logic into the vacuum thus formed and extended the field to which they applied.[94]

---

[89] J. A. Hobson, *The Crisis of Liberalism: New Issues of Democracy* (1909), pp. 172–3.
[90] Ibid., p. 93. See below, Chapter Four, pp. 149–50 for the radical contents of the term.
[91] L. T. Hobhouse, 'The Prospects of Liberalism', *CR*, vol. 93 (1908), 353.
[92] Hobhouse, *Democracy and Reaction*, p. 118.
[93] Cf. R. Rea, *Social Reform Versus Socialism* (1912), p. 10.
[94] Hobson, in a leader on Hobhouse's *Democracy and Reaction*, commented on this phenomenon: 'Cobden stood for freedom of opportunities as far as his outlook on the

Comparatively few observers[95] realised the underlying principle, the vivid conception of what is actually required by the common good as against the dominant interest, which connected the old and new in spirit and intention.[96]

The continuity and progress of liberal thought were, according to Hobhouse, an aspect of the emergence of the great religious and ethical systems which all aimed at a rational guidance of life towards its supreme end. This end, both of public and of private ethics, was 'the development of human faculty in orderly co-operation'.[97] Here was another avenue along which liberal principles moved towards a new concept of society: the theory of the ethical progress of humanity. It adumbrated a process by which

there arises by degrees the ideal of collective humanity, self-determining in its progress, as the supreme object of human activity, and the final standard by which the laws of conduct should be judged. The establishment of such an ideal, to which as a fact the historical development of the moral consciousness points, is the goal to which the mind, in its effort to master the conditions of existence, necessarily strives...[98]

Social reform became the expression of the central ethico-political maxims of Western civilization when applied to the social structure. The spirit of progress, asserted Hobhouse, was impelled by the pressure of events to attack existing social institutions and to ensure, by changing the conditions of social life, development towards the objective of collective rather than

circumstances of the time carried; we, with wider outlook on new circumstances, can express the inner continuity of Liberalism in larger measures of constructive policy.' (*MG*, 28.11.1904.)

[95] The exception was in Hobhouse's opinion T. H. Green. Hobhouse quoted from Green's *Liberal Legislation* a passage (pp. 6–7) which included the following: 'The passion for improving mankind, in its ultimate object, does not vary. But the immediate object of reformers, and the forms of persuasion by which they seek to advance them, vary much in different generations. To a hasty observer they might even seem contradictory... Only those who will think a little longer about it can discern the same old cause of social good against class interests, for which, under altered names, Liberals are fighting now as they were fifty years ago.' But of course Green would not have gone so far as to accept socialism as one of the altered names of liberalism.

[96] Hobhouse, *Democracy and Reaction*, p. 11.

[97] Ibid., pp. 107, 51–2.

[98] Ibid., p. 108. Hobhouse's treatment of this subject is examined in greater detail on pp. 66–70 and in Chapter Three, pp. 85–7.

individual humanity.[99] Through the ethical conception of the community as an organization of rationally co-operating individuals, the liberal belief in unimpeded development of individual faculty was complemented by a collectivism expressing mutual responsibility and social solidarity.

Similar views to those held by Hobhouse on the emergence of a social-liberalism could be found among other advanced progressives. Chiozza Money claimed of collectivism that it was

chiefly introduced by men who, esteeming themselves individualists, and calling themselves variously Liberals, Radicals, Conservatives, Unionists, found by practical experience that man is a social animal, and that, wherever two or three men are gathered together for mutual help, Socialism is in the midst of them. A crusade against Socialism would be a crusade against the better part of human nature...[100]

Indeed, no less a figure than Sidney Webb wrote:

...much of what is claimed as the progress of socialism might be equally well described as a merely empirical development from the principles of Canning, Peel, Bentham, and Gladstone... opinions will differ... as to the extent to which the vociferous efforts of the organised and avowed socialists are a cause, or merely an effect, of the general movement of thought.[101]

How Webb reconciled this statement with the rationale of the ostensibly successful Fabian policy of permeation is not clear.

The connection between socialist tendencies and the liberal tradition was seen to be greatly strengthened through the example of the high priest of liberalism, Mill. The fact that Mill gave utterance in his later years to views he regarded as socialistic was, one is tempted to say, a stroke of luck for those trying to make a case for liberal continuity. In his 'Chapters on Socialism', published posthumously in 1879, ten years after they had been written, Mill had indicted society for failing to implement the ideal of distributive justice, had called for the accommodation of social institutions to the altered state of

---

[99] Ibid., pp. 116–17.

[100] C. Money, 'Liberalism, Socialism, and the Master of Elibank', op. cit. 10. Cf. also R. G. Davis, 'Individualism and Socialism, and Liberty', *WR*, vol. 178 (1912), 144, 150–1.

[101] S. Webb, 'Modern Social Movements' in *The Cambridge Modern History of the World*, XII (Cambridge, 1910), p. 760.

human society and had concluded that the various schemes for managing the productive resources of the country by public instead of private agency had a case for a trial.[102] Progressives had further fastened upon the quotations from his writings that eventually became famous through repetition—the first preferring Communism to society's present injustices,[103] the second explaining his conception of socialism as a combination of individual liberty, common ownership, and equal participation in the benefits of combined labour.[104]

Hobhouse called this exposition 'the best summary statement of Liberal Socialism that we possess'.[105] Chiozza Money cited it as an example of aspiration to a socialist ideal.[106] Hobson, in an article commemorating the centenary of Mill's birth, remarked on Mill's transformation from theoretic Individualist to socialist as a result of his awareness of the need for social reconstruction. As Hobson saw it, Mill's '"Socialism" and the accompanying political disillusionment of his later years were the inevitable product of the thought of a new age which had left philosophic radicalism a generation behind it'.[107] Even Ball, whose moderate Socialism was still outside the sphere of liberalism, stated: 'As regards my own position in relation to Socialism, I am content to be a follower of Mill, from whom I learned my first lessons in Socialism as well as in Liberalism.'[108]

A further bond between liberalism and socialism was forged via the mediating factor of Christianity: '[Socialism] presents the sensitive modern man with the idea of pity, on which his religion is founded...', wrote the *Nation*.[109] And Dilke remarked that 'there is no doubt floating in the air a great deal of that kind of Socialism which Prince Bismarck has excellently defined as "practical Christianity"'.[110] The chief organization embodying this bond was the Christian Social Union, most of whose members were prominent liberals. Their journal *The*

[102] J. S. Mill, 'Chapters on Socialism', *FR*, vol. 25 (1879), 226, 220, 525.
[103] Mill, *Principles of Political Economy*, p. 358.
[104] J. S. Mill, *Autobiography* (O.U.P., 1924), p. 196.
[105] Hobhouse, *Liberalism*, p. 62.
[106] C. Money, 'Liberalism, Socialism, and the Master of Elibank', op. cit. 14.
[107] J. A. Hobson, 'John Stuart Mill', *Speaker*, 26.5.1906.
[108] Ball, 'Individualism and Socialism', 234–5.
[109] 'Attractiveness in Politics', *Nation*, 3.8.1907.
[110] Dilke, 'A Radical Programme', op. cit., 13–14, 159.

Commonwealth, edited by H. Scott Holland—a self-styled liberal[111]—with the assistance of C. F. G. Masterman, the author, journalist, Liberal M.P., and practising reformer, was a mouthpiece of progressive liberal opinions.

All this is not to maintain that liberals invariably regarded liberalism and socialism as positioned on a continuum on which movement from one pole to the other was inevitable. A small number of liberal intellectuals perceived it thus and directed their efforts to showing the light to their fellow liberals. Other progressive liberals saw it as an external change which liberalism was now undergoing for diverse reasons. But the mere fact that it was they, not only self-proclaimed 'official' Socialists, who urged liberals to adopt what they saw as new ideas, was in itself significant. For by remaining at the same time steadfast liberals they proved in practice the logical compatibility of liberalism and socialism. The point to be made is not that liberalism was uninfluenced by Socialist theories external to it, but that such influence was not essential to the rise of social-liberalism. At the very most, as one commentator on party politics asserted: '... not the least conspicuous achievement of Socialism is that it has to a great extent succeeded in infusing its spirit into the Liberal party and educated that party to a just appreciation of their own principles.'[112]

Of considerable importance was the illumination the *Speaker* gave to the subject. Already in 1890 it stated categorically: 'We must assimilate Socialism; if "Liberal" is not to become a mere shibboleth ... we must take from Socialism what is good and reject what is bad or doubtful.' But then it went on, in contrast to many other liberals, to list specifically what it understood as the essence of socialism:[113] democracy at work, moved by a profound dissatisfaction with the existing distribution of wealth and a keen sense of inequalities, 'bent upon turning its power into hard cash—things useful, solid, and good to enjoy: into short hours, high wages, and light taxes'.[114] Not only most Socialists proper, but Idealists and ethically con-

[111] Book review by H. S. Holland, *Commonwealth*, vol. 11 (1906), 91.
[112] J. G. Godard, 'The Liberal Débâcle', *WR*, 158 (1902), 603.
[113] This was always to be differentiated from dogmatic Socialism, considered patently un-English by the *Speaker* ('Co-operation and Social Progress', 27.5.1893).
[114] 'The Socialism of Non-Socialists', *Speaker*, 10.5.1890.

scious liberals would have abhorred such a materialistic definition. But in its way this idea of a good society illustrated the integration of the new liberalism into the mental climate of the nineteenth century. Together with a continuing accentuation of the Victorian faith in the production of wealth as the key to the nation's prosperity, and a concept of man as motivated by tangible interests, there was joined a social policy which in its details and in its Millian belief in redistribution offered what the *Speaker* called a 'Socialism of Non-Socialists'. These views voiced the thoughts of many perplexed liberals who saw the problem as one of adjustment of old principles to an extent which amounted to their substantial modification. Not all delved deep enough into the essence of liberal principles to find the connecting threads. But even if, for the sake of argument only, notions of social justice and social action were foreign to the body of liberal thought, the vital question would yet remain—how would liberals absorb them into their own beliefs and how would they re-emerge after being processed by the liberal mentality?

3. THE ROLE OF THE STATE: LIBERTY AND WELFARE

A. *A Clarification of Ends*

In 1903—by which time the ethical element in social reform was more lucidly comprehended—an attempted answer to the above question was proffered in an editorial in the liberal social-reformist *Independent Review*:[115]

The future lies with those who can elicit and apply to actual life what is fruitful in the new ideas, and can combine it with those elements in our past inheritance that are still living and productive of good; who can, as occasion calls, determine the limits within which the community may interfere with advantage; who can discern the directions in which it may be to the interest of all for the corporate action of State or municipality to replace private initiative; and who can, at the same time, both safeguard and extend each man's full freedom of action where it does not clash with the common welfare, and can ensure that

---

[115] On its editorial council were C. F. G. Masterman, G. M. Trevelyan, F. W. Hirst, and G. Lowes Dickinson. It appeared from 1903 to 1907 and was then transformed into the *Albany Review* which appeared for a further year under the editorship of C. R. Buxton.

individual enterprise is neither thwarted nor impaired, but merely guided into those channels in which it can produce its best results.[116]

Here, then, was the central liberal preoccupation, then as now: not only, as it sometimes is put, to resolve in theory and practice the constant tension between individual and social needs, but to reconcile the two prime human ends, freedom and welfare. To regard nineteenth-century England, from the ideological viewpoint, merely as the arena in which the idea of freedom unfolded, as has often been the case, is insufficient.[117] Nor is the ideological flavour of the era caught by outlining a transition from 'negative' to 'positive' liberty.[118] If the spirit of the age has to be captured, it seems more useful to do so by establishing the two ideals of liberty and welfare as being simultaneously predominant in progressive English thought. From a liberal angle, the ideological history of the nineteenth century should be depicted as a constant encroachment of the idea of welfare (material and other) on the idea of freedom from intervention, during which process both ideas became cognizant of each other to the extent of incorporating mutual elements as necessary components.

As has already been noted in the previous chapter, the utilitarian creed had aimed at the attainment of happiness rather than liberty.[119] This could, as with Jevons, imply a principle that no true liberal could wholeheartedly endorse: 'The liberty of the subject is only the means towards an end; it is not itself the end; hence, when it fails to produce the desired end, it may be set aside, and other means employed.'[120] But the other side of the coin was presented by the *Speaker*. True, it agreed, general opinion was very much nearer the socialist than the Individualist ideal on the question—what may the state do? But

---

[116] Editorial, 'A Plea for a Programme', *IR*, vol. 1 (1903), 4.

[117] Cf. G. Watson, *The English Ideology. Studies in the Language of Victorian Politics* (1973).

[118] A contention made for example in G. de Ruggiero, *The History of European Liberalism*, pp. 350–7; Laski, 'The Leaders of Collectivist Thought', op. cit., p. 418.

[119] Though happiness and welfare are by no means identical, the link is an obvious one inasmuch as both refer to a state of well-being. Bentham himself used 'happiness' loosely (*An Introduction to the Principles of Morals and Legislation*, ed. with an introduction by Wilfred Harrison (Oxford, 1948), p. 126) to include terms such as 'benefit' and 'good', the latter often synonymous with welfare.

[120] Jevons, op. cit., pp. 12, 13.

it was up to the utilitarian method to fix the point beyond which individual character and energy would be endangered.[121]

The utilitarian influence helped liberals realize that, though liberty could not be set aside, neither could it be regarded as a sole and exclusive end. That manifesto of liberty itself, Mill's famous essay, clearly pointed to an appreciation of liberty as a means to 'pursuing our own good in our own way', to 'the mental well-being of mankind'.[122] But liberty was an essential means. Happiness according to Mill was composed of many parts, one of the principal ones being the free development of individuality. Hence liberty was desired as part of happiness[123] and was consequently a component of the end as well as a means to it. While Mill transcended the implications of pure utilitarianism by insisting on the indispensability of liberty, liberty was analytically separated from happiness or welfare, a separation which, as the emergence of English social policy demonstrates, had historical roots as well. The possibilities incumbent in such an analysis were ignored by those successors to Mill who saw the way to human happiness through removing hindrances to liberty alone, rather than through removing hindrances to welfare as well. It was Spencer who grasped the difference precisely, though he criticized it as a dangerous confusion: '. . . it has happened that popular good has come to be sought by Liberals, not as an end to be indirectly gained by relaxations of restraints, but as the end to be directly gained.'[124] But Spencer would not admit that welfare could be achieved simultaneously by both methods, and that neither need be detrimental to individual liberty.

If both liberty and welfare were acknowledged human ends, the agent which secured the first might be set to achieve the second. The main issue round which the practical question of liberty revolved, namely state intervention, could be extended to the less pejorative state 'activity'. An activist state bent on implementing ethical conceptions of welfare was no novel thing, as Rae claimed when explaining his 'English doctrine of

---

[121] 'A Test for Socialism', *Speaker*, 1.4.1893.
[122] Mill, *On Liberty*, pp. 74–5, 111.
[123] J. S. Mill, *Utilitarianism* (1910 edn.), p. 35; *On Liberty*, p. 115. See also Ritchie, *The Principles of State Interference*, pp. 87 ff., and A. Ryan, *J. S. Mill*, (1974), p. 133.
[124] Spencer, *The Man Versus the State*, p. 70.

social politics'. The task of the state had all along been 'to promote the mental and moral elevation of the people; the chief end of Government being to establish not liberty alone, but every other necessary security for rational progress.'[125] This meant securing

for every man as effectively as it can those essentials of all rational and humane living which are really every man's right, because without them he would be something less than man, his manhood would be wanting, maimed, mutilated, deformed, incapable of fulfilling the ends of its being.[126]

B. *Green's Idealism Eclipsed*

The search for new theories or formulae became a main concern of liberal thought in its attempt to fill the vacuum caused by the demise of the minimalist theory of the state, while avoiding the pitfalls of the maximalist state. Contrary, however, to some scholarly opinions,[127] it was not T. H. Green who pioneered a new liberal conception of state action, as the following reflections on Green's political thought should clarify.

It has already been maintained in the previous chapter that the philosophical school of Idealism was not an essential link in the transformation of liberal thought and that its influence lay in supplying a motivation to social service. On the general level neo-Hegelian thought was anathema to most Englishmen, who were at the time not only hostile to abstract conceptual systems but were growing increasingly suspicious of anything with German origins. Hobhouse himself, though a pupil of Green's, reinforced those fears in his much quoted remark:

---

[125] Rae, 'State Socialism and Social Reform', 436.

[126] Ibid., 438.

[127] See e.g. A. B. Ulam, *Philosophical Foundations of English Socialism* (Harvard U.P., 1951), pp. 28, 38–40; D. Thomson (ed.), *Political Ideas* (Penguin Books, 1969), pp. 198–9; E. M. Burns, *Ideas in Conflict* (1963), p. 251; C. Brinton, *English Political Thought in the 19th Century* (Harper Torchbooks, New York, 1962), pp. 300–1. This point is corroborated by Richter: 'When Green spoke of "positive freedom" he did not commit himself to any use of state power beyond that in fact advocated by Gladstone and Bright. Unfortunately some historians of political theory have stumbled into the trap set by Dicey so long ago: they have called Green a "collectivist", implying by that term, the advocacy of extensive governmental action, or a presumption in favour of action by the community as a whole to achieve goods regarded as essential to its members.' (M. Richter, *The Politics of Conscience: T. H. Green and his Age*, pp. 341–2.)

For thirty years and more English thought has been subject... to powerful influences from abroad. The Rhine has flowed into the Thames... known locally as the Isis, and from the Isis the stream of German idealism has been diffused over the academical world of Great Britain.

And though the school of Green—owing to its ethical conclusions—would have been absolved from the charge, Hobhouse alleged that 'in the main, the idealistic movement has swelled the current of retrogression'.[128] In fact, his accusation that Idealist thought was on a level unintelligible to 'the humble, prosaic inductions and deductions of the plain man' applied to all varieties of Idealist thinking, Green included.[129] Outside a very small circle, the thought and word patterns of Idealist logic and analysis were completely alien to modes of expression of British intellectuals and in particular to most intellectuals active in reformulating liberal thought. Even Hobson, who had an important role to play *vis-à-vis* Idealism, 'dismissed the dialectical method as a frivolous pedantry'.[130]

As to Green in particular, he had no doubt a significant contribution to make by way of his concept of 'positive liberty', which became a fashionable watch-word of the new liberal credo. But it has not usually been realized that Green's political ideas and his practical understanding of the methods of safeguarding positive liberty were firmly rooted in the liberalism of his day and in no way transcended it. In other words, Idealist precepts when applied to political practice were not much different from current ideas on the moral function of the state, and can in no way be singled out as harbingers of a new liberalism. Quite apart from the collectivism espoused by advanced liberals which was the function of a new concept of society owing little to Idealism, the securing of powers for men to do or enjoy something worth doing or enjoying[131] was not basically different from what Rae, who cannot be suspected of affinity with Idealism, had to say, or from Mill's treatment of individuality and happiness.[132]

[128] L. T. Hobhouse, 'The Intellectual Reaction', *Speaker*, 8.2.1902.
[129] See e.g. L. T. Hobhouse, *The Metaphysical Theory of the State* (1918), pp. 24, 122 for Hobhouse's reservations concerning Green.
[130] Brailsford, *The Life-Work of J. A. Hobson* (1948), p. 6.
[131] Green, *Liberal Legislation and Freedom of Contract*, pp. 9–10.
[132] Cf. K. R. Hoover, 'Liberalism and the Idealist Philosophy of Thomas Hill Green', *Western Political Quarterly*, vol. 26 (1973), 560, n. 27.

The two points that have always appeared central to Green's transformation of liberal thought are the notion of the common good and the concept of the removal of hindrances to the power of individuals to contribute to the common good. An examination of both concepts establishes that in actual fact they were far removed from advanced liberal theory. True, the common good seemed to posit a conception of community based on interest in other persons as ends in themselves, and on the well-being of others as part of the well-being of each.[133] But Green did not really anchor the common good in concrete social behaviour or express it in acts of social legislation. As Plamenatz has shown, the common good was in fact the promotion of the self-perfection of the members of the community. As this is consequent to a state of mind and as Green denied the existence of a will beyond the individual wills of the members of a society,[134] one cannot talk of a common good in a sense that significantly differs from the traditional liberal-utilitarian concern with general as against sectional interests.[135] Green did not distinguish between co-operation towards common but private ends and the pursuance of a common good.[136] At the most he postulated a harmony between individual and society on the basis of reason—a moral harmony in itself acceptable to new liberals, but lacking the scientific and 'empirical' backing they later gave it. This fell short of the movement in liberal theory to conceive of a social entity on which important aspects of individual life are predominantly, if not entirely, dependent. As Richter has remarked: 'Green as a political theorist was unusually explicit in limiting real personality to individual men, while he denied it to their nationality, humanity or any other abstraction.'[137] But it was precisely from such supra-

---

[133] T. H. Green, *Prolegomena to Ethics* (Oxford, 1924 edn.), paras. 199–201.

[134] T. H. Green, 'On the Different Senses of "Freedom" as Applied to Will and to the Moral Progress of Man' in *Lectures on the Principles of Political Obligation*, pp. 10, 14; *Prolegomena to Ethics*, paras. 182–4.

[135] See quotation from Green's *Liberal Legislation and Freedom of Contract*, in n. 95 to p. 48 above.

[136] J. P. Plamenatz, *Consent, Freedom and Political Obligation* (2nd ed., Oxford, 1968), pp. 67, 72, 81. See also Richter, op. cit., p. 255.

[137] Richter, op. cit., p. 207. Cf. Hoover, 'Liberalism and the Idealist Philosophy of Thomas Hill Green', op. cit., 562, 564, and J. Rodman, 'What is Living and What is Dead in the Political Philosophy of T. H. Green', *Western Political Quarterly*, vol. 26 (1973), 576, n. 30.

individual notions—be they abstractions or not—that the new liberalism derived its new concepts of society.

As to the role Green accorded to the state: the progressiveness of the idea of 'removal of obstacles'[138]—while theoretically indefinitely expandable—must hinge upon the question, hindrances to what? Here again Green turns out to be a traditionalist, both in theory and in the practical examples he gave. He clearly was thinking in terms that advanced liberals would have defined as Individualistic. State action was to be employed to remove hindrances to the development of individual character, in the sense of an independent, self-respecting, responsible, self-helping individual,[139] and this was linked to an appreciation of moral actions as necessarily spontaneous, an appreciation that negated what Green termed 'paternal government'.[140] In the actual social reforms he advocated, the emphasis was on 'old liberal' measures such as greater access to land and temperance reform,[141] not in themselves necessitating radical state intervention or collectivism.

Ritchie, though also an Idealist, was much more of a key figure in the adaptation of liberal thought. Together with Green he agreed that morality could not be commanded by law. He also reiterated Green's opinion that the state should maintain conditions to enable members to exercise their faculties freely. But he went beyond Green in the importance he attributed to the state as reformer of human minds. Whereas Green had warned that 'to attempt a restraining law in advance of the social sentiment necessary to give real effect to it, is always a mistake',[142] Ritchie alleged that laws 'may produce those opinions and sentiments which go to the furtherance of morality'.[143] Indeed, among the Idealists it was Ritchie, not Green, who assisted most in formulating a new liberal theory of the state—and this by departing from the English Idealist tradition which, in the case of Bosanquet even more than of Green, restricted the role of the state. Not only did Ritchie

[138] Green, *Lectures on the Principles of Political Obligation*, para. 209.
[139] Cf. Richter, op. cit., p. 296. For a discussion on the changing role of 'character' in advanced liberal thought, see below, Chapter Five.
[140] Green, *Lectures on the Principles of Political Obligation*, paras. 18, 209.
[141] Ibid., paras. 228–32; *Liberal Legislation and Freedom of Contract*, pp. 15–22.
[142] Green, *Liberal Legislation and Freedom of Contract*, p. 20.
[143] D. G. Ritchie, *The Moral Function of the State* (1887), p. 8.

reharness imaginatively the organic analogy to cope with the
need for a new liberal concept of society, as shall be shown in the
next chapter, but he combined a utilitarian approach to state
action with a belief in the moral function of the state far beyond
that which most Individualists would have permitted. This he
accomplished by altering the Benthamite formula into 'the
vaguer but less misleading one: "Will [state action] tend to the
greater well-being, physical, intellectual, moral, of mankind, or
at least of that portion of mankind which we can practically
take into account?"'[144] There was, he emphasized, no evil in
compulsion and interference *per se*.[145]

As the complex nature of the social problem was revealed, the
hindrances to be overcome increased in number and the
challenges to the state multiplied. Hobson observed that it was
not clear 'that the limitation implied by the restricted function
of "hindering hindrances" really negates any of the positive
good works which the most advanced State Socialists require
from the State'. Such a limitation was, in Hobson's opinion, a
typical weakness of all social theories. It was

the show of a distinction which, in practice, has to yield place to some
quite fluid consideration of general utility. It was the same with
Professor Green's statement; when he sought to apply his principles to
any concrete case of conduct, the utilitarianism which he had
repudiated returned to do the work.[146]

The question of state action was not, however, only that of
continuously removing newly discovered hindrances to individual development. The new liberalism would have accepted
the guidelines Brougham Villiers offered to liberals in 1904, in a
book hailed by the *Westminster Review* as 'one of the most
inspiring political manifestoes we have seen for many years'.[147]
He saw the work of the state in removing hindrances to a public
spirit—'a thing organic and living'. He denied the existence of
a boundary line 'between the so-called "spheres" of private and

[144] Ritchie, *The Principles of State Interference*, p. 107.
[145] Ritchie, *The Moral Function of the State*, p. 9.
[146] J. A. Hobson, 'The Philosophy of the State', *EW*, 1.9.1900 (Review of Bosanquet's *The Philosophical Theory of the State*).
[147] Book Review, *WR*, vol. 162 (1904), 580.

public enterprise'. Public spirit and public enterprise were
mutually interdependent as soul and body of the collective
life—the second was the external manifestation of the first.[148]
Collective enthusiasm was created by removing hindrances to
expressions of collective life rather than individual perfection.
Villiers arrived at the conclusion not as a disciple of Idealism,
but as an ethical evolutionist. His advocacy of state socialism
and collectivism was due to a much more social concept of
personality than Green had entertained.

C. Suspicion of the State

The tension between the idea of an individual anchored in a
social entity and the concept of an individual will did not cease
to perplex liberals. This philosophical inconclusiveness often
coincided with deep-rooted liberal misgivings about the power
of the state which ran parallel to an awareness of its poten-
tialities. Indeed, a certain suspicion of the state was common to
many liberals. They were all of course averse to revolutionary
socialism, and its utilization of the state, as being contrary to
human nature. But a number of liberals voiced doubts as to the
desirability of any form of state socialism. Rae based his whole
argument on the distinction between 'the modern German
theory of State Socialism' and the English theory by which 'the
State, though not Socialist, is very frankly social reformer'. The
danger of state socialism appeared to arise precisely when
departures occurred from the old lines of social policy, for it
was then that individual initiative and development were
threatened:

The Socialism of the present time extends the State's intervention
from those industrial undertakings it is fitted to manage well to all
industrial undertakings whatever, and from establishing securities for
the full use of men's energies to attempting to equalise in some way the
results of their use of them.[149]

The old liberal attitude with its precept of self-help and its
concomitant voluntarism[150] remained all along an integral

---

[148] B. Villiers, [F. J. Shaw], *The Opportunity of Liberalism* (1904), pp. 61–3.
[149] Rae, 'State Socialism and Social Reform', 435, 439.
[150] Cf. L. Stephen, 'The Good Old Cause', *NC*, vol. 51 (1902), 16–17.

part of the liberal concept of individuality, preferred to state
help whenever possible. Invoking state aid when combination
could protect was a bad tendency of socialism, observed
Haldane. Indeed, encouraging working men to use Parliament
to achieve their aims would result in a decay of Trade-
Unionism.[151] He also reiterated the warning against the state
interfering with motivation for industry. Even a social reformist
liberal such as Barnett was worried about the influence of state
socialism on individuality. He conceded that there was much in
the socialist ideal for warmth, guidance, and safety, yet it
offered no place for the man who wanted to be himself.[152]

The pages of the *Westminster Review* were often a typical
reflection of the right of liberal centre fears of state socialism.[153]
As a contributor fervently wrote, conjuring up what was known
as the 'bogey of socialism':

... the old individualistic Liberalism is threatened by a torrent of
socialistic and democratic legislation which may indeed sweep away
many abuses but which may also bring in its tide a mass of
cumbersome and despotic restrictions ... If, however, in the transition
we are to avoid a despotism more potent and more irresistible than
that of the Caesars, and a social system more iniquitous than the *ancien
régime*; if we would escape the horrors of revolution and reaction in
their most insiduous and dangerous, because always in a democratic,
form, the freedom of the individual must be jealously guarded and
preserved.[154]

Other items in the staple vocabulary of these 'conservative'
liberals were their abhorrence of confiscation expressed in their
constant reassertion of private property,[155] and their qualms

[151] Haldane, 'The Liberal Creed', *CR*, vol. 54 (1888), 168. It could also result in the
waiving of another liberal rule, the repudiation of class legislation.

[152] Barnett, 'Social Reform', 35.

[153] For a statement reflecting editorial policy, see leader 'Liberalism and Socialism',
WR, vol. 166 (1906), 486–7.

[154] F. V. Fisher, 'Social Democracy and Liberty', *WR*, vol. 141 (1894), 651.
Fisher, later active in the Social Democratic Party, the Socialist National Defence
League, the British Worker's League, and editor of *British Citizen*, was associated with
the Liberal party and a member of the Eighty Club from 1898 until 1906.

[155] See e.g. F. Thomasson, 'Political Principles', *WR*, vol. 155 (1901), 368. It is worth
noting that Hobhouse resigned from the political editorship of the *Tribune*, the liberal
daily of which Thomasson was the proprietor, because of differences between them on
the nature of liberalism. See J. A. Hobson and M. Ginsberg, *L. T. Hobhouse* (1931), pp.
44–5.

about bureaucratic mismanagement and corruption.[156] Even the *Speaker*, at heart sympathetic to social reform, ruled out its implementation via the road of the paternal state, which stereotyped its working men as a semi-eleemosynary and dependent caste—this being the 'root idea' of socialism.[157] It might be interesting to examine, as an illustration of the increasingly salient differences of opinion among liberals, the discussion centring round a book published in 1897 by 'Six Oxford Men'.[158] This was a collection of essays purporting to justify liberalism in the names of Benthamite democracy and political idealism as against socialism and collectivism. The authors set the tone of the book by proudly reprinting a message of encouragement from Gladstone, who wished well 'to all the efforts you may make on behalf of individual freedom and independence as opposed to what is termed Collectivism'.[159] One of the contentions of the essayists was that none of the reform measures undertaken by the state had any relation to socialist ideals. As F. W. Hirst wrote, it was through the doctrine of economic waste that the strictly materialistic, as distinguished from the moral, justification had to be maintained for all social legislation promoted by the Liberal party. The aim of such legislation was 'to prevent men, women, or children from suffering in their capacity of wealth producers'.[160] This nineteenth-century notion of man reduced to the role of producer was in direct contrast both to the socialist and to the Ruskinian concept of man. On a slightly less extreme plane, J. A. Simon admitted that there was a large sphere of Labour

---

[156] e.g. W. L. Blease, *A Short History of English Liberalism* (1913), p. 334; Armsden, 'First Principles of Social Reform', op. cit. 642.

[157] 'Are We All Socialists Now?', *Speaker*, 13.5.1893. The Liberal Imperialist leaders, for instance, among whose main aims was 'a new Liberal ideology based on a constructive policy of social reforms', exhibited in fact a most unimaginative and conservative approach to social issues. See H. C. G. Matthew, *The Liberal Imperialists: The Ideas and Politics of a Post-Gladstonian Élite* (Oxford, 1973), pp. 8, 69, 235–42. Cf. also Asquith's speech at Ladybank (19.10.1907), reported in the *Tribune*, 21.10.1907, and the *Tribune*'s leader of the same day.

[158] *Essays in Liberalism* by Six Oxford Men (1897). The Six were H. Belloc, F. W. Hirst, J. A. Simon, J. L. Hammond, P. J. MacDonell, and J. S. Phillimore.

[159] Ibid., Preface, x. Asquith had refused to write a preface because of the polemical nature of the book as a declaration of war against collectivism, though he did not find himself in substantial disagreement with the authors. See F. W. Hirst, *In the Golden Days* (1947), p. 157.

[160] 'Liberalism and Wealth', *Essays in Liberalism*, p. 69.

legislation where state interference was approved alike by scientific Socialists and by traditional liberals. 'But', he went on to emphasize, 'this *coincidence* is no more than a casual agreement, and it is entirely gratuitous to assume that reforms which both schools of theorists are agreed to welcome can be justified only from the Socialist point of view.'[161] The fatal flaw of Socialism, argued Simon, was the failure to distinguish between the municipalization of a natural monopoly and of an ordinary competitive trade. For him the former, in addition to factory laws, was the limit of state intervention.[162]

The reviewer of the *Speaker*—at that time exhibiting an editorial policy torn between advocating social reform and attempting to reconcile labour on the one hand, and a repugnance from collectivism on the other—welcomed it as a 'refreshing' book. He saw in it a protest against a 'wishy-washy' collectivism that had resulted in the Liberal defeat of 1895, 'due to the prejudice entertained by owners of property against the philosophic palliation of the predatory instinct in mankind'.[163] But otherwise the book was not very favourably received by liberals, thus putting paid to the *Speaker*'s hopes that 'what Oxford thinks to-day England will think to-morrow'. The *Daily News* wrote a rather frivolous review, in itself significant of the regard in which such opinions were held by advanced liberals, which delighted in exposing the essays as unwittingly furnishing the materials for a socialist evangel. It noted that 'all recent indications seemed to have proved that the social dangers from Collectivism are apt to be over-rated' and that the essays were falsifying the socialist ideal by denying the existence within its framework of individual enterprise.[164] Indeed, *Essays in Liberalism* opened itself to attack primarily because it lumped all socialists together and did not trouble to differentiate between the various accepted uses of the term.

The *Daily Chronicle*, though more restrained in its criticism, took the essays to task on their narrow definition of socialism as 'a system of public policy which, under the pretext of satisfying men's bodily wants by a rigid system of State organisation,

---

[161] 'Liberals and Labour', op. cit., pp. 111–112 (my italics).
[162] Ibid., p. 112.
[163] 'Liberalism at Oxford', *Speaker*, 10.4.1897.
[164] 'Six Oxford Men', *Daily News*, 2.4.1897. Cf. below p. 72 n. 210.

would deprive them of personal initiative, of the power of realising the individual will'.[165] If this were the case, said the newspaper, liberals would oppose socialism without question. 'Opportunity for all, but ... "the tools to him who can handle them"' was the formula expressing the new political idea taking hold of Oxford youth. Yet this, maintained the *Chronicle*, evaded the economic issue, since

What is really wanted is that, on the one hand, the average Socialist should discard his false ethics and half-baked metaphysics, or rather denial of metaphysics, his hedonism, his materialism, and see that personality is the highest aim of the world effort, while on the other hand, the too narrow Liberal should shed his rooted conviction that there is no real economic problem ...[166]

It is noteworthy that the editor of the *Chronicle*, Massingham, must have considered this review too mild, for another evaluation of the *Essays* appeared elsewhere over his initials, which began rather devastatingly: 'We have heard of a society which set about to restore the Middle Ages by half-guinea subscriptions; and now six Oxford men issue a book intended to bring back the Older Liberalism at three-and-six a copy.' Such an approach to collectivism, decided Massingham, was either culpable ignorance or wilful misrepresentation.[167] Indeed, he must have assumed that a more collectivist liberalism was by then common intellectual property and knowledge, for he was content to expose the views of the essayists with only a mere allusion to an alternative. A defence of liberty alone was no longer acceptable to an age in which the challenge of catering to human welfare loomed larger than any other.

[165] Leader, *Daily Chronicle*, 2.4.1897.
[166] Ibid.
[167] H.W.M., review, *Commonwealth*, vol. 2 (1897), 162–3. Significantly, one topic fastened upon both by Massingham and by the *Daily News* was Hirst's endorsement of natural monopolies alone as subject for state intervention. They thus recognized that liberalism had advanced beyond the preliminary stages of a progressive social policy (see pp. 44–5 above). Massingham accused Hirst of ignoring private capitalist monopolies; the *News* saw in Hirst's use of the theory of natural monopolies an excuse for preventing the label 'socialist' from being attached to Hirst himself. Hirst got into difficulties when he expressed equal antagonism to class monopoly and state monopoly. For a Fabian critique of *Essays in Liberalism* see Ball, 'Socialism and Individualism'; Hirst's reply and Ball's rejoinder appeared in the *Economic Review* (vol. 8) under the title 'Individualism and Socialism', in April 1898, pp. 225–35.

4. INTERVENTION AND INDIVIDUALITY—STRIKING THE BALANCE

The doubts concerning state socialism continued to be expressed to a certain extent by more progressive liberals, though in moderate form. The starting-point was the same: to establish the social agencies and institutions through which moral and just communal life could be attained. Herbert Samuel attempted to put the case for progressive liberals by stating that the first principle of liberals led to a policy of social reform to be furthered by state action.[168] He was however vague in the role he accorded the state, at times appearing to prefer voluntary associations,[169] at times construing the new liberalism as 'a school that favours a large use of the powers of the State',[170] though the formula he adopted was state assistance rather than state interference. The new role of the state, which was due not merely to changes in the minds of men but to its increased competence, would have to be limited so as not to injure liberty and self-reliance.[171] In practice, however, Samuel was unable to offer guidelines to such delimitation. His rather lame excuse was that liberalism was no stereotyped collection of fixed principles but a living force applying to the changing phases of national life.[172] This indecision, as Massingham wryly remarked, would hardly convert anybody to liberalism.[173]

A new confidence in the state did eventually take the place of the customary hostility, though always in the form of a guarded optimism. As Ritchie maintained, doubts concerning direct state engagement in economic production did not rule out 'the advisability of immediate State-action to secure the health and the intelligence of the community and a fair chance for its moral progress'.[174] The test, as another liberal saw it, was empirical: 'If such State-interference as we see has on the whole done well,

---

[168] H. Samuel, *Liberalism*, p. 11. It was remarkable at the time that a general work on liberalism should have 'Social Reform' for its second chapter.

[169] H. Samuel, 'Social Reform', in Members of the Eighty Club, *The Liberal View* (1904), p. 158.

[170] H. Samuel, 'The Independent Labour Party', 258.

[171] Samuel, *Liberalism*, pp. 22–3, 29.

[172] Ibid., p. 31.

[173] H. W. Massingham, 'From Doubting Castle', *Speaker*, 15.3.1902.

[174] Ritchie, *The Moral Function of the State*, p. 16.

the balance must be struck in its favour.'[175] For many of those who had a 'vision of society' it was simply a case of using the only instrument for attaining it. C. R. Buxton believed that social progress would not advance towards such a vision without 'an extension of State activity, far wider than any we have yet experienced'. Appealing to the state was essential to the cause of reform for 'the power behind all this machinery is enormous. Here at least is an organization which can grip and grapple with social evils'.[176] And Hobson, who more than most recognized the great value of action through the state, claimed quite apart from this that the state could furnish a security obtainable in no other way.[177]

A. The State as Supreme Ethical Framework

A more sophisticated synthesis between individual and social claims was attempted by Hobhouse. More than any other new liberal theorist, Hobhouse was a disciple of Green's and it is precisely in those aspects of his thought which are basically a repetition of Green's ideas that Hobhouse is least satisfactory. Hobhouse, too, adhered both to the concept of the 'common good' and to the ethical end of individual self-perfection. To attain both—in other words, 'to reconcile the rule of right with the principle of the public welfare'—was for him 'the supreme end of social theory'.[178] This could be achieved, according to Green and Hobhouse, because man was essentially a rational being and his spiritual development tended towards a unity between rational private goods, this being the common good. Elaborating on Green's ideas, Hobhouse noted that the fundamental rights of a human being were a condition of the free development of the individual's personality as a moral being. He denied the assertion of absolute rights as independent of the common welfare—because rights were relative to the well-being of society and were to be interpreted only within the

[175] A. F. Robbins, *Practical Politics or the Liberalism of To-Day* (1888), p. 180.

[176] C. R. Buxton, 'A Vision of England', *IR*, vol. 7 (1905), 156, 151. But again, state machinery was not to be divorced from 'the vital influence of individual contact' (152). See Chapter Five below. Cf. also W. M. Lightbody, 'Socialism and Social Reform', *WR*, vol. 167 (1907), 294.

[177] J. A. Hobson, 'Old Age Pensions. II. The Responsibility of the State to the Aged Poor', *SR*, vol. 1 (1908), 297.

[178] Hobhouse, *Democracy and Reaction*, p. 131.

context of social life. Conversely, the community had rights pertaining to the maintenance of its common life, but they were best served when individual personality was developed to the utmost, i.e. when its moral rights were upheld.[179] This was the expression of Hobhouse's idea of harmony between man and man.

Hobhouse's theory, however, was not solely a development of Green's, as some scholars have been wont to claim.[180] There was firstly a difference between Hobhouse's notion of harmony and Green's concept of unity. Hobhouse's harmony among developed individual personalities postulated a common good which could exist apart from, and even in contradiction to, a man's partial good.[181] This was not only a question of Hobhouse's greater alertness to the cases in which compulsion was necessary, cases that demanded that the social conscience override the individual conscience,[182] nor was it merely an increased awareness of the spheres in which human rights had to be asserted, though both these points have to be made. Rather, Hobhouse held a different view of the nature of the common good, despite his confused and confusing assertions to the contrary. Ginsberg has pointed out that, in contra-distinction to Green, Hobhouse never considered society to be the manifestation of a metaphysical spiritual principle alone. It represented an empirical truth as well.[183] The growth of mind could be observed empirically, for mind was a mode of reality.[184] Beyond this, however, there was an unresolved ambiguity about the notion of mind and its bearing on social theory. On the one hand Hobhouse repeatedly stressed that society exists in individuals; that only individuals, not society, have a distinct personality; that there is no thought except in the mind of an individual thinker; and that there was no such thing as a unitary social mind or will.[185] On the other hand he

---

[179] Ibid., pp. 124–6.
[180] e.g. G. de Ruggiero, op. cit., p. 155.
[181] Cf. Hobson and Ginsberg, op. cit., pp. 184–5.
[182] Hobhouse, *Liberalism*, p. 79.
[183] Hobson and Ginsberg, op. cit., pp. 101–2; M. Ginsberg, *Reason and Unreason in Society* (1947), pp. 45–6.
[184] This is a main theme of Hobhouse's *Mind in Evolution* (1901) and *Development and Purpose* (1913).
[185] Hobhouse, *Social Evolution and Political Theory*, pp. 85, 94, 96–7; *Liberalism*, p. 68.

claimed that in its advanced stages of development, mind
obtained a unified, self-directing force of its own and that the
sum of thought in existence was more than any thought that
existed in the head of any individual.[186] Society did have 'a
certain collective life and character' and there was something
called the common will which was the sole means of realizing
the common good.[187] He finally ended on an inconclusive note:
'Whether this unity would be less inadequately described as a
Central Mind or as a pervading spirit, and whether such a
category as Personality is fitly applicable to it, I cannot here
seek to determine.'[188] Moreover, whereas for Green society was
already implicit in the consciousness of others as ends, Hobhouse by means of his organic conception of society saw the
essence of social life in social interaction and relationships.[189]

There is therefore no clear-cut answer in Hobhouse's writings
to the question: can one or can one not anchor the community
to a separate entity or to distinctly observable phenomena? As
Ginsberg remarked, Hobhouse had a spiritual conception of the
social bond,[190] one that was entirely dependent on rational,
ethical behaviour, even if such behaviour could be studied
empirically. It was Hobson's opinion that

Progress of personality as a harmonious development of the interplay
of individual and social motives was the key to the social thinking of
Hobhouse. His stress on personality as the end and object of all social
processes carried a denial of any group or social mind other than the
orderly interplay of individual minds and reduced such a term as
'esprit de corps' to a personal feeling common to the members of a co-
operative group.[191]

On the issue of communal or state action, however, Hobhouse adopted a position notably different from Green's. In line
with the ongoing restatement of liberal essentials, Hobhouse
maintained that freedom was not the sole foundation of a true
social philosophy: 'On the contrary, freedom is only one side of

---

[186] 'The Philosophy of Development' in Hobhouse, *Sociology and Philosophy*, pp. 325–6
(essay first published in 1924); *Social Evolution and Political Theory*, p. 94.
[187] Hobhouse, *Liberalism*, pp. 68, 71–2.
[188] Hobhouse, 'The Philosophy of Development', *Sociology and Philosophy*, p. 327. For a
further elaboration of this issue see the next Chapter.
[189] Hobhouse, *Liberalism*, p. 71; *Social Evolution and Political Theory*, p. 85.
[190] Hobson and Ginsberg, op. cit., p. 196.
[191] Hobson, *Confessions of an Economic Heretic*, pp. 76–7.

social life. Mutual aid is not less important than mutual forbearance, the theory of collective action no less fundamental than the theory of personal freedom.'[192] If the ethical progress of society was towards greater social solidarity and rationality, collective, i.e. state, action was merely the best expression of the moral and spiritual interests of its members.[193] Hobhouse, like all liberals, never undervalued the importance of voluntary action, nor did he overlook the fact that society was composed of multitudinous groups and institutions[194] But collectivism was necessary because 'it is a simple principle of applied ethics that responsibility should be commensurate with power'.[195] The state had the means, and therefore the responsibility, to realize the ethical life. On the broadest level, this activist notion of the state was 'no modern "Socialist fad", but is as old as Aristotle, holding with him that the State "comes into being that men may live, but exists that they may live well"'.[196] The function of the state was in one sense that of compulsion—to secure conditions necessary for the common good. Primarily, though, the state was cast in the role of intelligent regulator of forces essential to the welfare of the community, of controller rather than owner.[197]

The issue could also be represented as one of the development of organization, which was, as Hobhouse asserted, an aspect of progress itself.[198] The extension of social reform by means of the state was to be motivated and occasioned by an increased awareness of the complexity of conditions vital to the free development of personality. Such development, as with Mill, remained the standard by which the life of the community was evaluated. Hobhouse always objected to the increase of governmental power *per se*, as transforming a means into an end. The state was to be used for ethical, i.e. human, ends.[199] Rather than a question of encroachments on liberty, it was one of

---

[192] Hobhouse, *Liberalism*, p. 67.
[193] Hobhouse, *Social Evolution and Political Theory*, p. 188.
[194] Hobhouse, *Liberalism*, pp. 118–19; *Social Evolution and Political Theory*, p. 89.
[195] Hobhouse, *Liberalism*, p. 86.
[196] L. T. Hobhouse, *The Labour Movement* (1893), p. 53.
[197] Ibid., pp. 53–4; *Liberalism*, p. 108.
[198] Hobhouse, 'The Ethical Basis of Collectivism', *International Journal of Ethics*, vol. 8 (1898), 145; *Democracy and Reaction*, pp. 110–22.
[199] Hobhouse, 'The Ethical Basis of Collectivism', 143–4.

reorganizing restraints, because society's close-knit structure
has accordingly allowed the development of certain nodes, or perhaps
certain connecting fibres, to cut which is to destroy life while to
ligature them is to induce temporary paralysis. This being so, society
itself, through its own direct organs of government, is being compelled, apart from any Collectivist theory, to exercise a closer and
more effective control over all that passes at these vital spots...[200]

Hobhouse thus helped to shift liberal thought towards an
enhanced comprehension of the social aspects of individual
personality and action, and towards a growing reliance on and
confidence in the state's ability to contribute towards the
common good. But both in practice and in theory he stopped
short of the summit of liberal potential. His practical proposals,
especially his exaggerated early faith in Co-operation, did not
always place him in the ranks of the most advanced liberal
reformers. When they did—in his later writings, via the
columns of the *Manchester Guardian*, and as adviser to Lloyd
George on the land question—they seemed to echo Hobson's
more elaborate socio-economic analyses. Even more, his
theoretical cautiousness did not endow him with the best
qualities for creating the new synthesis liberalism was sorely in
need of. Indeed, the point to be made is that on the basis of its
ethical conceptions alone advanced liberalism did not develop
new theories quickly enough. It was, as we shall see, the
empirical-biological argument that really propelled liberal
thought over the boundaries of its traditional limitations. Still,
even in the terms and concepts of this chapter more could have
been said. It was Hobson who put into words what had been on
the tips of his colleagues' tongues.

B. *The Idea of the Minimum: A Division of Functions*

The definition Hobson supplied of the role of the state was the
most succinct of the new liberal formulations:

The public, it is said, should undertake such works as it is best capable
of administering; it should undertake works which are required for
supplying the common necessities of the people; it should undertake
such works as, if left to private enterprise, are prone to abuse, by
reason of high or irregular prices, or by causing danger to the public or
to the workers engaged in them.[201]

[200] L. T. Hobhouse, 'The Conditions of Permanent Peace', leader, *MG*, 21.8.1911.
[201] Hobson, *The Social Problem*, p. 175.

It was on the question of directly supplying common social needs that Hobson went beyond the commonplace liberal position as regards state interference and entered the most advanced ranks of liberal theorists. On some issues it was actually difficult to pinpoint distinctions between Hobson and the Fabians as to what the state was to undertake. In fact, Hobson adopted Webb's 'four-fold path of socialism' when describing the policy 'to the furtherance of which most Liberals are committed'.[202] But when Webb spoke of a 'fourfold path of collective administration of public services, collective regulation of private industry, collective taxation of unearned income, and collective provision for the dependent sections of the community', he had himself described it as an empirical extension of liberalism.[203] Hobson's concept of a minimum standard of life was related to Webb's but surpassed it.[204] It included not only mere food, clothing and shelter but 'good air, large sanitary houses, plenty of wholesome, well-cooked food, adequate changes of clothing for our climate, ample opportunities of recreation' and moreover, 'art, music, travel, education, social intercourse'.[205]

For Hobson, physical, moral, and intellectual aspects of well-being were all closely interconnected. However, as the physiological attributes of human nature were constant they could be dealt with uniformly and quantitatively, whereas the other aspects of human life were artistic, creative and qualitative, and allowed for no standardization.[206] Here, as Hobhouse later interpreted it, was scope for 'a kind of partnership between the individual and the community, the State affording a certain basis of material well-being on which it is left to the individual to build by his own efforts the fabric of his independence, comfort and even wealth'.[207] Industrial developments and 'the reign of the machine' had rendered a great service to humanity, contended Hobson, by taking over much heavy, dull, and degrading work. It was machinery, then, that by

---

[202] J. A. Hobson, 'The Four-Fold Path of Socialism', *Nation*, 30.11.1907.
[203] S. Webb, 'Modern Social Movements', p. 760. Cf. p. 49 above.
[204] Hobson, *Work and Wealth*, p. 168.
[205] Hobson, *The Social Problem*, pp. 78–9.
[206] Ibid., p. 105.
[207] L. T. Hobhouse, 'The Contending Forces', *English Review*, vol. 4 (1909–10), 368. Hobson, as we shall see, went beyond the idea of a partnership.

performing the routine processes of industry could supply basic common necessities, thus liberating man's productive tastes and faculties.[208] This led to the following delimitation: 'The radical antithesis which underlies the antagonism of Socialism and Individualism in its industrial application is the antithesis of Machinery and Art.'[209] What Hobson envisaged was not a substitution of socialism for individualism but a distribution of labour between the two. Individuality would be preserved on a plane where it could find adequate expression. In fact, as he reminded his readers, this was not only the social philosophy of liberalism, for 'Most, if not all, avowed Socialists would be prepared to stake the value of their Socialism upon the single test of its active promotion of individuality in freedom of life, and in the fuller satisfaction of those needs which give distinction to the individual.'[210] But the balance had shifted. Starting out from new social conceptions, Hobson felt obliged to point out the old liberal commonplaces to a readership perhaps forgetful of the purpose of it all. The structure of the following passage is more indicative than anything else of the distance liberalism had travelled by the end of Victoria's reign. 'Man is not only one with his fellows, but also one by himself; not merely a partaker of common humanity, but an individual with nature and conditions which evolve tastes and needs that are his, and his alone.'[211] The state, by undertaking routine industries, would enable the social will to find in that work its self-

[208] Hobson, *Work and Wealth*, p. 76. L. G. Chiozza Money, in his famous *Riches and Poverty* (1905), conjured up a similar vision in which the organization of production and distribution would enable men to turn to uplifting individual work (p. 325).

[209] Hobson, *The Social Problem*, p. 180. An identical view was expressed by Hobson's colleague, W. Clarke. Cf. 'The Limits of Collectivism', *CR*, vol. 63 (1893), 24–43.

[210] Hobson, *The Social Problem*, p.183. This merits comparison with S. Ball's observation that 'the whole point of Socialism is missed if it does not somehow or other raise the wage-earner's power and character as an individual...' But the conclusion of Ball's sentence is: 'which it does to the extent of recognizing him as a citizen of a co-operative industrial community' ('Socialism and Individualism', 503). This conception of individuality as defined merely by social role and action was not acceptable to a liberal, not even to the more sophisticated formulae of Hobson which will be examined in the next chapter. Ball took exception, when reviewing Hobson's *The Crisis of Liberalism*, to the latter's statement on p. 93: 'Liberalism will probably retain its distinction from Socialism, in taking for its chief test of policy the freedom of the individual citizen rather than the strength of the State...' (review, *ER*, vol. 20 (1910), 218–19), and accused Hobson of regarding the individual rather than the citizen as the unit of his political thinking.

[211] Hobson, *The Social Problem*, p. 182.

realization.[212] But original talent, art, spiritual life—these could never be socialized; 'the essentially individual character of [an artist's] work is crushed and thwarted by externally imposed conditions of social service'.[213] Hobson's aesthetic approach to individual creativity even had affinities to the Marxist end-product: 'An artist must produce the whole of a product—a product with a unity; it must be the direct expression of his personal skill, directed to the individual work in hand. The first of these conditions negates division of labour; the second, machinery.'[214] The innovatory capacity imperative for social progress depended on a cultivation of individuality. But although Hobson often transcended the realm of political possibilities when directing his social liberalism on the path of its own logic, it was significant that this 'higher' sphere was to retain its competitive aspects. Competition was yet an indispensable component of the liberal *Weltanschauung*. Indeed, in the short run Hobson did not anticipate, nor did he advocate, fundamental changes in the capitalist structure of society.[215] On the contrary, he upheld a principle that 'differs from the broader Socialist theory, in that it recognises the full rights of individuals in a competitive society'—including complete freedom in private enterprise, with the exception of specific state monopolies, and without prejudicing the satisfaction of minimum human needs.[216] But even ultimately, once all common needs had been socialized, competition in the spheres of individual production would be beneficial as it would engender a genuine rivalry in excellence of work. Such competition would not set up antagonisms between the individual and the social good,[217] because competition would have been removed from a level where it might have injurious effects. Liberal essentials had thus been preserved in a crucial manner: the principle of rendering unto society what was society's—in itself a socialistic one but deducible from liberal

[212] Hobson, *Work and Wealth*, p. 305.

[213] Hobson, *The Social Problem*, p. 244. It was again the error of the socialist, Hobson insisted, to disparage the importance of the individual will and incentive in industry ('Are Riches the Wages of Efficiency?', *Nation*, 9.11.1907).

[214] Hobson, *The Social Problem*, p. 181.

[215] See pp. 45–6 above.

[216] Hobson, 'The Taxation of Monopolies', 25–6.

[217] J. A. Hobson, 'Of Labour', in Rev. J. E. Hand (ed.), *Good Citizenship* (1899), p. 106.

tenets—did not threaten the unwavering adherence to a more central liberal principle, that of individuality. But this was now expressed in a form which did not clash with accepted precepts of social justice.

Above all, the conception of social life entertained by Hobson and other advanced liberals entailed an ethical transformation of society towards a rational humanitarianism in which each man would be treated as an end. Hobson insisted that 'both concrete reforms, and methods of attaining them, must strengthen the moral character of individuals, and must be direct feeders of a spirit of ethical democracy, which shall bind individuals and classes by a conscious bond of moral fellowship.'[218] And Hobhouse demanded that any economic reform introduce 'a new spirit into industry—a feeling for the common good, a readiness to forego personal advantage for the general gain, a recognition of mutual dependence'.[219]

In their idea of society as an ethical entity, the new liberals fastened upon a theme which drew together a wide spectrum of progressives. The material and economic reforms requisite to mitigate social distress were deemed inseparable from, though logically and temporally consequent to, the infusion of a new spirit into social life—a sense of community and mutuality which encompassed all members of society irrespective of their concrete situation. Liberals, Idealists, Christians, Positivists, could all subscribe to a vision of society which was considered to be the only meaningful solution to the current social ills. Advanced liberals restored the notions of the ethical mainstream, out of which liberalism itself had sprung, to their position of ultimate guide, framework, and essence of human conduct, but in doing so did not repudiate their own specifically liberal tradition. Indeed, there was no question of such a repudiation—the authentic spirit of liberalism was conceived of as an ethical one, in which individual and social aims were complementary, harmonious, or even identical. The transition was by no means a smooth one, inasmuch as tensions, hostilities, and preconceptions within the liberal tradition were deeply rooted and perhaps not completely eradicable. However,

---

[218] Hobson, 'The Ethics of Industrialism', pp. 98, 105–6.

[219] Hobhouse, *The Labour Movement*, pp. 4–5. For an expression of such ideals in dialogue form see G. Lowes Dickinson, *Justice and Liberty* (1907).

liberal social thought not only rejuvenated its ethical elements but moved towards a general theory of social life within which it sought to resolve the old difficulties. The 'condition of the people' question became basically one of extending the concept of community to the 'periphery', of the full incorporation of newly articulate and conscious sections into society. By 1907, when the impact of the sizeable group of keen and innovative liberal intellects was already being felt, Hobson could state that 'the real revolution is in the minds of men'. It was, he maintained, no 'violent breach of continuity' with liberal traditions, the novelty being rather in the strength of the faith and the size of the remedies.[220]

New ideas, new conceptions, a new spirit—these could not be dictated. They were to be the reaction of independent, rational minds to the human environment, and liberty was vital to their budding. Mind would fashion matter so that the conditions for mind's further development would be established. A profitable and never-ceasing interplay would be set into motion. Here indeed was the optimism of progress.

The new liberal conception of society was not, however, grounded only on a reinterpretation of ethical duties of man to man, and this is why the above discussion of Hobson's ideas does not do justice to his ideological synthesis and to his notion of community. Other liberal theorists as well bestowed an added dimension on their principles through a more scientific comprehension of the fabric of society. That fabric was woven, new liberals would contend, not merely out of moral values but out of empirically demonstrable facts. The claim that biology supported ethics, and the integration of both within the liberal outlook, vastly increased the persuasive power of the liberal argument. It is to a consideration of the role of biology in liberal social thought that we now turn.

[220] J. A. Hobson, 'Socialism in Liberalism', *Nation*, 12.10.1907. Reprinted in Hobson, *The Crisis of Liberalism.*

III

Biology, Evolution and Liberal Collectivism

I. THE NATURAL LAWS OF SOCIAL LIFE

DURING the nineteenth century the interplay between scientific discovery and social thought reached epic proportions. Theories of development and evolution could apply concurrently to the natural and the social sciences, and they were consequently responsible, to a hitherto unprecedented extent, for a co-ordination and overlapping of those two branches of human knowledge. The natural sciences had discovered apparently definitive laws that dominated thinking in other fields as well and demanded total commitment from all empirico-rationally minded people. Social thought appeared to be well on the way to becoming one particular manifestation of a general cosmology.

The revival of the concept of evolution was the prime contribution of biology to nineteenth-century civilization. Undoubtedly, any socio-political theory failing to come to terms with evolutionary thought would have lost its intellectual credibility and its vitality as a solution to the great questions of the time. It is not surprising, then, that the liberal thinkers who gave liberalism a new lease of life turned to biology and evolution for inspiration, argumentation, and verification.

The names most obviously connected with the revolution in the modes and foci of nineteenth-century English thought are, first and foremost, Darwin, and then Spencer and Malthus. The fact that the theories of all three were associated—in varying degrees of accuracy—with conservative, reactionary, or amoral conclusions pertaining to social nature and social policy has often blinded scholars to the fundamental patterns of thinking which they bequeathed to the whole spectrum of social thought.

It will be the special concern of this chapter to examine the adoption of their ideas by liberal thinkers and the ways through which these ideas were set to work for a progressive-liberal theory of society.

The immediate outcome of Malthus's writings was to throw into sharp relief the population question, which in one form or another overshadowed nineteenth-century social thought.[1] The issue of human multiplication focused simultaneous attention on two spheres: it served as a reminder that man was subject to the same biological laws that existed in the animal kingdom, a truth many moralists chose to ignore or alluded to vaguely; and it emphasized the problem of supplying basic human needs under conditions of scarcity, which was one way of formulating the Social Question. Malthus's biological determinism, with its sense of impending catastrophe, promoted an ethos of social irresponsibility, for social aid negated social survival. To exchange the principle of conflict for one of mutual help would be unnatural and hence disastrous, for by rescuing the losers one would only make the boat sink more quickly. Malthus thus emerged as the principal ideologue of the school of thought opposed to poor-relief and to alleviating the condition of the distressed. True, the question of improving the human race as a method of social reform, which is the subject of Chapter Five, owed its inception to the breakthrough effected by Malthus in placing problems of human regeneration before the public eye. But it was not the threatened deluge of numbers that perturbed new liberals in this case. Rather, as part of a general shift of focus of late-Victorian, in contrast to mid-Victorian, ethics, quantitative issues were making way for qualitative ones.

The other two figures in the crystallization of evolutionary theory were Darwin and Spencer. Advanced liberals constituted no exception in holding that, intellectually, the second half of the nineteenth century was the age of those two leading thinkers.[2] Yet the main question to be asked is, what could they offer the new liberalism? Both men were associated with socio-

---

[1] See T. Kirkup, *A History of Socialism*, 3rd ed. (1906), p. 296; R. M. Young, 'Malthus and the Evolutionists: The Common Context of Biological and Social Theory', *Past and Present*, no. 43, (1969), 110–11.

[2] L. T. Hobhouse, leader, *MG*, 9.12.1903.

political trends of thought which became increasingly remote from, if not downright opposed to, the mainstream of liberal thought. If Malthus had considered attempts at ameliorating the human condition as hastening the Fall, Spencer saw them as tampering with a natural balance that should best be left alone. His optimistic faith in the ability of society to evolve spontaneously into a harmonic body of co-operating individuals was coupled with adherence to a radical brand of *laissez-faire* which by the end of the century was so absurdly out of tune with current thinking as to discredit him in general. Darwin, in turn, though he had left the question of the direction of social evolution entirely open, had borrowed from Malthus and from Spencer ideas that attached his name to that school of thought which saw human existence as a relentless and continuous struggle for life resulting in what Spencer called the 'survival of the fittest'. But progressive liberal thinkers, Hobhouse and Hobson in particular, while in bitter conflict with these offshoots, fastened upon Darwin's essential message and knew how to value Spencer despite his political views. As Hobhouse explained:

Darwin's great achievement was to show for the first time, by means of the theory of Natural Selection, that the Evolution principle might be made to harmonise and illuminate a vast mass of otherwise disconnected and unintelligible facts of organic life. Spencer's achievement was to show that the same principle could be made the connecting link of all the sciences, and in particular of all the sciences that deal with living beings, and by its aid to construct a philosophy not, as philosophy too often is, opposed to science, but itself the sum or synthesis of the sciences.[3]

It was the search for a unifying principle which could explain, give meaning to, and ultimately direct human progress that appealed to these liberals intent upon finding criteria by which human welfare could be estimated and society reformed. The quest for general laws, if not a whole system, by which society would eventually be reconstituted, was part of the optimistic positivism which they inherited.[4]

Beyond a general theory of progress, and the law of natural selection, the implications of evolution for politics and ethics

[3] Ibid.
[4] L. T. Hobhouse, leader, 'The Darwinian Theory', *MG*, 1.7.1908.

were tremendous. As Hobson noted of Spencer: 'His most revolutionary work was the extension of evolutionary thought to this newly-conquered realm [of human sciences]. Man is henceforth part of nature.'[5] The age-old philosophical dualism between man and nature appeared to be terminated. The ascending belief in the unity of knowledge meant that 'we are all Spencerians to-day, whether we like it or not'.[6] Significantly, it was not T. H. Green but Spencer's *The Study of Sociology* that was a prime influence on the shaping of Hobson's mind, showing him how scientific methods could be applied to the study of social life.[7] Hobson was aware, of course, that Spencer's political thought did not give full expression to his concept of unity, but explained away this failure in consistency by the fact that Spencer had committed himself politically at too early a stage in his mental development, before his politics could have evolved from his science.[8] This was not, of course, a satisfactory explanation. Not only contrary politico-ethical predispositions, but incompatibilities in theories of evolution and of social structure caused the divergence between Spencer and the new liberalism, as shall be shown below.

2. THE CONTROVERSIALITY OF SOCIAL DARWINISM

The influence of Darwinian theory on late Victorian social thought has been considered almost entirely in terms of the conflict version of Social Darwinism. It is only in recent years that attention has been drawn to other implications of Darwinism for social thought.[9] In two of the Darwinian variations, in fact, the struggle for survival was ruled out. As G. Himmelfarb has observed, Social Darwinism could be expanded to include inter-species struggle that, for the sake of its efficiency, suppressed intra-species conflict; or it could relate to a conception of evolution that stressed the growing role co-operation

[5] J. A. Hobson, 'Herbert Spencer', *SPM*, vol. 9 (1904), 51.
[6] Ibid. 51, 49. Spencer had 'more clearly, more fully, and more effectively re-stated the truth of the Unity of Things and Thoughts than any other man' (55).
[7] H. N. Brailsford, *The Life-Work of J. A. Hobson* (1948), p. 5. See Hobson's autobiography, *Confessions of an Economic Heretic*, p. 23.
[8] Hobson, 'Herbert Spencer', 52.
[9] R. J. Halliday, 'Social Darwinism: A Definition', *Victorian Studies*, vol. 14 (1971), 390–5.

played in the lives of more developed species.[10] Peel and Semmel, however, commit the error of viewing the 'external' (inter-species) type of Social Darwinism as that occupying 'the central position in collectivist Darwinism' which they regard primarily as 'the natural idiom of social imperialism'.[11] This ignores the increasing weight being given to the co-operative-altruistic version of Darwinism in progressive social thought. Indeed, the sway of Social Darwinism[12] upon liberal minds was steadily on the decline, so that by the Boer War it was associated mainly with anti-liberal tendencies.

The socio-biological argument opposed to Social Darwinism maintained that natural processes of development were leading to increased co-operation which replaced the evolutionary mechanism of competition. That this could be proved by Darwinian methods was of immense importance in legitimizing the new direction liberal thought was taking. Even among plants and animals co-operation appeared to be prominent. The evolutionary process inevitably led to altruism, which itself was reasonable. The struggle for life was mitigated among higher types. The conclusion was one that advanced liberals were increasingly adopting: '... the law underlying the evolutionary process makes for collectivism, and ... there is a deeper significance in the old saying that man is a "social animal" than we have as yet realised'.[13] Natural science was verifying the

---

[10] G. Himmelfarb, *Victorian Minds* (1970), pp. 321-7.

[11] J. D. Y. Peel, *Herbert Spencer: The Evolution of a Sociologist* (1971), pp. 235-6; B. Semmel, *Imperialism and Social Reform* (1960), *passim*. I cannot accept Semmel's basic framework, in which he regards internal Social Darwinism as 'a bulwark of Liberalism', challenged by external Social Darwinism, seen by Semmel as attached to the new collectivist spirit of the eighties. Firstly, this disregards the other socio-biological ideologies. Collectivism in internal affairs was much more closely linked to a socio-biological rejection of Social Darwinism as struggle. Social reform did not primarily enter liberalism via imperialism. Secondly, it is mistaken—in a book dealing with the years 1895-1914—to identify liberalism with Cobdenism and with a belief in the struggle for existence and *laissez-faire*. The battle at the end of the century, as far as liberalism was concerned, was not between 'social-imperialism and Cobdenite liberalism'—for the liberal mainstream dissociated itself from both (see especially Semmel, p. 31).

[12] I prefer to use 'Social Darwinism' in conjunction with the notions of struggle and competition. Cf. also J. A. Rogers's usage of 'Social Darwinism' v. 'Reform Darwinism' ('Darwinism and Social Darwinism', *Journal of the History of Ideas*, vol. 32 (1972), 267).

[13] R. Didden, 'Individualism or Collectivism? Which Way Does Evolution Point?', *WR*, vol. 149 (1898), 660-1.

new ethical understanding of socialism and its concomitant of joint social action.

Two almost simultaneous events helped to speed the new liberal ideology on its course: T. H. Huxley's 1893 Romanes Lecture entitled 'Evolution and Ethics', and Benjamin Kidd's 1894 bestseller *Social Evolution*, both of which sparked off lively intellectual debates. Huxley had already dismissed Spencer's attempt to derive *laissez-faire* from biological analogy over twenty years before,[14] and came to occupy a central position between 'Anarchic Individualism' and 'Regimental Socialism', claiming that state intervention was a matter to be determined by circumstances. Indeed, the higher and more complex the organization of the social body, the larger the category of acts that ceased to be merely self-regarding.[15] Competition and struggle as an exclusive social ethic were repudiated by Huxley. In his Romanes Lecture he attacked the Social Darwinists for advancing the doctrine of the survival of the fittest as a universal process applying to social as well as to biological evolution. In an oft-quoted passage he offered his alternative position: 'Social progress means a checking of the cosmic process at every step, and the substitution for it of another, which may be called the ethical process; the end of which is not the survival of those who may happen to be the fittest, in respect of the whole of the conditions which obtain, but of those who are ethically the best.'[16] This sentence created quite a stir among the evolutionary naturalists, who had a strong following among progressive liberals. While obviously agreeing with Huxley's rejection of the struggle for survival as explaining social development, they could not accept the antithesis between cosmic and ethical processes, nor could they accept Huxley's arbitrary super-imposition of ethical values on the cosmic process, despite his cautious hope in man's ability to subdue nature. As the liberal daily *Westminster Gazette* observed, one could not but be struck 'by the curious turn which thought appears to be taking at the close of the century. There is a general rounding upon progress ... now comes Professor Huxley to tell us that the fine thing we have called evolution is

[14] T. H. Huxley, 'Administrative Nihilism', *FR*, vol. 10 (1871).
[15] T. H. Huxley, *Social Diseases and Worse Remedies* (1891), pp. 43–4.
[16] T. H. Huxley, *Evolution and Ethics*, Romanes Lecture (Oxford, 1893), p. 33.

in absolute conflict with our aspirations towards a new heaven and a new earth.'[17]

Most progressive liberals accused Huxley of having done an injustice to the essential ethicality of man by reintroducing the dualism between nature and mind. Ethical fitness itself was one of the conditions that determined survival.[18] Huxley's outlook was understandably regarded by ethical evolutionists as a non-evolutionary argument, since it negated continuity of development in so far as man was concerned.

Kidd offered an original variation on the struggle for survival theme. While accepting that progress depended on the existence of rivalry and selection among individuals, he granted that maximum human development could only be attained by subordinating individual to social interests. However, the group activity and consequent social efficiency towards which evolution proceeded could be endangered by the rational preference of individuals for their present welfare over the future interests of the race, manifesting itself in a tendency towards socialism. This was avoided by the intervention of religion which supplied a super-rational sanction for altruism—defined as the interests of the race. By justifying social legislation Christianity created the conditions for an equality of opportunity which would admit all to the rivalry of life and refine the efficiency of such rivalry.[19] Here was the ultimate ideology of social efficiency—the pseudo-scientific term then embarking upon a fashionable career to last until World War I—for the fittest were those most successful when competition started from the same point.

Some of the older liberals believed Kidd's doctrine to adumbrate a 'Philosophy of Liberalism'. The *Speaker* described Kidd's specific contribution as drawing the line between liberalism and socialism and reinstating competition as a

[17] 'Professor Huxley on Original Sin', leader, *WG*, 19.5.1893. See also 'Professor Huxley at Oxford', *Speaker*, 27.5.1893.

[18] J. A. Hobson, *John Ruskin Social Reformer* (1898), p. 104. In all fairness to Huxley it is worth noticing that his critics tended to overlook a partial retraction of his position in a footnote to his lecture: 'Of course, strictly speaking, social life and the ethical process, in virtue of which it advances towards perfection, are part and parcel of the general process of evolution, just as the gregarious habit of innumerable plants and animals, which has been of immense advantage to them, is so.' (*Evolution and Ethics*, p. 56, n. 19.)

[19] B. Kidd, *Social Evolution* (1894), pp. 62–7, 85, 141, 153–5.

fundamental principle of social life: 'The movements of modern Liberalism, falsely called Socialistic, are all directed to making the terms of the competition fairer and increasing the number of competitors . . .'[20] The liberal *Daily Chronicle* considered *Social Evolution* to be one of the most important sociological treatises in a long time, and declared: 'Mr. Kidd's work is thus an apologia for the body of doctrine to which *The Daily Chronicle* bears diurnal witness—the new social and political faith, reinforced by the newer Christian spirit and interpretation.'[21] But it regretted the antagonism of faith and intellect and, further, questioned Kidd's optimism as regards the inevitable path of progress. In fact, though, it was a leader in this liberal-progressive newspaper that went so far as to praise Kidd's 'remarkable' book for insisting that education and intellectual culture must always be subordinate to ethical and religious feeling; that western progress was ethical, not intellectual.[22]

However, the chorus of progressive protests against Kidd, both on biological and on ethical grounds, was equally in evidence. Co-operation was seen by them not as a means to improved competition but as a substitute for it. Kidd's appeal to those who placed self-reliance above everything is obvious, for the basic ethos of self-reliance was preserved in combination with what seemed to be a very humane attitude to social evils.[23] But his idea of welfare, in contrast to the new liberal one, subsisted on two time levels: an inclusive, universal approach towards the welfare of the masses up to the point where they could compete efficiently with all, and insensibility to problems of individual welfare once this point was passed. As a writer in *The Commonwealth* noted, it was a 'startling reversal' of the social reformist ideal concerning peace and harmony, substituting instead an ideal which would work rivalry up to the highest pitch.[24]

When Kidd stated that human progress could not be rational, he appeared to contravene the basic assumption of all

[20] 'Towards a Philosophy of Liberalism', *Speaker*, 10.3.1894.
[21] 'The True Path of Progress', *Daily Chronicle*, 10.3.1894.
[22] Leader, *Daily Chronicle*, 9.10.1894.
[23] Kidd, op. cit., p. 217.
[24] M. Carta Sturge, 'Kidd's "Social Evolution"', *Commonwealth*, vol. 1 (1896), 231–3. See also W. H. Fremantle, 'Individualists and Socialists', *NC*, vol. 41 (1897), 312–13, 319.

progressive forces since the enlightenment. It was in this sense that Kidd was essentially illiberal. In effect, Kidd's reason was really the Hobbesian 'reasoning'[25] or in other words, unenlightened self-interest, a mere sequence of materialistic cause and effect.[26] Hobson suggested the more progressive 'enlightened utilitarian' and even 'idealist' interpretation of reason while accusing Kidd of excluding moral forces from his concept of 'rational':

The man who reasonably seeks his own interest will (in a socially efficient race) conform to such rules of conduct as make for the welfare of the race, because such conduct will give him most satisfaction, or, to use the language of a school who mistrust utilitarian language, because such conduct contributes to the realization of his rational self.[27]

Hobson was aware of the subtle distortions Kidd had inserted into basic liberal-democratic notions. While welcoming Kidd's 'vigorous assertion of the claim of the wider social organism upon the conduct of the several generations ...', he put more faith in the capacity of the individual to understand and act according to those interests. Hobson therefore denied any antagonism between the true interests of the individual and society, even on the level of conscious, rational behaviour. Ethical conduct, he asserted, could be openly justified and did not have to enter by the back door under false disguises.[28] Hobson also rejected the quantitative social efficiency in favour of an increase in the quality of life and the development of a higher individualism.

An important question of consequence to democratic theory emerged, one which had ramifications for social reform thought a decade later. Was it democratic in spirit to admit the grievances of the masses but to overrule them on the ground of long-term considerations of the good of future generations? Was it not part of the doctrine of self-determination that each generation had the privilege of defining and discovering its own good irrespective of previous or future goods? Kidd's alternative

[25] See M. Oakeshott, Introduction to Hobbes's *Leviathan* (Oxford, 1946), p. xx.

[26] B. Kidd, 'Social Evolution', *NC*, vol. 37 (1895), 231.

[27] J. A. Hobson, 'Mr. Kidd's "Social Evolution"', *American Journal of Sociology*, vol. 1 (1895), 303.

[28] Ibid., 302, 312.

was illiberal inasmuch as he removed the element of choice from human action or, rather, circumvented choice by tracing the inevitable development of irrational religion—the only alternative to which was self-destruction. The old problem had arisen once again—whether the will and interests of the people were those of any given moment or those that, owing to their shortcomings, they were unable to comprehend. Democracy, in Kidd's hands, was an instrument of social efficiency, detached from its ethical function as the optimal expression of the dignity of man.

A pattern had been established over the Kidd controversy. On the one hand was a conception of welfare which acknowledged the need for aiding people to achieve basic conditions of living, but did so with the ultimate aim of enabling them 'to stand on their own feet'. In fact, Kidd's future-oriented theory blended into the Spartan 'Protestant Ethic' in its stress on deferment of satisfaction.[29] The opposite ideal of the new liberals was that which saw welfare as immediately desirable and attainable, inasmuch as existing distress was an evil in itself which could not be mitigated by visions of future happiness. Social responsibility was therefore concrete and direct, and altruism was to be applied to one's fellow-men as a moral end *per se*. This view did not necessarily imply a defective and partial conception of society. It could retain an appreciation of the worth of the individual while concurrently acting for the good of society as a whole, as long as it postulated the potential ability of the individual to perceive the interest of the whole, both in 'space' and in time.

3. ORTHOGENIC EVOLUTION: REFORM VERSUS DETERMINISM

The fullest statement of ethical evolutionism leading to collectivism was that of Hobhouse. He was initially even more suspicious of biological argument than of German Idealism. Its reactionary implications militated against social justice as well as postulating beliefs concerning race and inheritance which negated the efficacy of social and institutional improvement to which Hobhouse was pledged.[30]

[29] Though that ethic stressed the planned deferment of satisfaction and was consequently a defence of the *rationalistic* capitalist way of life.

[30] Hobhouse, *Democracy and Reaction*, pp. 83–4, 88.

To this misuse of biology Hobhouse had two answers. The first was that the doctrine of equality—the ethical principle on which society should be based and towards the realization of which social reform should be directed—was not touched by biological theory. Rather, it could be maintained on the ground that human beings enjoyed certain fundamental rights *qua* human beings. Instead of being a simple restatement of the 'natural rights' argument, this viewpoint regarded rights as existing solely in society and depending on social recognition.[31] The second answer was an attempt to demonstrate, even more emphatically than many of Hobhouse's progressive contemporaries had done, that biological evolution did not necessarily proceed by a struggle for existence. Some types of evolution did, but they did not lead to more advanced forms of life. Moreover, Hobhouse posited a correlation between ethics and evolution:

Before we apply biological conceptions to social affairs, we generally suppose that the highest ethics is that which expresses the completest mutual sympathy and the most highly evolved society, that in which the efforts of its members are most completely coordinated to common ends, in which discord is most fully subdued to harmony.[32]

In contradistinction to Huxley's imposition of mind on nature, Hobhouse treated mind as a factor in evolution inasmuch as it determined the behaviour of the individual and the development of the species. It could be proved empirically that, when applied to the study of society, orthogenic evolution consisted of the evolution of mind. Science thus came to the aid of ethics. The only meaningful way in which a concept of progress could be used, argued Hobhouse, was by accepting that mind was higher than matter. Mere fitness to survive was not a sign of superiority. Because the development of mind was natural to human beings and eventually led to the establishment of ethico-rational ideals, reformers who insisted on applying ethics to politics were justified as against materialists for whom ethical consciousness was a by-product doomed to failure.[33] The development of mind enabled the individual to grasp that he was acting within the framework of human society.

[31] Hobhouse, *Social Evolution and Political Theory*, p. 197; *Democracy and Reaction*, p. 89.
[32] Hobhouse, *Social Evolution and Political Theory*, p. 23.
[33] Hobhouse, *Democracy and Reaction*, p. 116.

The turning-point in the evolution of thought, as I conceive it, is reached when the conception of the development of humanity enters into explicit consciousness as the directing principle of human endeavour ... In particular, it can be seen to be the conception necessary to give consistency and unity of aim to the vastly increased power of controlling the conditions, external and internal, of life, which the advance of knowledge is constantly yielding to mankind.[34]

Although Hobhouse had a conception of mind very similar to the Idealist one,[35] he stressed its historical and empirical, rather than its logical, development. Yet a protective, defensive stance towards liberal ethical values detracted from his ability to innovate in liberal theory. Unlike Hobson, his fear of the political uses of biology overrode persistent attempts on his part to see its positive implications for society, a shortcoming also manifest in Hobhouse's attitude to Idealism. Yet Hobhouse's social thought was not only a negative reaction to biology. After all he emphasized the existence of co-operation in many forms of nature, thus linking biology to his ethics. He examined the evolution of mind as a concrete, scientifically demonstrable fact. It was a description of human characteristics as much as biology was. It was also an attempt to discover explanatory laws concerning human behaviour in society in terms of the life-history of a species. To that degree, sociology was an extension of nineteenth-century biological thought. As Hobhouse admitted, 'we are bound to regard biology and all the physical sciences as one of the roots of sociology, for notwithstanding all that has been said, man is an animal, and as an animal he does fall within the sphere of biological enquiry.'[36]

The realization that physical determinants were a vital aspect of human and social behaviour was at the time a breakthrough in social theory. Hobhouse was only half-consciously enunciating a discovery with revolutionary impact on social reform. It was left to others to consolidate this connection. Thus Dyer could formulate the far-reaching claim, the implications of which will be clarified in later chapters:

... a knowledge of biology is necessary to guide us in sociological investigations ... it explains the true nature and limits of competition,

[34] Hobhouse, *Social Evolution and Political Theory*, pp. 155–6.
[35] Hobhouse, *Development and Purpose*, pp. xix, 197–8.
[36] Hobhouse, 'The Roots of Modern Sociology' (1907), in *Sociology and Philosophy*, p. 13.

and of the necessity for co-operation in different forms and for the division of labour. It indicates the functions of trade unions, and justifies the demand for a fair, or at least a minimum, rate of wages. It imparts the knowledge necessary for the solution of the problems connected with the population question, and it shows the necessity for a thorough change in our system of land tenure, so that the most may be made of our national resources in the interests of the people.[37]

Hobhouse was also unquestionably committing an injustice by his hostile generalizations about biologists. He held that their belief in the struggle for existence caused them to entertain doubts about social reform; indeed, convinced them that social reform was self-defeating.[38] W. Bateson, one of the leading biologists of the period, certainly held a different view. He denied that biological science sanctioned free competition for the means of subsistence. As soon as social organization commenced, he asserted, competition occurred between societies and not between individuals; whereas within societies, provision was made for all members of the community.[39] Though most new liberals rejected this external Social-Darwinism, it did not involve a struggle for existence from the national standpoint. Another biologist, G. A. Paley, gave further encouragement to social reformers by upholding Weismann's theory as against Lamarck's and enlarging on its socio-political implications. The Lamarckian theory—that human characteristics were acquired and that such acquisitions could be inherited—would have supported an aristocratic view of politics. If the results of culture were handed down, the children of the rich would be superior. The assumption behind this was Spencer's (who tenaciously adhered to Lamarckianism long after it had gone out of scientific fashion), namely, that the adaptation of humans to their environment was a natural process of equilibration which precluded social intervention. In contrast, Weismann's influence on social and political theories was tremendous. If the continuity of germ plasm was established irrespective of the life-history of the parents, it meant that there was as good material in the lower classes as in any other. And since in one respect environment did have a role in

---

[37] Dyer, *The Evolution of Industry*, pp. 43–4.
[38] Hobhouse, *Social Evolution and Political Theory*, pp. 20–5.
[39] W. Bateson, *Biological Fact and the Structure of Society* (1912), pp. 24–5.

Weismann's theory, in that the germ cells depended on the parent body for their existence, here was an argument in favour of guaranteeing the well-being of all. 'Therefore the social reformer is perfectly justified in hoping that there are as many refined natures at the bottom of the social scale who would develop in [a] more fortunate environment.'[40]

The central issue, however, contained in Hobhouse's conception of social process revolved round the question of necessitarian evolution (a determinism evident in Idealism as well) as opposed to social self-determination. The consequences of this question had direct bearing on the entire subject of reform. Put at its simplest: if nature was ethical, if the dualism between spirit and matter was non-existent, and if the law of evolution was an inevitable law of development, then the social reformer was superfluous. This kind of deterministic optimism was apparent in Spencer's writings. For him, the evolutionary process was the teleological unfolding of the principles of sociality and altruism, provided the natural adaptive activity of individuals was not hampered.[41] The new liberals held of course a similar notion of the social end-product, but allocated to mind a decisive role in its attainment. Whereas Spencer saw little room for ideas and for thought as motivating change—in other words, he denied essentially human characteristics a place in the evolutionary process[42]—the new liberals came to deduce their collectivist conception of society precisely via the operation of mind. Here Hobhouse's theory was crucial. Mind was not there merely to speed up the march of nature towards co-operation, but was itself a natural phenomenon and hence the rational self-direction of society through mind was part of the 'natural' evolutionary process. This theory coalesced with the ethical-collectivist currents of liberalism in two ways. The question of mind functioning on a social level, as a mechanism of social adaptation, highlighted the important issue of society

[40] G. A. Paley, 'Biology and Politics', New Quarterly, vol. 1 (1907), 122–31. This interpretation was adopted by liberal social reformers in direct contradiction to the opposite conclusion which could be drawn, namely, that Lamarckianism encouraged social reformers to change the environment, whereas Weismannism rendered all reform useless, a conclusion found, e.g., in Semmel, op. cit., p. 45.

[41] H. Spencer, The Study of Sociology (1907 edn.), p. 341; Peel, op. cit., p. 139; E. Barker, Political Thought in England 1848 to 1914 (1963), p. 96.

[42] Peel, op cit., pp. 75, 244.

as a conscious entity.[43] Furthermore, it legitimized the task of the social reformer who, by showing ways through which man could rationally control and change his environment and himself, was taking an active part in evolution.

This viewpoint was succinctly expressed by Ritchie, whose writings on these issues influenced a whole generation of reformers. Unlike Hobhouse, Ritchie preferred to adhere to some version of social struggle and competition. He attempted to assimilate the conviction of new liberals like Hobson, who regarded competition as valuable once removed to a level where it could have no harmful effects, into an evolutionary perspective. The crucial difference introduced into natural evolution was, for him as for Hobhouse, the appearance of consciousness. Consciousness meant not only the awareness of the struggle for existence and a critical attitude towards it, but a deliberate choice of certain ideas among those generally available and through them the adoption of new habits.[44] That process was natural rather than imposed:

The process by which we accept and reject opinion is not merely *analogous to* natural selection. It is that same process in a higher sphere, though we may prefer to call it 'the dialectic movement of thought' or by some other term which is free from biological associations. The element of consciousness differentiates intellectual selection from biological natural selection ...[45]

In this one passage Ritchie managed to square the central liberal tenet of freedom of choice with the Darwinian biological discovery of natural selection. The one element which the Darwinian hypothesis lacked manifestly (though not latently)[46]—*rational* choice—was added by the introduction of consciousness.

For new liberals, the role of the social reformer was not deterministic precisely because mind and will involved choice and could involve error as well. Ritchie maintained that the social reformer was destined for a greater role than mere reverence for history. Although the Universal Reason worked

[43] See Chapter Two, p. 46 and this chapter, *infra*, on the general will.
[44] D. G. Ritchie, *Darwinism and Politics* (1889), pp. 22–33.
[45] D. G. Ritchie, 'Evolution and Democracy', in S. Coit (ed.), *Ethical Democracy: Essays in Social Dynamics* (1900), p. 7.
[46] As Ritchie had observed in *Darwin and Hegel* (1893), p. 58.

unconsciously, it was sometimes immediate, in the form of inspiration.[47] Hence the social reformer became pioneer and propagandist of the true consciousness. The evolution of mind was a catalyst of social progress. It was inevitable but at the same time controllable by the individual will. The reformer, by arousing individual minds to an awareness of their social nature, by providing a rational concept of society, was eliciting the ethical potential from the members of society. He could not, however, merely impose his particular opinions, for mind was self-determining. In the last resort ethical social reform was a question of will, whether individual or social.[48] Hobhouse himself had recognized this, not only in his insistence on free choice as the condition of development, but explicitly when, accepting the Darwinian denial of unilinear evolution, he went on to rebut 'the theory of continuous automatic inevitable progress'.[49] Nevertheless, Hobhouse did not appreciate that the social reformer's idea of ethicality would have to *compete* with other ideas which were blocking the way towards a conscious, scientific, and universal social philosophy.[50]

The keen positivism of theorists like Ritchie and Hobson was reflected in their faith in the power of the reformer to elicit change from society.[51] This positivist inclination reached its apex with Fabians like Ball and S. Webb (and one must remember that Ritchie himself was a Fabian until 1893) who likewise, despite their professed 'socialism', did not rule out competition. Holding an even greater conviction in the possibility of manipulating society to achieve ethical ends, they could combine acceptance of evolutionary theory with a confidence in human ability to *control* competition.[52]

Like the new liberals, Webb believed that man himself held

[47] D. G. Ritchie, *Philosophical Studies* (1905), p. 261.

[48] Hobson would have opted for the latter interpretation. See below. Cf. also Villiers, *The Opportunity of Liberalism*, p. 62.

[49] Hobhouse, *Social Evolution and Political Theory*, pp. 199–200, 160.

[50] Hobhouse, 'Democracy and Empire', *Speaker*, 18.10.1902.

[51] Hobson wrote: 'The social reformer who does not "form" is not doing his best. There must be more and more of the enthusiasm of "making" . . .' ('The World We Make', *SPM*, vol. 12 (1907), 83). See also S. A. Barnett, 'Social Reform', *IR*, vol. 1 (1903–4), 28; H. Jones, *The Working Faith of the Social Reformer*, pp. 215–16, and review by Hobhouse, 'A Social Reformer's Faith', leader, *MG*, 17.5.1910; Hobson, *The Social Problem*, p. 283; D. G. Ritchie, *Natural Rights* (1894), pp. 112–13.

[52] S. Webb, 'The Policy of the National Minimum', *IR*, vol. 3 (1904), 173.

the key to social progress. He differed from them in accepting Huxley's evolutionary viewpoint[53] and, consequently, his confidence in manipulation was greater than Ritchie's or Hobson's. For was not a theory which postulated an external substitution of 'regulated co-ordination' for 'blind anarchic competition' very much in line with the Fabians' sense of mission? Here again the tension between 'natural' evolution and 'artificial' change is evident. The anti-Huxley stance was fundamentally more conducive to liberal ideals, being less elitist and placing more value on the inherent mental and moral equipment of the common man.

For the new liberals, social reform ceased to be solely a question of removing hindrances, of adjusting social evils, of redressing wrongs; in sum, of occasional intervention to restore nature's balance. The operation of mind was regarded as continuous and dynamic. It was an endless quest, dictated by the ethicality and rationality of man, aimed at controlling his physical and human environment. Concurrently, the meaning of social reform was extended from concern mainly with the physical alleviation of poverty and, at most, the creation of ethical motivation for such concern, to a change in orientation towards society and social values. Social reform in this sense was not restricted to the improvement of conditions in which certain individuals and groups were living. Rather, it was a concept that applied universally to all members of society regardless of their material, class, or power situation. It was a desire to change their perception and understanding of the social relationship by realizing the rational and ethical potential that could unite all individuals, by realizing that co-operation was a fact of social life. Though Green had no doubt contributed towards this shift in focus from form to spirit, Hobhouse gave the best possible statement of this approach when using primarily the concept of evolution. This ethical evolutionary perspective was also expressed by Brougham Villiers whose ideas on social reform were more radical than Hobhouse's. He too believed that 'the general trend of human evolution is towards an ever wider and closer solidarity' and that civiliz-ation progressed towards the displacement of disorganization

---

[53] S. Webb, 'The Basis of Socialism—Historic', in G. B. Shaw (ed.), *Fabian Essays* (1889), p. 60.

and instinct by organization and reason.[54] In its new dimension, social reform was equated with social progress.

Collectivism was for Hobhouse just another way of saying that human behaviour was increasingly directed by the individual's consciousness that he was part of society. The aim and spirit of this collectivism was a social harmony which entailed self-sacrifice and altruism, to be realized in the here and now. Any scheme of social welfare had to satisfy the moral consciousness—the conceptions of justice, equality, and liberty.[55] In itself, this was only a restatement of old liberal precepts—a fact which Hobhouse would not have denied for a moment. In practice, though, as will be seen later on, Hobhouse gave these precepts a very wide interpretation commensurate with his belief in progress and the development of organization and co-operation. But his brand of collectivism never implied more than harmony and co-ordination between individual and social claims. Even Ritchie insisted that biological principles did not signify any merger of the two, thus exhibiting the liberal fear of a monolithic society. Just as evolutionary principles prevented an underestimation of the value and need for cohesion,

the significance of differentiation in development may guard us against the monotonous rigidity of some collectivist ideals, which provide no sufficient scope for individual initiative and no sufficient security against the crystallisation that means decay and death to societies.[56]

Dyer certainly was on firm ground when he asserted that biology was replacing political economy as the scientific basis of politics and ethics.[57] This observation receives further corroboration from the uses of organicism in liberal thought, which shed more light on the issues dealt with in this section.

[54] Villiers, *The Opportunity of Liberalism*, p. 79. Cf. also Hobson, *John Ruskin Social Reformer*, p. 18.

[55] L. T. Hobhouse, 'The Ethical Basis of Collectivism', *International Journal of Ethics*, vol. 8 (1898), 150–1.

[56] D. G. Ritchie, 'Evolution and Democracy', in S. Coit (ed.), *Ethical Democracy*, pp. 2–3.

[57] Dyer, *The Evolution of Industry*, pp. 1, 10.

4. LIBERAL ORGANICISM

Society conceived of as an organism is an idea virtually as old as political thought itself. However, the claim that, in addition to the notion of evolution, the social organism was the second biological concept profoundly to influence late-Victorian liberalism calls for some explanation. The political uses of organicism were as a rule anything but liberal. The theorists we are concerned with encountered the idea through Comte and through Idealism, both sources having contributed to its renewed popularity and diffusion among nineteenth-century social thinkers. It had generally been used as a vague theoretical analogy between the human (or other animal) body and between social structure, function, and development. Its two basic premisses were: (1) The existence of mutual dependence between the parts of an autonomous entity, so that no part could exist separately from the others. (2) The relation between the whole and the parts, whereby the whole was not identical with the sum of the parts and had a will separate from and superior to the particular wills. As such, organicism had much in it to appeal to the Idealist bent of mind inasmuch as Idealism regarded the state as morally and logically prior to its members. Yet the new uses of organicism endorsed the specifically biological contents of the concept. Indeed, the Idealists often failed to realize the full implications of the terms they were borrowing from biology:

In the present age the most conspicuously advancing science is biology; and the categories of organism and evolution are freely transferred to philosophy with the great advantage of lifting it out of the more abstract conceptions of mathematics or mechanics, but too often with insufficient consciousness of what is being done ...[58]

The Idealist notion of organicism has often been interpreted as conservative, reactionary, or absolutist, apparently asserting the claims of society as against those of individuals. These political implications received confirmation from another quarter. In a rather different sense, 'organic' denoted 'natural', 'inherent', gradually growing and developing, and was probably the most common and established sense of the word. There

---

[58] Ritchie, *Darwin and Hegel*, p. 41.

was general agreement concerning, in J. M. Robertson's words, 'the quasi-biological fact ... that no society can stably pass through radical changes of structure and purpose in a generation'.[59] But here again, in the hands of the Burkeian conservative, the progressive faith in purposive change was rejected, the stress being put instead on continuity with the past and a fixed relationship or balance between the classes composing society.

The one figure in mid-nineteenth-century England who, while opposed to conservatism, viewed society as an organism and did so in what appeared to be a scientific and literal, rather than a symbolic, manner was Spencer. Similar to conservative usage, Spencer understood the social organism to be characterized by gradual adaptation and growth, which indicated that society was a natural phenomenon instead of the artifact the social contract theorists thought it was. But unlike conservative usage, growth implied change more than continuity, linked as it was to the notion of evolution. This was not the only feature of Spencer's organicism. What made it peculiar was his repudiation of one of the main points of the organic analogy— the existence of a central sensorium. Whereas the organism analogy was generally used in conjunction with higher organisms, Spencer drew parallels with lower ones.[60] The implications were obvious: not only did Spencer's understanding of evolutionary principles negate any wilful and purposive change on the part of the social organism, but for him consciousness existed only in individuals while the community as a whole had no corporate consciousness. For thus distorting the conventional organic analogy Spencer came under severe attack for inconsistency. Huxley noted that, if anything, the opposite conclusions were to be drawn from the analogy, namely, that the function of the state could not be negative.[61] And Ritchie and Hobson argued that Spencer was led to the false conclusion that 'as there is no social sensorium, it results that the welfare of the aggregate, considered apart from that of

---

[59] Robertson, *The Meaning of Liberalism*, p. 241.

[60] H. Spencer, 'The Social Organism', reprinted in *The Man Versus the State*, p. 205.

[61] Huxley, 'Administrative Nihilism'. For a general discussion of Spencer's organicism see W. H. Simon, 'Herbert Spencer and the "Social Organism"', *Journal of the History of Ideas*, vol. 21 (1960), 294–9.

the units, is not an end to be sought. The society exists for the benefit of its members, not its members for the benefit of the society.'[62]

This critique highlights the distance the new liberalism had travelled since Mill, for whom social progress was to be evaluated by the degree to which individuals were able to do with their own life, for their own benefit, what they chose, as long as they did not harm others or prevent them from doing the same. Not that the new liberals ignored the importance of individual freedom. But biological influences, and in particular a re-reading of the organic analogy, were instrumental in leading to new conclusions. Both evolution and organicism were interconnected inasmuch as they postulated the notion of a cohesive society, thus reinforcing those liberals who regarded society as an interdependent entity in which mutual responsibility was an ethical and practical necessity. But whereas the concept of evolution pointed towards increasing co-operation and continuous planned social improvements, organicism located the responsibility for and control over these developments squarely in the prime communal agency—the state. The new liberals offered a notion of organism unlike either the positivist-Spencerian or the Idealist-conservative one. Society was not a natural phenomenon that could not or should not be interfered with, but neither was it the artifact classical liberalism made it out to be.[63] As Ritchie explained: 'One suspects ... that the choice does not lie solely between "making" and "growing", and that social organisms differ from other organisms in having the remarkable property of making themselves; and the more developed they are, the more consciously do they make themselves.'[64] Consciousness and purposiveness—when translated into political terms—made the notion of organism point to an interventionist, i.e. self-regulatory, theory of government.[65] Government, by this view,

---

[62] Quoted in Ritchie, *The Principles of State Interference*, p. 17, from Spencer's *Principles of Sociology*. See also p. 22 and Hobson, 'Herbert Spencer', 52.

[63] Ritchie, *Natural Rights*, pp. 101–2 and *passim*. See also his *Darwin and Hegel*, p. 251.

[64] Ritchie, *The Principles of State Interference*, p. 49.

[65] Peel, op. cit., pp. 170–1, who contrasts conservative organicism with liberal mechanism (planning and manipulation), ignores this third possibility of self-determined growth which the new liberals attributed to their idea of the social organism.

could not be alien or external to society, being a manifestation of human rationality. To this extent, liberalism eschewed its nineteenth-century prejudices. That it did so while adhering to liberal fundamentals, first and foremost among which was a continued appreciation of individuality, will be shown in the remainder of this chapter.

A. Ritchie: Idealist Evolutionism

The role of the organism model in making liberalism consonant with Idealism as well as with the biological variant of positivism was of special importance for liberal theory. Liberalism remained a viable theory for social and political thinkers because it could establish its legitimacy in relation to the two dominant idea-currents of the English academic world. At the same time, it produced something that was an improvement upon the original formulations of either school and upon the methods by means of which these schools tackled social problems. Two men can be credited with this achievement, Ritchie and Hobson; the first laid the foundations for the new synthesis, whereas the second modified and expanded it into a framework of social thought.

Ritchie's starting-point was what he described as the hopeless controversy between 'Idealism' and 'materialism', between Hegelians and Darwinians. A consideration of both theories under the influence of Green on the one hand and scientific friends on the other, with the purpose of examining the concrete problems of ethics and politics, led him to what he termed Idealist Evolutionism.[66] The concept of the organism first demonstrated its usefulness for Ritchie in a consideration of the evolutionary process. He accepted the teleological perspective adopted by Idealists rather than straightforward evolutionary change.[67] The organism concept when applied to society produced the idea of purposive, directed, interdependent growth. The meeting-point between Hegel and Darwin was in that both had imposed rationality on seemingly non-rational phenomena. 'What distinguishes Darwin's theory from other theories of evolution is the kind of explanation it gives ...

---

[66] Ritchie, *Darwin and Hegel*, vii.
[67] Ibid., p. 47.

Darwin restores "final causes" to their proper place in science
...'[68]

The concept of organism, when used as a model of social growth, could thus reconcile Idealism and biological evolutionism through the part–whole relationship. Applied to ethics it meant that the end of the individual had to be a social end, a common good—that of the whole. As Scott Holland commented some years later, a belief in what Ritchie had called the evolution of the world as a rational purpose was necessary to give direction to social organization.[69] This was once again the quest for a total explanatory outlook on social life. It was not a simple teleological unfolding but—in Hegelian terms—a dialectical conflict and competition of thought and ideas. Indeed, the element of consciousness—an indispensable part of the Idealist terminology—was also an intervening factor of great importance in the evolutionary process. Although Ritchie was aware that society could be regarded as a plurality of organisms,[70] he maintained, in conjunction with Idealist theory:

It is as a State, *i.e.* as an ordered political society, that a social organism becomes most distinctly conscious of its existence as an organism and consequently most capable of regulating the tendencies, which if left to themselves, would make its history a merely natural process.[71]

However, unlike some conservative interpretations of Idealism, Ritchie was careful to stress that his was a dynamic perception of society that did not imply sanctification of what existed. The identification of the 'ought' with the 'is' was mistaken, and the tendency of interpreters of Hegel to read this into his dictum 'the real is the rational' bolstered reaction.[72] The social organism theory was not to be understood as justifying all growth. 'Morality is adequately determined as the *health* of the social organism.'[73] It therefore aspired in the Aristotelian sense

---

[68] Ritchie, *Darwin and Hegel*, p. 60.
[69] H. S. Holland, 'The Living Wage and the Kingdom of God', in *The Industrial Unrest and the Living Wage*. Converging Views of Social Reform, No. 2 (1914), p. 179.
[70] D. G. Ritchie, 'Social Evolution', *International Journal of Ethics*, vol. 6 (1896), 165–81.
[71] Ritchie, *The Moral Function of the State*, p. 6.
[72] Ritchie, *Darwin and Hegel*, pp. 68–9.
[73] Ritchie, *Philosophical Studies*, p. 267.

to the good life, not to mere life. 'Morality comes to mean the conscious and deliberate adoption of those feelings and acts and habits which are advantageous to the welfare of the community; and reflection makes it possible to alter the conception of what the community is, whose welfare is to be considered.'[74] Ethics could not be accounted for in terms of animal biology alone. To this extent Ritchie rejected the biological sense of organic growth. But he anchored his theory in biological processes by maintaining, contrary to Huxley's position, that 'natural selection is a perfectly adequate cause to account for the rise of morality'. Consequently, claimed Ritchie, 'in Ethics the theory of natural selection has vindicated all that has proved most permanently valuable in Utilitarianism'.[75]

Ritchie welcomed the concept of organism as helping political thinkers out of the confusions of individualism and because it was an aid to understanding how society functioned and developed. It was never supposed to be a fully adequate concept. But he improved upon the Idealists in making it more than an abstract explanatory device.[76] It was rooted in social and historical fact and its existence was borne out by biological theory. Moreover, it fortified a collectivist approach to social questions and justified an interventionist theory of the state. It powerfully reinforced the idea of social reform reflected in Hobhouse's writings—a continuous effort at social improvement. It was, furthermore, a synthesis of Idealism and biologism achieved by combining consciousness and competition. It remained for Hobson to complete Ritchie's synthesis between the two systems of thought, and to reconcile it with liberal principles.

B. Hobson: The Science and Art of Welfare

It has already been shown in the previous chapter that Hobson entertained a very comprehensive notion of human welfare, embracing physical, moral, and intellectual aspects of well-being. From the outset Hobson appended a third dimension to the uses of biology in the study of society. To the acceptance of evolutionary and organistic models he added a

[74] Ritchie, Darwin and Hegel, p. 63.
[75] Ibid., p. 62.
[76] As, e.g., in J. S. Mackenzie, An Introduction to Social Philosophy (Glasgow, 1890).

profound awareness of the centrality of the physical aspects of human and social behaviour. This arose from a rich and full appreciation of human nature and life which in itself might indicate why Hobson displayed affinities both to Idealism and to biologism. His total perspective on human life, though not of a Spencerian pretentiousness, came close to constituting a coherent general system, despite a number of inconsistencies.

The great influence on Hobson's thought in this direction was John Ruskin. It was originally as an innovator in the field of political economy—hitherto regarded by Hobson as an arid science[77]—that Ruskin first appealed to Hobson. Both thinkers expanded the subject-matter of economics far beyond its usual limits and interwove it with all fields that could contribute to human life. Hobson attributed to Ruskin the demolition of 'economic man' and the substituting for him of a conscious, rational, and emotional being. To this Ruskin had added the replacement of the money-standard of value by a vital standard.[78] The *Speaker* called this the 'true biology'. Ruskin, with the help of Hobson, had put that science in its proper place. 'For since biology is the art of living, it cannot help considering social conduct, and social conduct must be a branch of ethics, while money-making itself is but a branch of that branch.'[79] Ruskin's equation of wealth with life had after all revolutionized the nineteenth-century attitude to production and consumption, a theme which occupied Hobson in many of his economic writings, and which he expounded most fully in the pre-war period in his book *Work and Wealth*. The old attitude had expressed a preoccupation with the production of quantifiable wealth and a corresponding neglect of consumption which, all in all, was the end of the process—both chronologically and ethically.[80] But Ruskin insisted on all concrete wealth being estimated in relation to the vital cost of its production and the vital utility of its consumption,[81] i.e. by its power to sustain life, with the aim of establishing a general approach to the study of society, a 'full, final conception of Political Economy, as a

[77] Hobson, *Confessions of an Economic Heretic*, p. 55.
[78] Hobson, *John Ruskin Social Reformer*, pp. 75–7.
[79] 'Mr. Ruskin as a Social Teacher', *Speaker*, 12.11.1898.
[80] See Hobson, *The Social Problem*, pp. 45–50; *Work and Wealth*, passim.
[81] Hobson, *Work and Wealth*, p. 9.

science of human welfare, [which] includes within its scope not merely the processes by which men gain a livelihood, but all human efforts and satisfactions'.[82] For Hobson, this furnished 'the necessary hypothetical end or goal required to give meaning to Sociology as a science and to Social Progress as an art'.[83]

In his emphasis on the quality of consumption Hobson proceeded one step ahead of those progressive liberals whose critique of political economy made them focus their attention on mal-distribution as the cause of social maladies. Rather than look at one aspect of the economic process, Hobson's commitment to a total viewpoint compelled him to see the whole process as one. The value of any human activity could only be measured in terms of life. Cost was regarded as expenditure of life and utility its enrichment.[84] These terms varied, to be sure, according to the nature and intensity of the individual need; therefore redistribution in itself could not guarantee human welfare. Embodied in this approach was an obvious utilitarian perspective, in that all goods and activities were evaluated by their usefulness in sustaining life, as is evident from Hobson's approving quotation of Ruskin's posing of the social question: 'How can society consciously order the lives of its members so as to maintain the largest number of noble and happy human beings?'[85] But this was no Benthamite utilitarianism, being qualitative and, further, based on a standard of *social* utility, defined by Hobson as 'the social good regarded as the desirable goal of action'.[86] Unlike Ruskin, Hobson did not posit absolute and immutable principles of health and justice. He accepted the relativity of such values, and consequently the permanent flexibility of social reform, by acknowledging that the standard of life and the ethical standards derived from it were a question

[82] Hobson, *John Ruskin Social Reformer*, p. 74.

[83] Ibid., p. 87. Cf. also E. T. Cook, 'Ruskin and the New Liberalism', *New Liberal Review*, vol. 1 (1901), 18–25.

[84] Hobson, *The Social Problem*, pp. 47–50.

[85] Hobson, *John Ruskin Social Reformer*, p. 155. Hobson rephrased this query in a more sophisticated form: 'Given a number of human beings, with a certain development of physical and mental faculties and of social institutions, in command of given natural resources, how can they best utilize these powers for the attainment of the most complete satisfaction?' (*The Social Problem*, p. 7.)

[86] Hobson, *The Social Problem*, p. 64.

of subjective opinions, in that they depended on human evaluations.[87] Hobson considered Ruskin's presentation to lack the evolutionary viewpoint, which contributed the conception of an orderly and natural development of a standard of consumption, involving the conferring of value upon previously useless goods.[88] Yet, although substantively a dynamic concept, the very reference to social utility implied an objective standard independent of individual whims and partial views while based on a spreading consensus. Hobson's leap from the subjective to the objective was evidently the counterpart of the latent teleology contained in the evolutionary working out of final causes. But this involved operational difficulties concerning practical guidelines to action. By uniting the 'is' and the 'ought' Hobson confused, not facts and values, but present and future. How was one to know when the objective standard of social utility had been realized? Hobson vacillated, as he did not infrequently, between an ideal and its present manifestations, between an ultimate rational interpretation of social utility and its present indeterminacy owing to the multifariousness and uneven composition of current societies. The aim of his qualitative utilitarianism was, however, clear. There existed a social good, limited in time and space but sufficiently articulated and acceptable to serve as a framework for social action.

Hobson's concept of social utility, related to his idea of society as a prime ethical entity, received added justification from the idea of society as a social organism. Of all the liberal theorists who used the term 'social organism', Hobson gave it its fullest treatment and deepest analysis. At the same time, the strains attendant upon using such a concept to elucidate liberal theory are evident throughout his writings. That trend in organicism which tended, in Rousseauist terms, to construct a social will often opposed to individual wills, could be interpreted as reasserting the undesirable antagonism between man and society which liberal criticism had found to characterize the early utilitarianism. That such antagonism was anathema to new liberals needs no explanation, especially if coupled with a possible complete suppression of the individual will. This might explain certain hesitations of Hobson's in employing the social organism concept and the consequent tensions and inconsistencies in its use.

Organic welfare appeared to Hobson to be the best approximation to a vital standard of value, and that for three reasons. Firstly, it acknowledged the fact that the roots of human industrial activity were physical—'the expenditure and recoupment of physical energy'. Moreover, the gregarious instinct which cemented societies, though rationalized with the progress of the human mind, had biological roots.[89] In contrast to Victorian morality, material as well as spiritual needs were stressed.[90] Secondly, the organic point of view was a comprehensive one in that it evaluated economic activity with regard to its total effect upon human life. Reforms which applied to partial manifestations of individual (and for that matter, social) life were doomed to failure. Social reform had to proceed on all fronts in a co-ordinated manner,[91] and both specialization and the piecemeal approach were its enemies. Thirdly, it adequately described the essence of social life, for society was an organic structure and could only be understood 'as a group-life with a collective body, a collective consciousness and will, and capable of realising a collective vital end'.[92] This was the basis for a theory of society—specifically, for a notion of community—considered to be so lacking in liberal thought. That deficiency, so deeply felt by Barnett,[93] was remedied by the organic viewpoint which supplied both a scientific framework for the application of social reform and a means for evaluating and directing it.

Hobson, even more conclusively than Ritchie, spanned the gap between Idealism and biologism. It is not surprising that he

---

[89] Hobson, *Work and Wealth*, pp. 12–15. Hobhouse had already stated this in his *Mind in Evolution* (1901).

[90] '. . . for the practical reformer, the satisfaction of the lower material need is always more urgent and important than the satisfaction of a higher need, because the latter is historically non-existent, having as yet no soil out of which to grow'. (Hobson, *The Social Problem*, p. 82.)

[91] See below, Chapter Four, pp. 140–1.

[92] Hobson, *Work and Wealth*, p. 15 and *John Ruskin Social Reformer*, p. 155. Hobson admitted that the concept 'organism' was not an exact description of society but an explanatory device: '. . . it is more appropriate than any other concept, and some concept must be applied'. It was a question of intellectual expediency, dictated by the clearness and force of the term (*Work and Wealth*, pp. 15, 18).

[93] See Chapter Two, p. 41.

had much in common with Idealism. His preoccupation with values and ideas as realized in society, his endorsement of evolutionary ethics, his universalism, all point in that direction. He was an active Rationalist under the auspices of the Ethical Movement, which was host to Oxford Idealists as well. Although Hobson himself rejected Hegel's system and method, it is remarkable to what extent parallels can be found between the two,[94] that is, to what extent an unintended echoing of Idealist tenets emerged within the British liberal tradition, far out-distancing Green's personal contribution. Hobson, because he also appreciated the biological facets of human life, was eminently equipped for constructing a synthesis. One aspect of this synthesis was, as Hobson realized: 'It is not the least of Spencer's victories that he has forced evolution on the idealists—those who approach Unity from the other side.'[95] He agreed with Ritchie that reason and order were common to both schools of thought. Indeed, the Idealists now had biological proof of the advance of reason in the concrete world. However, Hobson's concept of organism, while bridging the gap between the social implications of Idealism and biologism, appeared to improve on both. He differentiated his concept of society from the Idealist one when he asserted that society was a vital structure, not exclusively a spiritual or ethical one.[96] Men entered body and soul into society and any separation of the two was meaningless. Nevertheless, Hobson was not sure which element in his social organism model he should stress more. This indecision was a question of finding the right balance between the uses of the model so as best to employ it in the service of liberal theory. Thus he stated elsewhere:

... whatever view we hold about Society on the physical plane ... it can, I think, be made quite clear that Society is rightly regarded as a moral rational organism in the sense that it has a common psychic life, character and purpose, which are not to be resolved into the life, character and purpose of its individual members.[97]

And although he observed that 'recent biological researches

[94] See M. Freeden, 'J. A. Hobson as a New Liberal Theorist: Some Aspects of his Social Thought Until 1914', *Journal of the History of Ideas*, vol. 34 (1973), esp. 423–6.
[95] Hobson, 'Herbert Spencer', 51.
[96] Hobson, *Work and Wealth*, p. 14.
[97] Hobson, 'The Re-Statement of Democracy', *CR*, vol. 81 (1902), 263. Reprinted in Hobson, *The Crisis of Liberalism*.

strengthen the tendency to regard Society as an organism even on its physical side',[98] he could elsewhere remark that 'biology has in the past been too arrogant in pressing distinctively physical implications of the term "organism" into the dawning science of sociology'.[99] Hobson therefore sometimes tended to use the term 'super-organic', which together with his search for unity of outlook were expressed in his belief in a new science of psycho-biology. He was convinced that 'the practical problems of the art of social reform have one root in physiology, one in psychology. A sane standard of work on the one hand, or of enjoyment on the other, can only be achieved by social reforms based ultimately on these related studies.'[100] The study of society was on the way to becoming a 'collective psycho-physics'.[101] Here, then, was the scientific foundation of community. Whether or not this involved an autonomously functioning entity was, however, a moot or even unclarified point among new liberals, as their treatment of the general will illustrates.

C. *The General Will: The Nucleus of Community?*

The differences between Hobhouse and Hobson revolved in the main around the degree to which they were willing to grant society an autonomous existence. Hobhouse had written that 'to speak of society as if it were a physical organism is a piece of mysticism, if indeed it is not quite meaningless'. He restricted himself to the limited idea of organism as denoting interdependence of the people constituting a society.[102] For Hobhouse, 'organic' was identical with 'harmonic' and related to the ability and willingness of the parts to co-operate with each other. Hobson considered this treatment of organic formulae to be inadequate:

I am disposed to think that Mr. Hobhouse does not carry his central organic mind quite far enough, as, for instance, when he says that 'there is no thought except in the mind of an individual thinker'. Nor am I certain that it is necessary to repudiate so confidently as he does

[98] Ibid., 262.

[99] Hobson, *Work and Wealth*, p. 17. See also Hobson, leader on Hobhouse's *Democracy and Reaction, MG*, 28.11.1904.

[100] Hobson, *The Social Problem*, p. 257.

[101] Hobson, *Work and Wealth*, p. 16.

[102] Hobhouse, *Social Evolution and Political Theory*, p. 87.

the existence of a social body corresponding with and related to the social mind ... we have no experience of the existence or the action of any sort of mind without the body.[103]

Hobhouse, as we have seen, was vague and undecided about the existence of a central mind. When he later moved towards identifying the organic with the purposive, the teleological, in his book *Development and Purpose*, this was welcomed by Hobson.[104] But although Hobhouse realized that purpose when applied to the social body postulated a central mind, he was unable to explain its relation to reality.[105]

The argument over the existence of a central mind was closely connected with the concept of the general will. Hobson used 'social will' interchangeably with 'general will' and regarded it as an obvious concomitant of organicism. Hobhouse distinguished between social will and general will, claiming that the latter was as a rule non-existent. '... when we speak of social thought, social will, or more generally of social mind, we neither imply a mystical psychic unity nor a fully achieved consciousness of the social life on the part of the component members of society.' Social mind simply denoted the mass of communicable ideas operative in a society, the result of interaction between individuals.[106] This issue was a constant bone of contention between the two theorists. It obviously enabled Hobson to proceed farther along the road towards a general conception of community than did Hobhouse. Hobhouse posited social development as dependent on the evolution of individual minds towards harmony and collective responsibility, whereas Hobson could insist that the germ of an ethical and wholesome society existed in the psycho-physical structure of any human group at all stages of development,[107] and that the nature of human thought was not separate but assimilated and fused through interaction into a common consciousness.[108] Hobson dismissed of course the false monadism of Benthamite

[103] Hobson, review of Hobhouse's *Social Evolution and Political Theory*, *MG*, 22.2.1912.
[104] Hobson, review of Hobhouse's *Development and Purpose*, *MG*, 22.4.1913.
[105] Hobhouse, *Development and Purpose*, pp. 324, 364–7.
[106] Hobhouse, *Social Evolution and Political Theory*, pp. 96–7. Cf. also Hobhouse, 'Ethics and Economics', review of Hobson's *Work and Wealth*, *MG*, 24.7.1914.
[107] Hobson, *Work and Wealth*, p. 350.
[108] Hobson, 'The Re-Statement of Democracy', 265.

utilitarianism:[109] 'If... the social will be taken merely to mean
the aggregate of feeling for the public good thus generated in the
separate wills, it may not suffice to support the common-
weal.'[110] The social will was rather an *esprit de corps* 'far
transcending the vision and the purpose even of the most
enlightened and altruistic member'.[111] It was an intrinsic
component of an emerging social consciousness wielded in
practical activity, resulting from processes of industrial co-
operation. Hobson saw no sense in talking in the abstract about
a general will and the spiritual solidarity of society without
anchoring that will in corporate institutions: '... every well-
ordered reform of economic structure is an expression of the
moral force of the community, the "general will" finding
embodiment in some stable and serviceable form of social
support'.[112] Social reform was seen to originate in a common
social will, not in the humanitarian conscience of isolated
reformers, or in the sectional particularistic viewpoint of a
group or class. Hence Hobson's criticism of Ruskin for the
latter's antithesis between individual and public effort:

It is perfectly true that every social reform requires that the individual
members of that society shall accept and respond to a moral appeal: it
is perfectly false that they can by moral action in their individual
capacity apply a social remedy. The separate action of individuals can
never attain a social end, simply because they are *ex hypothesi* not
acting as members of society. Social evils require social remedies.[113]

The general will was above all an empirical fact, an aspect of
the psychical relations between the members of a society.
Indeed, the contact between minds, maintained Hobson, was
far more intimate and constant than that between bodies.[114]
His empirical description of the origins and the nature of the
general will was a departure from the notions harboured by
some Oxford Idealists, in particular Bosanquet. Hobson's

---

[109] Hobson, *The Social Problem*, p. 254. See also Hobson, *Work and Wealth*, p. 302.

[110] Hobson, *Work and Wealth*, p. 302. Here Hobson can obviously be contrasted with Green.

[111] Ibid., p. 303.

[112] Hobson, *The Crisis of Liberalism*, p. 217.

[113] Hobson, *John Ruskin Social Reformer*, pp. 198–9. Cf. Hobson, *Work and Wealth*, p. 350.

[114] Hobson, 'The Re-Statement of Democracy', 263–4.

'general will' actually had roots in animal instincts. Once again the organism concept was proved to be no mere analogy.[115] However, in his notion of instinct evolving towards rationality Hobson was demonstrating an Idealist turn of mind, even if he added an emphasis on the physical origins of ethical behaviour. Hobson also occasionally sounded the plea for social efficiency when justifying conformity to the general will. By social efficiency he understood 'the desire of individuals to merge or subordinate their separate ends of individuality, and to act on the supposition that a common social end realized by the individual consciousness, is in itself desirable.'[116] Though such individual conduct was in part a matter of knowledge and of rational self-control, it did lead Hobson into difficulties when translating these ideas into practical terms. As will be seen, any political approach which raised social efficiency to the level of a desired end was bound to clash with a liberal philosophy which relegated efficiency to a bottom rung in the ladder of priorities and which, indeed, espoused ends and values that from many viewpoints would be 'inefficient'.[117]

But could the subordination of the individual will to the general will be avoided? Here Hobson was vague and imprecise in his use of terminology. In 1902 he wrote that 'the individual feeling, his will, his ends and interests, are not entirely merged in or sacrificed to the public feeling, will and ends, but over a certain area they are fused and identified'.[118] Some years later he criticized Ramsay MacDonald for almost the same ideas he had himself expressed, in terms reminiscent of Hobhouseian argument rather than his own. Reviewing MacDonald's *Socialism and Government*, Hobson wrote:

... we cannot go so far as Mr. Macdonald in his interpretation of the centralisation and specialisation involved in the organic treatment of society. In a healthy State individual wills, though co-operative, are not fused in a general will. It is for the preservation of a harmony between individual and collective wills and activities that we defend the policy of the referendum and of proportionate representation.[119]

---

[115] Hobson, *Work and Wealth*, p. 353.
[116] Hobson, *The Social Problem*, p. 263.
[117] See below, Chapter Five.
[118] Hobson, 'The Re-Statement of Democracy', 265.
[119] Hobson, 'Socialism and Government', review, *MG*, 27.12.1909.

But this was not typical Hobsonian language.[120] In the 1902 article Hobson specified the workings of the general will. He envisaged a government of experts—the educated and actively-governing classes—parallel to the nerve centre of an organism, acting as pivot to a feedback process. The cells had the right to convey information and advice to the centre which then formulated the policy that the cells had to carry out. Only as a last resort did Hobson concede that 'it is advantageous to the organism that ... rights of suggestion, protest, veto and revolt should be accorded to its members'.[121] This elitist model of government came under fire from the *Manchester Guardian*, who feared that Hobson had overstepped acceptable limits in denying individual rights and had in fact contradicted what he himself had recently written,[122] thus undermining the 'reciprocity, that tie of mutual obligation between the whole community and every individual member of it, which we take to be the central point of Mr. Hobson's own theory'. The newspaper reminded Hobson that to assert that the majority merely had to obey laws was untenable even from the organic perspective, let alone to the older generation of liberals:

Society may be an organism, but it is certainly not a machine in which the parts do not matter as long as the work gets done. On the contrary, because its life is the life of its members and nothing over and above, it rests on their individual character, initiative, energy, their tastes, their bent, their feelings—all that we sum up in the word personality.[123]

Perhaps this insistence on liberal fundamentals within the framework supplied by Hobson stimulated him into elucidating and modifying his views. At any rate, in following years he made a real effort to delve further into the organic model in search of a fortified liberal-democratic argumentation.

[120] It should be noted that the slight inconsistencies or changes of opinion displayed by Hobson cannot be explained as a development in time. He reprinted early articles of his years later in book form without any modifications. His understanding of organicism vacillated between physical and non-physical interpretations without a pattern. Most inconsistencies of Hobson's, not severe enough to disrupt the general coherence of his social thought, are better explained as reflections of the intellectual gropings and hammering-out of issues which typified the new liberals.

[121] Hobson, 'The Re-Statement of Democracy', 269–70.

[122] In *The Social Problem*, pp. 93–111. See below, Chapter Six.

[123] Leader, *MG*, 4.2.1902.

D. *The Reformulation of Liberalism*

The dangers involved in operationalizing the general will had been in the forefront of men's minds ever since the French Revolution had implemented Rousseau's dictum and had forced men to be free. The task of achieving a delicate balance between the individual and society became more than usually complicated with such concepts as a starting-point. The problem was how to reconcile the empirical freedom so valued by practical liberals with the rational freedom inculcated into them by ethical movements, Idealism and the moral implications of liberal theory itself. Hobson, as we have observed, was not always up to that task. The perspective dictated by the organism theory made him trifle at times with sacred liberal principles. Accordingly, he regarded maxims such as 'no taxation without representation' solely as a matter of expediency, because the conception of society as a moral organism negated the old democratic idea of every member's right to the same power of determining social actions. Likewise, he considered as absurd from his viewpoint the tenet that 'every man's life is of equal value to Society'.[124] Instead of that he repeatedly postulated the old socialist slogan 'from each according to his powers, to each according to his needs' as the full organic formula, and even saw Mill as having felt his way towards this notion of political and economic justice.[125]

Nevertheless, Hobson succeeded in establishing a formula which preserved the integrity of liberal tenets within the organic framework, as the following passage demonstrates:

The unity of ... socio-industrial life is not a unity of mere fusion in which the individual virtually disappears, but a federal unity in which the rights and interests of the individual shall be conserved for him by the federation. The federal government, however, conserves these individual rights, not, as the individualist maintains, because it exists for no other purpose than to do so. It conserves them because it also recognises that an area of individual liberty is conducive to the health of the collective life. Its federal nature rests on a recognition alike of individual and social ends, or, speaking more accurately, of social ends

[124] Hobson, 'The Re-Statement of Democracy', 266–7.
[125] Ibid., 268. Robertson also adopted the maxim for liberal theory (*The Meaning of Liberalism*, pp. 152–3).

that are directly attained by social action and of those that are realised in individuals.[126]

Hobson envisaged a society which, by its concerted action, encouraged and engendered the development of individual capabilities. But society did not exist for this purpose, as some old liberals would have maintained. Society encouraged individual development because society itself was the beneficiary. That alone was the *raison d'être* of individualism. Here was a very fine attempt at laying down a new basic liberal formula to replace the antiquated maxims of J. S. Mill concerning self- and other-regarding actions. It was probably the most adequate theoretical expression of the change of perspective that had emerged within liberalism. It displayed an ingenious combination of innovation and traditionalism as far as liberalism was concerned: the innovating aspect of the formula being the priority of social aims and interests over individual ones; the traditional aspect being the retention of the liberal belief in the highest and most harmonious development of the individual. Thus were individualism and collectivism inseparably intertwined.

It can of course be claimed that this formula did not change the substance of liberalism in the least, but that it merely altered the perspective from which society was regarded, the rationale of individual activity. Individualism would flourish as before, the only difference being that the liberal theorist could explain away its manifestations as ultimately geared towards the good of society, and only incidentally benefiting the actor. This could be the gist of such a sentence: 'Scope must remain, in the interests of society itself, for the legitimate play of individuality. The well-ordered society will utilise the *energies of egoism* in fruitful fields of individual activity.'[127] Conversely, it could be said that evaluation of human activity solely in terms of the social good divested individuality of any meaning. This flexibility of interpretation should be thought of more as a strength than a weakness. For in a time of changing concepts, ideas and social facts, it was more applicable and more vital than the Millian dogmas. In its fragile balance, it symbolized the tension

[126] Hobson, *Work and Wealth*, p. 304.
[127] Ibid., p. 291 (my italics).

between individual and social claims, a tension now possibly occupying the minds of men more than ever before.[128] Hobson exhibited clear signs of this tension in his attitude to Mill. Not only did he reject the distinction between self- and other-regarding conduct, but he accepted the legitimacy of conduct adversely affecting others: 'A certain amount of injury to existing social order must remain the perpetual price of progress.'[129] But it was precisely this injury that vindicated eccentricity. Following Ritchie,[130] Hobson maintained that to force natural instincts into certain grooves was a neglect of the teachings of evolution about the mode of progress. Most eccentricities and extravagances had to be regarded from the standpoint of social progress, as experiments in life, and here 'Modern biology and its companion science psychology enforce most powerfully the plea of J. S. Mill'.[131]

The liberal outlook in Hobson's approach is brought out more strikingly when compared to Webb's interpretation of organicism. In *Fabian Essays*, published in 1889, Webb wrote:

... we must take even more care to improve the social organism of which we form part, than to perfect our own individual developments. Or rather, the perfect and fitting development of each individual is not necessarily the utmost and highest cultivation of his own personality, but the filling, in the best possible way, of his humble function in the great social machine.[132]

Thus Webb, who was one of the first to realize the importance of the 'new scientific conception of the Social Organism'— apparently under Ritchie's influence, whom he quoted—failed to grasp the subtleties of the term or to accord within its framework a place to individual liberty. Ritchie himself, however, was preoccupied with this question and tried to equate the perfection of character with the existence of the

[128] Dyer had outlined the position already in 1890, when he defined true socialism as a state 'in which each, while retaining his individual liberty, will remember that he is only a unit in a great organization, the welfare of which is of much more importance than his own personal advance either in wealth or position'. (H. Dyer, *Christianity and Social Problems* (Glasgow, 1890), p. 11.)

[129] Hobson, 'Character and Society', in P. L. Parker (ed.), *Character and Life* (1912), p. 96.

[130] See above, p. 93.

[131] Hobson, 'Character and Society', in P. L. Parker (ed.), *Character and Life*, pp. 94–5.

[132] S. Webb, 'The Basis of Socialism. Historic', in *Fabian Essays*, p. 58.

social organism. This was possible with a concept of character that included the attribute of concern for the well-being of others, and with a concept of the social organism that encompassed the whole of mankind, thus avoiding internecine strife.[133] Ritchie, too, concluded that the organic analogy taught that 'in a healthy body all the parts may develop together'. The government and the individual could both gain in strength, not at each other's expense.[134] An identical opinion was expressed by Brougham Villiers.[135] Liberal inferences from the metaphor of the biological organism were also drawn by Hobhouse, in line with his notion of harmony:

... the life of the body is not perfected by suppressing the life of the cells, but by maintaining it at its highest point of efficiency. Nor is the organism developed by reducing the cells to a uniform type, but rather by allowing each type to vary on its own lines, provided always that the several variations are in the end mutually compatible.[136]

Hobson himself was increasingly aware of the fact that, although in principle community, and indeed some aspects of liberal theory, did not necessarily imply democracy, it had become virtually impossible to be undemocratic without being illiberal. He came to regard biology as justifying the importance of participation, for if there was any class deprived of all obligation to take part in government, it was doomed to political disease through the atrophy of a human function. 'The body politic will become diseased and suffer if any of its members is deprived of all participation in government ...'[137] Hobson now repudiated H. G. Wells's idea of an aristocratic 'wise' rule because of its inevitable damage to society. The proper functioning of society depended on the expression of every man's thoughts, feelings, and interests in acts of public government.[138] In effect, Hobson conceived of the general will as playing freely through the state, checking abuses of social

[133] Ritchie, *Philosophical Studies*, pp. 322–3.
[134] Ritchie, *The Principles of State Interference*, p. 24.
[135] B. Villiers, *The Socialist Movement in England* (1908), pp. 291–2.
[136] Hobhouse, *Social Evolution and Political Theory*, p. 90.
[137] Hobson, 'The New Aristocracy of Mr. Wells', *CR*, vol. 89 (1906), 496.
[138] Ibid. Cf. also W. Clarke, 'Liberalism and Social Reform', in W. Bliss (ed.), *The Encyclopedia of Social Reform* (New York, 1897), p. 812, who saw the future success of liberalism dependent on realizing the idea of participation. Many English social thinkers collaborated on the encyclopedia, which also had an English supplement.

power at every stage. The state was an instrument for the co-operative action of individual citizens, rather than an organ of class interest. The question of a civic spirit was mainly one of education, by means of which the real harmony of the industrial and political systems would become evident. But the demand for such education would have to originate with the people themselves.[139]

The imagery of health and disease within the context of organicism was quite prevalent throughout the period. Ritchie had considered indifference to politics a symptom of disease for the same reasons as Hobson: '... the constitution of a country in its every fibre should be such an organism as to give a genuine and healthy expression to the "general will" or spirit of the community.'[140] But it was not only a question of exercising the human spirit. The human body had to be provided for as well. This was seen by the biologist Bateson as justifying a policy of social reform incorporating some type of socialism:

Just as the body needs its humbler organs, so a community needs its lower grades, and just as the body decays if even the humblest organs starve, so it is necessary for society adequately to ensure the maintenance of all its constituent members so long as they are contributing to its support.[141]

Brougham Villiers elaborated on this point: 'The lives of men are so bound up with one another in the complex web of society, that it is impossible for social want or disease in any part of the body politic not, in the long run, to bring ruin to others.' Those diseases, both physical and moral, would be handed on and eventually destroy the nation, unless the power of the state was employed to combat this phenomenon.[142] Social reform was immediately and urgently necessary on the basis of the organic perception of society, as a sort of continuous 'maintenance-work' upon the various elements constituting it. That perception was a powerful reinforcer of 'state socialism' and of the action of individuals for their own betterment via the central social organs. This approach modified the liberal suspicion of

---

[139] Hobson, 'State Interference', SPM, vol. 13 (1908), 78–9; also 'Political Ethics of Socialism', SPM, vol. 13 (1908), 128–31.
[140] Ritchie, The Moral Function of the State, pp. 11–12.
[141] Bateson, op. cit., p. 25.
[142] Villiers, The Opportunity of Liberalism, pp. 24, 30–1.

the state and tended to restore confidence in it. As Villiers explained:

A State that is closely in touch with the whole people, and whose action enters largely into their lives ... becomes a thing, separation from which is to the individual neither desirable nor conceivable. It is not something outside of and alien to the individual life, but the means by which that life can alone attain full freedom of expression, the effective agent of the Nation, the organ of its collective will.[143]

This persuasion, despite its similarities to Idealism, was the natural and logical conclusion of the progressive biological thought of the period. Villiers, like many other advanced liberals, had arrived at an expanded and more radical expression of Green's social philosophy by means of the concepts of 'evolution' and 'organism'.

The developments in liberal social theory that have been surveyed in the last two chapters cannot be regarded as other than a major intellectual contribution both to liberalism and to the social thought of the era. This contribution has been somewhat overlooked in the plethora of new ideas then being launched and worked out—the various streams of socialism, social psychology, and pluralism. There is no reason to apportion less importance to the resuscitation of liberalism which, as will be made clearer in the following chapters, has left a heritage at least as solid as the others. The dual anchorage of liberalism both in the positivist and in the Idealist traditions must be seen as the key to its successful transformation or reinterpretation. A shift in focus occurred from concern with the individual as such to concern with the nature of the social relationship. Here ethical socialism was corroborated by biological science. The movement in the new liberalism towards an identifiable organic social entity, which at the very least could not be resolved into the actions of its members as individuals, if it was not a distinct psycho-physical being, made out the strongest possible case for regarding society as a community and as a creator of social values and property. But this concept of society did not, as it might have, necessitate a compromise on liberal essentials. Indeed, these too were reinforced by science: liberty, individual perfection, and

[143] Ibid., p. 84.

variation were prerequisites and attributes of social 'health' in the widest sense. With the emergence of mind as the primary factor in human evolution, competition ceased to be related to a struggle for existence and, though not eliminated, was removed to the sphere of intangible spiritual goods. Collectivism and individualism were related in a scientifically struck balance, by nature more of a synthesis than a compromise.

The 'vision of society' liberals were engaged in formulating was a dynamic conception involving conscious acts of human will to preserve the ethical constitution of society. It was not conservative because a constant innovatory and adaptive effort was needed to realize the potential and natural ethicality of man. That intellectual effort, too, was part of human nature. The state was conceived of as a self-regulatory instrument of ethical consciousness. This dispensed with the idea of an external superimposed institution but, though similar to Idealist formulae, never meant adopting the view that the state was identical with a rational society. Rather, it encompassed a general utilitarian notion of corporate action consequent on the need to maintain a high level of social health. Liberalism achieved a totality and unity of perspective that fully merits its designation as a social philosophy. A new deeper understanding of human nature resulted in a broad concept of welfare and, as we shall now see, profoundly influenced the ideas embodied in the notion of social reform.

IV

The Nature of Liberal Social Reform

IF ideology be defined as action-oriented political theorizing,
there needs be an intervening stage between the moulding of a
socio-political *Weltanschauung*—the concern of the two previous
chapters—and the drawing-up of detailed suggestions for
legislative and administrative measures. This chapter examines
the middle range of ideological activity. It consists of the
translation of general categories of social and politico-
philosophical analysis and deontology concerning human
nature and social processes into a time- and space-bound
application. It also necessitates the extension of the circle of
theoreticians and ideologues to include participants who, while
perhaps less sophisticated in their over-all perceptions and
exactitude of formulation, are closer to the realities of the
situation in which they operate. Late-Victorian and Edwardian
England were the particular scenes in which the theoretical
changes of liberalism were worked out in relation to current
political and economic problems, and in which a mental
climate was created from which all progressive practitioners of
social reform were to draw. The crystallization of new attitudes
towards social life, the infusion of a heightened awareness of
communal ends, and the recognition of the changing role social
institutions, in particular the state, would be called upon to
play, were reflected in the emergence of social reform as one of
the most prominent terms of progressive politics and ideology.
Ethics and evolution contributed towards a profound change in
the content of social reform, as has already been shown, and it
now became the dominant item of the new liberal policy, the
link between the emerging liberal social philosophy and the
concrete steps the politicians were now urged to undertake.

When considering the wider circle of new liberals, one cannot expect to find, concerning the meaning of social reform,
the same unity and consistency of thought described in the

previous chapter. To begin with, there was probably only one
notion on which consensus prevailed, namely that reform
implied gradualism. The remainder of the problems arising
from the term 'social reform' were at first unanswered, often
even unrecognized: did it involve a reshaping of society in
general, progress to a new form or return to a good one; or was it
just a repair of damage to existing form which, once set right,
would continue functioning faultlessly as it was supposed to?
Moreover, the meaning of 'social' in this connection was just as
vague. Sometimes it was merely synonymous with improving
the economic condition of certain groups; at other times it
applied to primary social processes; yet again it meant all that
was not included in political reform. It was used to refer to social
relations, social evils, and social structure. However, two main
conceptions of social reform became salient among liberals in
the closing years of the nineteenth century. On the one hand
was the established interpretation of social reform: the restorative notion of rendering help to individuals and groups
that were at a disadvantage—basically material—with respect
to their fellow citizens. On the other was a desire to regenerate
or redesign society in such a way as to realize ethical values
among *all* its members. Within these two frameworks were a
multitude of variations. But interchange and refinement of ideas
prevented any crucial polarization among liberal thinkers and
gradually led to the predominance of the second concept over the
first, or perhaps—the incorporation of the first concept in the
second.

I. BEYOND A POLICY FOR THE DISADVANTAGED

Originally the demand for social reform had arisen out of an
increased awareness of the plight of the poor and as such had
simply entailed doing something about it. At first, as Hobson
saw it, the pure humanitarianism of the early nineteenth
century was philanthropy directed to individual cases of
suffering, together with an 'utter absence of all feeling that
anything is wrong with the general working of the industrial
system'.[1] What was lacking was an appreciation of the 'condition of the people' in relation to its economic causes. At a later

[1] J. A. Hobson, 'The Ethics of Industrialism', in S. Coit (ed.), *Ethical Democracy:
Essays in Social Dynamics* (1900), p. 84.

stage movements arose which sensed moral defects and highlighted social questions concerning the operation of factories,
mines, sanitation, and the Poor Law. But they as well were too
sentimental, limited, and concrete, in Hobson's opinion, to be
successful. The measures they advocated were to be 'regarded
primarily as a progress along a line of least resistance before the
pressure of humanitarian sentiment'.[2] Hobson maintained that
personal kindness, charity, and humanitarianism could do no
more than promote palliatives. All such forces were in-
efficacious when unguided by larger principles of social justice.

Hobson's ideas, however, were too advanced in relation to
the prevailing mood of most liberals. Dilke interpreted the
'condition of the people' issue as referring to the majority of the
community, the wage-earners,[3] though he assumed that eventually, even if not yet, those questions would come to concern
the entire people. For Dilke, who may serve as a typical
example of the standard liberal-radical approach to social
reform, it was the duty of the community to give a fair chance to
every man, and to sweep away obstacles to the free course of
nature when beneficial to the individual. The failure of
unrestricted competition meant also organizing the force of the
state in the interest of the weak.[4] According to this view, social
reform was directed at grievances of the working section of the
population, acting in their particular interest. It was hence
obviously regarded by many as promoting class interests. The
fact that this class constituted the majority only serves to
underline that state action on behalf of the majority was
considered to be a new departure. Secondly, it put forward a
limited ideal of equality of opportunity—the removal of
hindrances to unfettered human behaviour within certain
confines.

Though the practical removal of hindrances was a restorative
rather than a regenerative approach,[5] the question of aiding the
poor had by the end of the 1880s passed the stage of mere

[2] Ibid., p. 85.
[3] C. W. Dilke, 'A Radical Programme', NR, vol. 3 (1890), 2–3.
[4] Ibid. 158.
[5] Cf. J. G. Rogers, 'Is the Liberal Party in Collapse?', NC, vol. 43 (1898), 151. And
the extreme position was outlined as late as 1909 by the Individualist M.P. H. Cox: 'We
cannot therefore hope to remould society. The most we can do is to amend here and
there the worst evils, to curb this vice, to remove that impediment to progress. This is
true social reform...' ('The Budget of 1909', NC, vol. 65 (1909), 916).

humanitarianism. It now involved a certain method of dealing with the distress of the working classes. One of the elder generation of liberals, G. W. E. Russell, had written already in 1883 that the Liberal party had a special duty to deal with matters affecting the food, health, housing, amusement, and culture of the working classes, the end of liberalism being the creation of better moral and physical surroundings for the mass of the citizenry.[6] Assuming these to be the prime targets of social reform, the recurring refrain of progressive reformers was that they could be achieved primarily, if not wholly, by means which would secure a larger amount of material equality in society. Thus the 'materialistic' doctrine of redistribution of wealth was the initial reply of liberals to the problem of achieving the social good. This was of course not an exclusively liberal doctrine. The less extreme among the official Socialists espoused it as did the Fabians and Joseph Chamberlain.[7] As Atherley-Jones saw it, the essence of social reforms was in that 'without violence to persons or shock to the principles of public morality, there may be compassed for our people a wider diffusion of physical comfort, *and thus* a loftier standard of national morality. This is the new Liberalism.'[8] The possibility of redistribution must have immediately come to the mind of any intelligent observer bent on seeking remedies to the social problem. The question is rather, as it has been throughout these pages, what the liberal theorists did with it.

A potential tension existed in the liberal approach to redistribution, because from a narrow point of view it could be seen as a sectional policy, whereas one of the repeated liberal dogmas was the 'cause of social good against class interests'.[9] At first this tension was hardly evident, usually arising in cases where the cause of labour—as a political movement, not a social agglomerate—was mistakenly identified with aiding the work-

[6] G. W. E. Russell, 'The New Liberalism: A Response', *NC*, vol. 26 (1889), 496.

[7] See, e.g., H. H. Champion, 'The Labour "Platform" at the Next Election', *NC*, vol. 30 (1891), 1037; S. Webb, 'What Mr. Gladstone Ought to Do. V', *FR*, vol. 53 (1893); J. Chamberlain, 'The Labour Question', *NC*, vol. 32 (1892), 677.

[8] L. A. Atherley-Jones, 'The New Liberalism', *NC*, vol. 26 (1889), 192 (my italics).

[9] T. H. Green, *Liberal Legislation and Freedom of Contract*, p. 7. Traces of this tension were observed by C. F. G. Masterman in the malaise of the Liberal government of 1906, which appeared 'specially anxious to promote legislation which will obviously benefit one section of the community without exciting compensating anger in any other'. ('Politics in Transition', *NC*, vol. 63 (1908), 9.)

ing classes. The Radical ideal, however, as Haldane remarked, was equality, and there is no doubt that Radicalism impressed upon liberalism that no interpretation of freedom was tenable that did not include some striving towards equality, however vaguely perceived. The state, claimed Haldane, had to be supplied 'with the means of in some measure modifying the advantages which one man gets over another, and the inequalities of fortune which must always arise from diversity of natural capacity'.[10] Once more, the justice of such measures was seen to be the protection of the weak against the strong, indeed the forestalling of the struggle for existence. The diversity of natural capacity was not, of course, regarded by liberals as a regrettable and inevitable evil. As one liberal wrote, liberalism was not communistic in the sense of bringing about equal distribution of wealth. It was instead concerned with the removal of inequality due to privilege, and with securing to all the same opportunities and rights.[11] In fact, a Radical doctrine was smoothly integrated into the grand liberal tradition, as Robertson explained: '... the saying that the spirit of Liberalism makes for "equality of opportunity to all"... would be a logical paraphrase or extension of the general motto of past Liberalism, namely, "war on privilege".'[12] This is another example of the mechanism of conceptual extension by which liberalism adjusted itself to current demands. For, as we have seen, by the end of the century equality of opportunity was a term given very wide leeway. It entailed more and more sweeping measures of reform to attain it. Among old liberals, more often than not, the word 'equitable' rather than 'equal' was used together with the word 'distribution'.[13] Once again, Mill was evoked to demonstrate the continuity of liberal social thought in the demand for more equitable distribution of wealth. But Mill's use of 'equitable' was by the 1890s only mildly radical. It involved taxation of ground values, enfranchisement of leaseholds, graduated inheritance duties, and a very unclear statement as to shorter

[10] R. B. Haldane, 'The Liberal Creed', *CR*, vol. 54 (1888), 467.
[11] J. G. Godard, 'The Liberal Débâcle', *WR*, vol. 158 (1902), 603. For a further discussion, see below, pp. 167-9.
[12] J. M. Robertson, *The Future of Liberalism*, pp. 14-15.
[13] G. Allen, 'Individualism and Socialism', *CR*, vol. 55 (1889), 738.

working hours.[14] The liberals who referred to the vague 'equitable distribution' seemed to be using it to avoid explicit commitment to those progressive tendencies of their fellow liberals that were too advanced for them.[15] The new liberal was usually to be recognized by his preference for the slightly more suggestive, though flexible, 'more equal distribution of wealth'.[16]

Though arguments from 'Bismarckian' assumptions were occasionally heard—aiming at the preservation of social stability by improving the condition of actual and potential malcontents[17]—they never became more than a minor key as far as English liberals were concerned. The case for the working classes was usually argued on grounds of moral regeneration and the recognition of solidarity of interests.[18] This already signified an approximation towards equality. There was, moreover, a growing realization that the social and economic evils undermining the general well-being could not be dealt with by legislative methods alone.[19] The stress on moral factors in social reform which most progressive liberals adopted was however entirely different from the moral approach of organized charity which, as will be noted in the next chapter, put forward as the basis of reform individual character rather than altruism or a general will. Moreover, whereas in the early years of the period examined the ethical, regenerative interpretation of social reform existed all along as a secondary theme side by side with the major restorative function, the transformation of

[14] F. Dolman, 'Political Economy and Social Reform: A Protest', *WR*, vol. 133 (1890), 638–9.

[15] See E. Latham, 'A Negative Ideal', *ER*, vol. 22 (1912).

[16] A clear-cut distinction cannot of course be made, but the tendency was certainly there. Compare, e.g., Touchstone, 'Will the Liberals Repent?', *WR*, vol. 151 (1899), with the opening editorial of the *Independent Review* (1903). The first was a right-of-centre liberal who talked about 'means to facilitate the equable distribution of the total earnings' (613) within the context of Kidd's doctrines (see below, p. 159). The *Independent Review* emphasized more equal distribution within the context of an advanced social platform ('A Plea for a Programme', *IR*, vol. 1 (1903), 11, 15). As time went on, redistribution received more precise operational definitions.

[17] See W. Graham, *The Social Problem: In its Economical, Moral, and Political Aspects* (1886), pp. 8, 15–17; Atherley-Jones, 'Liberalism and Social Reform: A Warning', *NR*, vol. 9 (1893), 629; 'How the State Can Help Commerce', *Speaker*, 5.12.1903.

[18] Graham, op. cit., pp. 343–7, 373.

[19] G. Vere Benson, 'The Social Problem', *WR*, vol. 128 (1887), 612 (a review of Graham's book). Cf. also S. A. Barnett, 'Sensationalism in Social Reform', *NC*, vol. 19 (1886), 289.

liberalism lay in the reversal of those roles; the ethical approach buttressed by biology became comprehensive and dominant, whereas the question of aiding underprivileged sections—although more immediately urgent—was reduced to one element in that conception. This transformation roughly paralleled the shift in relative weight given to material and spiritual elements in social reform. Material factors remained indispensable but were no longer regarded as a cure-all.

When social reform was regarded simply as an easing of the condition of the working classes—as it generally was until the end of the Victorian age—that too was not a clear-cut affair. The *Speaker* saw in the tame brand of socialism it advocated 'an attempt to confer upon the poor and the multitude the advantages which the *bourgeoisie* has in every country wrested from the Crown and nobles'.[20] In other words, the issue at stake was the desire of the poor to be incorporated into the middle class and to share its tangible fruits of victory. The *Speaker* was in its early years rather hesitant about endorsing new social ends and means for attaining them. It did, though, talk of 'refreshing dreams' and 'distinctly new ideals' when praising the new Radicalism for its incursions into dark corners haunted by socialist and communist bogies. But those ideals were so general as to be obvious—freedom for all, comfort for all, a happy childhood for all, and full participation by all in every innocent pleasure of life.[21] The nearest the *Speaker* came to a general social conception was, not surprisingly, when discussing municipal socialism. It was easier to appreciate in such a framework that social reform should function not for the benefit of a class but for the community.[22]

A question of great importance loomed behind these discussions: the relationship between social reform and liberal policy towards labour. For as the *Speaker* clarified in the same article, the Liberal party was the party of reform and the champion of the cause for labour, but it was not the Socialist party. It would never 'impose needless and arbitrary fetters upon the freedom of the individual under the pretence of

---

[20] 'The Socialism of Non-Socialists', *Speaker*, 10.5.1890.
[21] 'The Old and New Radicals', *Speaker*, 14.2.1891.
[22] 'Men and Measures', *Speaker*, 30.7.1892.

benefiting the mass'.[23] The liberals, committed as they were to supporting the masses as against the classes, were divided on what course to adopt *vis-à-vis* the claims of labour. Most liberals were aware by 1890 that the vast electoral power now in the hands of the working class was on the verge of becoming a dominant factor in British political life. A growing number were coming to the radical conclusion that redistribution was justified on the principle that the working class was to be the administrator of the wealth it produced. This meant in fact 'equality of social conditions' or a greater share of the national product.[24] But liberals were undecided as to the political role organized labour should play. In 1891 the *Speaker* still believed that the workers were 'by no means inaccessible to cordial advances from the ruling classes'. What was needed to win them over was an increased use of political methods as an instrument of social good. The temper of the workers was 'resolute for a larger, more liberal social atmosphere' and it was up to liberalism to step in as their leader.[25] By 1892 the *Speaker* was writing: 'The Liberal party has reached a point at which the consideration of the claims of Labour takes precedence of all others... What working men agree upon, the Liberal party will, in all probability, make a part of its programme.'[26] Yet at the same time the weekly resisted a separate Labour party. It believed that Labour should work through the two great parties and was particularly incensed by the Fabian Society's demand to run fifty independent labour members.[27] A more moderate line was taken by those liberals who began advocating the establishment of separate labour candidates. As the *Manchester Guardian* saw it, the readiest way for the Liberal party to give practical aid to the labour movement was by admitting to a much larger scale the claims of labour candidates. By not rejecting labour candidates who differed from views of liberal politics, 'the first step, and a long one, will have been taken towards that blending of the older Liberalism with the new aspirations of the labouring masses out of which the party of

[23] Ibid.
[24] Atherley-Jones, 'Liberalism and Social Reform: A Warning', 629, 633.
[25] 'Labour-Day Lessons', *Speaker*, 2.5.1891.
[26] 'A Labour Party', *Speaker*, 2.1.1892.
[27] See, e.g., 'Liberalism and the Working-Man', *Speaker*, 25.2.1893; 'The Fabian Squib', *Speaker*, 4.11.1893; 'Gleanings from Criticism', *Speaker*, 9.12.1893.

progress of the future must spring'.[28] Many progressives conceived of a party which would unite all progressive forces and organizations, whether under the wings of the Liberal party[29] or a new body.[30] Among new liberals this mood was dominant until the end of the 1890s for they regarded it as the organizational concomitant of a social reform policy with a special but not exclusive appeal to the working class. Most liberals would therefore have endorsed Samuel's summing-up, that 'a Labour party which was not Socialist would have no right to remain independent', now that the new liberalism was pursuing an active policy of social reform.[31]

Only Hobson consistently showed an aversion to the support of a weaker class as opposed to society as a whole. He criticized the bulk of existing social reform legislation as 'chiefly inspired by the intention of protecting certain sections of the working classes'.[32] Of course, the social organism model taught Hobson that to benefit the part meant to benefit the whole but, as he warned: 'though society is evidently benefited by such social work, a chief and special benefit is conferred upon some particular persons or class; and this latter consideration is a more and more important determinant of extensions of State activity.'[33] Hobson of course did not object to such legislation *per se*. He was afraid of its misuse in the form of unintelligent humanitarianism or open particularism to protect sectional weakness instead of protecting society. It was a question of difference in intent rather than in action. Reform measures could seemingly be applied to the benefit of certain groups only as long as 'these services are directed and intended less to fill the deficiencies of a class than to protect and improve the social organism as a whole'.[34]

The majority of liberals would not have understood why Hobson went to the hair-splitting length of establishing particularism on the basis of motive for, as Hobson himself admitted, there could be a close identity between the two types of

[28] Leader, *MG*, 11.5.1894.
[29] R. B. Haldane, 'The New Liberalism', *PR*, vol. 1 (1896), 134, 138–9.
[30] H. Dyer, 'The Future of Politics', *WR*, vol. 145 (1896), 2.
[31] H. Samuel, 'The Independent Labour Party', *PR*, vol. 1 (1896), 258–9.
[32] Hobson, *The Social Problem*, p. 196.
[33] Ibid., p. 197.
[34] Hobson, *The Science of Wealth* (1911), p. 220.

legislation. The distinction was however a vital one because social reform was becoming for new liberals a question both of ethical awareness and of scientific knowledge. Without a *consciousness* of the nature of social life and a new social spirit which would pervade public life, the notion of social reform was defective. Once an over-all understanding of the constitution of society was the propelling force of social action, it would be legitimate and proper to aid the working class. Hobhouse had already realized this in 1892, though he lacked Hobson's sensitivity to possible pitfalls in misguided social action:

If Liberals wish to avoid the formation of a sectional party of Labour, they must get rid of the taint of sectionalism themselves. They cannot ride two horses. Either they must stand on middle-class interests—and then they cannot complain if they lose the support of working men— or they rest on broad *national interests*, of which . . . the greatest and most pressing is the improvement of the condition of the working millions . . .[35]

This is one of the earliest expressions of regarding the cause of the working class as the cause of all, rather than as an act of abstract justice or of political exigency.[36] This perspective was later incorporated into the framework of the organic metaphor by Samuel when justifying redistribution:

. . . all expenditure which succeeds in improving the part benefits, not that part alone, but the whole of the community, and this is why all sections may justly be called upon to share the cost of measures which in their direct and immediate application touch only the well-being of the poorer.[37]

As the quotations from Hobhouse and Samuel show, liberals preferred to justify measures of social reform on grounds of promoting the common interest than on the parallel path open to them—the democratic argument of the will of the majority demanding reform. The roots of a sense of community could be traced to Mill's forebodings about the tyranny of the majority.

[35] 'Labour and Liberalism', letter to the editor by L.T.H., *Speaker*, 9.1.1892 (my italics).
[36] This point had been made by Socialists such as H. H. Champion, op. cit. 1037: '. . . from a truly patriotic point of view the welfare of the working classes is of the highest national importance', but a general awareness of this issue resulted probably only from the 'physical deterioration' findings after the Boer War.
[37] H. Samuel, *Liberalism*, p. 185.

The stress on interest rather than right had the additional advantage of being more palatable to endowed minorities.

The advance to more comprehensive notions of welfare proceeded on parallel lines. It was occasioned by the evolutionary and Idealist perspectives of theorists like Hobhouse and Samuel. It was seen as a logical extension of liberalism to cope with the socio-political demands of the enfranchised classes. Even plain and simple redistributionists who saw the central goal of the liberal to diminish the inequalities between rich and poor through the action of government, without looking too deeply into philosophical justifications, were coming to see this policy as progress 'towards a more and more highly organised social order'[38]—a goal that could not be seen as solely restorative. For the new liberals, redistribution was seen as part of a more general process. They now emphasized the motive behind it, as Hobhouse explained:

The true aim of social progress is not so much to make one class richer, as to purify and brighten the life of the whole community by seizing on the best conceptions of social order that are afloat within it and translating them into political or economic institutions.[39]

This entailed primarily an educational effort, as Hobson wrote in 1899:

The true economy of reform consists in recognising the futility of direct forcible assaults upon deep-rooted habits, and in directing more and more energy to the general educative work of intellectual and moral enlightenment, which alone is really 'radical', because it alone reaches the roots of national character, from which all large changes of national conduct proceed.[40]

Abetted by evolutionary and organic perspectives, liberalism was approaching a synthetic view of social reform which enabled it to 'recognise the conditions of healthy social development'.[41] As Dyer claimed in an oft-used slogan, what was demanded of future politicians was not simply 'the maximum amount of material wealth, but the realisation of

[38] A. Hoare, 'Liberalism in the Twentieth Century', *World's Work*, vol. 1 (1902–3), 85.
[39] L. T. Hobhouse, 'The Foreign Policy of Collectivism', *ER*, vol. 9 (1899), 211.
[40] J. A. Hobson, 'The Pace of Progress', *EW*, 13.5.1899.
[41] Dyer, 'The Future of Politics', op. cit. 5.

human welfare'.[42] This reflected the new belief that, although the social question was originally an economic one, the change in the subject-matter and aims of economics transformed the entire method of dealing with social issues.

2. WEALTH, WELFARE, AND WASTE

The motto 'from wealth to welfare' as descriptive of the transformation of liberalism at the turn of the century would certainly be an oversimplification, if not a false juxtaposition of terms. Wealth was not necessarily opposed to welfare, nor was the transition from exalting the one to promoting the other a direct or self-evident one. It would be more correct to say that there was a shift in emphasis, in the first place, from production to distribution. The mid-century view had been that ever-increasing production and prosperity would be the best way of securing plenty for all. But this exclusive belief in material improvements and prosperity as permanent factors in social evolution had led to a more unequal social structure which aggravated the social problem.[43] The emergence of re-distribution towards the end of the century as the main item in a social reform policy, was a challenge to the belief of those who thought wealth could be attained via the Empire, to the 'pious confidence that increase of British trade and consequent influx of wealth will remove all discontent...'.[44] The Liberal party, and indeed liberalism in general did not, however, execute a volte-face as far as production was concerned. At most, as Haldane remarked, liberalism looked as much to distribution as to production.[45]

Most liberals insisted on retaining the emphasis on wealth and production as the essential financial source of a social reform policy.[46] This was often linked to the old liberal view which understood social reform in terms of material comfort and therefore demanded greater productivity even at the risk of widening inequality. But even new liberals were maintaining

[42] Ibid. 2.
[43] See, e.g., R. G. Davis, 'Individualism and Socialism, and Liberty', *WR*, vol. 178 (1912), 148–9.
[44] C. F. G. Masterman, 'Realities at Home' in *The Heart of the Empire* (1901), p. 4.
[45] Haldane, 'The New Liberalism', 136.
[46] Hoare, op. cit. 86; Rae, 'State Socialism and Social Reform', *CR*, vol. 58 (1890), 441.

that production and accumulation of wealth were vital to social well-being. They obviously realized the truism that you could not redistribute without previously having produced. These liberals were thinking about redistribution in more sophisticated terms than simply transferring the wealth of the rich to the pockets of the poor—as some of the more vulgar statements of Chamberlain and Lloyd George would have it.[47] The change that had occurred was, as another social reformer, G. F. Millin, explained, a consequence of the fundamental principle of liberalism—the promotion of the welfare of the whole population—having been attained in fact, not only stated in theory. Whereas in the past the public welfare had been promoted indirectly through the capitalist employer, the new revelation was in finding ways to promote it directly.[48]

The question became one of a permanent reorganization of the economic system with a view to channelling the resources of the nation in the right direction. With such schemes in mind new liberals such as Robertson could insist on state aid being administered within a system that would add to the amount of real wealth;[49] and Samuel could write that the new liberals 'do not consider that their aims are inconsistent with the encouragement of enterprise and the development of commerce, and believe that it is as necessary to maintain the volume of production as it is to improve its distribution'.[50] Brougham Villiers stated explicitly that he wanted the problem of the poor to be solved through their contributing usefully to the national wealth, rather than by a greater division of the wealth already possessed by the better-off, i.e. through the support of others.[51] There was a hint here of the traditional preoccupation with self-reliance.

Wealth was, after all, an essential precondition to welfare, even if it had ceased to be an end in itself. But Ruskin's influence had been at work to extend the new liberal notion of wealth beyond the mere preoccupation with efficient production: '... the economic activities of the people should be expressed in

[47] This was implied by Chamberlain's 'ransom' doctrine and by Lloyd George's 'Limehouse' speech in 1909.

[48] G. F. Millin, 'The New Liberalism', *FR*, vol. 69 (1901), 638.

[49] J. M. Robertson, 'The Right to Work', *SPM*, vol. 14 (1909), 53.

[50] Samuel, 'The Independent Labour Party', 258.

[51] B. Villiers, *The Opportunity of Liberalism*, pp. 75–6.

terms of human beings *and* prosperity, instead of prosperity only. In short, national prosperity would be "cashed" for the benefit of the whole of the people.'[52] However, the key question was: 'are we to have a higher standard of life and of comfort and a lower national income?'[53] This was simply the old problem of either having the cake or eating it. Intelligent liberals at the turn of the century understood it was imperative to dissociate social reform from identification solely with the latter process. Social reform was a product of a well-to-do society, and in turn it contributed substantially to that society's continuing and expanding prosperity.[54] The efficiency of a society organized for the production of wealth could become the index of its ability to solve the social problem. In fact, as the 'under-consumptionist' theories had shown, material comfort was not necessarily opposed to a higher national income—a jarring note perhaps in the ears of Max Weber's puritan capitalist and, indeed, in those of many of the leading economists of the day, but one increasingly heard by new liberals relying on Hobson's economics.

Hobson had criticized mal-distribution not only on moral grounds, but on economic ones, and had accordingly supplied the firm scientific basis for redistribution which social reformers had been looking for. He denied the validity of the sacrosanct principle of thrift, which during the Victorian era had combined the insistence on a strong and independent character with the economic foundation of capitalism. The cyclical crises of the capitalist system, with their consequent unemployment and distress, he saw as a result of under-consumption—a lack of demand for goods which caused a standstill of capital and labour. The way out of these crises was to redistribute the power to consume which at present was in the hands of those who had already used it to saturation point. Hobson was all for the working classes increasing their consumption, raising their standard of material and intellectual comfort, so that fuller and more regular employment would ensue.[55] This line of reasoning was adopted by other important liberal theorists such as

[52] A Radical of '85 'Liberalism without Ideas: A Few Notes', *WR*, vol. 169 (1908), 139.
[53] Ibid., 145.
[54] Cf. also Chapter Six, pp. 238–44.
[55] J. A. Hobson, *The Evolution of Modern Capitalism* (1894), pp. 288, 375–6, and *passim*.

Robertson,[56] and was taken up by leading liberal organs such as the *Speaker* and *Nation*.[57]

The economic importance of consumption was of course linked to the appreciation of the vital utility of consumption discussed in the previous chapter. A small number of liberals continued further along the road leading from the relative importance of production through that of distribution, and located the main factors of welfare in sound consumption. Ruskin and Hobson had always regarded redistribution as a means to ensure a high quality of consumption. As Hobson explained when deliberating on the living wage, economic efficiency—though necessary—did not presuppose that the end of man was the production of material forms of wealth. A living wage would also have to provide the wholesome and pleasant elements of customary consumption.[58] This point was developed by the *Independent Review* which, admitting that the poor were not always the best judges of the uses of wealth, conferred upon the state a double duty—not only to redistribute but to 'influence the lives of the recipients as to fit them to enjoy their new privileges'.[59]

There was a further sense in which it was incorrect to speak of a direct transition from wealth to welfare. This was a growing cognizance of the intervening factor of waste in social and industrial organization. As was becoming clear, waste was the other side of the coin of wealth. Many liberals were moved to consider, under the impact of the poverty and misery around them currently being brought to light, that the question was not so much the promotion of wealth as the prevention of the squandering and misuse of available resources, including human ones. Perhaps it was in this sense that efficiency became

[56] J. M. Robertson had developed a similar economic theory in the early 1890s, at about the same time Hobson was formulating his, and like Hobson, had made it an integral part of a social programme (see below, Chapter Six, p. 201). See, e.g., *The Fallacy of Saving* (1892). Robertson thought it essential to the independence of the labourer that the poor spend more. This was the only way to break the economic power of the 'idle' classes (pp. 120–1).

[57] The *Speaker*, for example, endorsed the under-consumption theory outlined in Hobson's 'important volume, *The Social Problem*'. It realized that all redistribution measures were in fact a distribution of the power to consume. ('Mr. Bryce on a Liberal Programme', *Speaker*, 28.1.1905.)

[58] J. A. Hobson, 'A Living Wage', *Commonwealth*, vol. 1 (1896), 128–9.

[59] 'A Plea for a Programme', *IR*, 15–16.

a desirable end for advanced liberals—efficiency not as signifying a society geared to an external measure of success, to race
and empire, but as denoting a society that could rationally
apply means towards the moral end of its own well-being.
Ritchie was one of the first to state that 'the history of progress is
the record of a gradual diminution of *waste*'.[60] Waste resulted
from unchecked competition and was mainly typical of lower
organisms. It manifested itself as 'all one great problem of
distribution'.[61] The state, thought Ritchie, was the chief
instrument by which waste could be prevented by setting free
the individual from the mere conditions of life and making
culture possible. 'An ideal State would be one in which there
was no waste at all of the lives, and intellects, and souls of
individual men and women.'[62]

Essentially, this approach employed a different perspective to
examine the social question. As the *Speaker* made clear:

What we want to know in these days is not so much what averages of
national prosperity we can secure, but what are the weak spots in our
system, what are the proportions, and what the occupations that
subsist on 10s. a week or less, what are the wages of sweating, what are
the possibilities, by combination or by other means, of righting what is
wrong.[63]

It is also evident from this quotation that focusing on waste
could lend itself to the restorative interpretation of reform.
Hobson was the one who developed the preoccupation with
waste from merely, as the *Speaker* implied, a question of ironing
out dents in the system to a conception of social organization.
His entire socio-economic structure can be seen from this angle.
Influenced on this point by Ritchie, Hobson believed that 'the
Social Question will find its essential unity in the problem how
to deal with human waste'.[64] Waste was in evidence in the
industrial system wherever one looked. Many people were
unemployed, others were overworking or underworking,
others again were not doing what they were best suited to do, or
what was in the interest of society they should do. The same was

---

[60] D. G. Ritchie, *The Principles of State Interference*, p. 50.
[61] Ritchie, *Darwinism and Politics*, p. 60.
[62] Ritchie, *The Principles of State Interference*, p. 50.
[63] 'The Wages of Labour', *Speaker*, 28.9.1895.
[64] Hobson, *The Social Problem*, p. 7.

true in the intellectual and spiritual fields, although there waste was less avoidable, because less controllable and less essential to social preservation.[65]

Other liberals also began to evaluate the social system in terms of waste. Masterman, concerned with the effects of social disorder, described this viewpoint as questioning 'the justice of a social order which condemns common humanity to a region of random endeavour; which accepts the destruction of so much "by-product", when that "by-product" is the endowment and natural happiness of so many men and women and children....'.[66] The problem of unemployment was regarded as a waste of skilled and efficient labour[67] and the national network of labour exchanges set up in 1909 was seen as a way of avoiding such waste.[68] Writing about the land question in 1913, the *Nation* remarked: '... the nation cannot afford the waste in life, liberty, happiness, and food that follows from the existing system'.[69] As critics of the new liberalism remarked, the utilitarian and Ruskinian notion of maximization was being abandoned, and the nourishing of the greatest number of happy human beings was replaced by another goal: 'that the State may have to apologize for the smallest possible number of unfortunates and poor'. Thus the abolition of poverty and distress at any cost was in danger of becoming the popular ideal instead of the diffusion of plenty.[70] It was precisely this 'inverse utilitarianism' that symbolized the change in the liberal perspective. Both sides of the coin were now being appreciated. A gradual shift in emphasis was taking place in the direction of a Ruskinian qualitative concept of human life, without abandoning the old stress on production, but while recognizing an ethical responsibility for all. An attempt was made to demonstrate scientifically that redistribution and consumption of wealth were indispensable elements in attaining social welfare, that 'investment' in material human improvement was not only ethically desirable but economically healthier. Social reform

---

[65] Ibid., pp. 8–16; *Work and Wealth*, p. 120.

[66] C. F. G. Masterman, 'Towards a Civilisation', *IR*, vol. 2 (1904), 499.

[67] 'Towards a Social Policy. IX. The Problem of the Unemployed', *Speaker*, 17.12.1904.

[68] 'Insurance and Unemployment', *Nation*, 29.5.1909.

[69] 'The Land Policy', *Nation*, 25.10.1913.

[70] Latham, op. cit. 417–19.

was discarding its reputation as a necessary evil. Liberals were seeking welfare first of all in an organized, systematic, and scientific attempt to cope with the manifestations of 'illth' before turning towards the natural and interconnected sequel—the reorganization of human and natural resources.

3. LIBERAL FINANCE AND SOCIAL REFORM

A major tool in the hands of liberal reformers—indeed for a time the only one of significance[71]—was financial policy. As many of the reform measures contemplated had to do with redistribution and material aid, this was to be expected. By the end of the 1880s liberals had not gone far beyond the rules laid down by Mill. Their guidelines were a taxation policy deduced from the 'unearned increment' theory and the second item in the liberal trinity of 'Peace, Retrenchment, Reform'. To begin with, taxation was regarded as a necessary evil—an encroachment upon individual property needed to finance essential governmental activities. This attitude was only slowly beginning to change under the pressure of Radical reformers but there were still a number of voices opposed to direct taxation, on the grounds that no man should be taxed to pay for another man's needs.[72] At a much later date the *Westminster Review* mounted a campaign against direct taxation rather than the taxing or rating of ground values. Land values were in the Review's opinion the sole just and proper source of public revenue, for they related to the only property created by the public. The income tax, as indeed all taxes on wealth, was a 'robber tax'.[73] Even Haldane, displaying the liberal's respect for private enterprise, expressed fears that the income tax would interfere with motives for industry.[74] But taxing unearned increment and unearned incomes fitted in perfectly with the aim of preserving individual effort, for what was unearned did not owe to the incentive of the owner. In such a category were

[71] The attitude of the House of Lords to social reform caused the liberals to believe (until 1909) that the Liberal Government was master in its own house only in matters of finance. Consequently, 'to financial reform accordingly the party is now looking for those constructive, organic measures by which alone so great a democratic majority can justify its existence'. ('The Cost of Old-Age Pensions', *Nation*, 30.11.1907.)

[72] Allen, op. cit. 738.

[73] 'The Month', *WR*, vol. 165 (1906), 224–5, 333–4.

[74] R. B. Haldane, 'The Liberal Creed', 467.

both death duties and the increasing value of land due to development and scarcity. Imposing taxes on high incomes was also justified from this perspective.

However, most liberals were prepared to go further and to recommend a general graduated income tax, which was just another way of taxing high incomes. The absorption by taxation of large concentrations of wealth was thought to be a question of eliminating an idle class and dispersing economic power, as well as one of abstract justice.[75] Graduated taxation was also derivable from the classic maxim of Adam Smith and Mill—equality of sacrifice. This principle assumed that all citizens could bear taxation in proportion to their ability to pay, although most liberals would have agreed with Robertson in fixing a limit—necessary for a minimum of comfort—below which none would be taxed.[76] Robertson delved into the ethics of taxation in a number of his writings in the early 1890s, linking taxation with a general conception of mutual social relations. He insisted on maintaining a strong connection between income received and service rendered to society. This necessitated, in his opinion, a digression from mathematical equality of sacrifice. Recipients of unearned incomes would therefore have to pay a larger proportion of taxes than other citizens. Beyond the plain redistributionary principle, moral and economic, taxation could be interpreted as symbolizing an act of participation in the social system, a reminder that individual and social interests were interlinked. Robertson, who conceived of society as a network of mutual obligations, was therefore interested in imposing a direct income tax on the working classes as well as other classes. Provided they attained a minimum level of living, for instance through old-age pensions and similar reforms, 'such a tax would represent their specific contribution to the national burdens, and would constitute by far the best *quid pro quo* as against their pensions. It would be a

[75] Dilke, op. cit. 252.
[76] J. M. Robertson, *Modern Humanists*, Epilogue, pp. 264–5. 'Equality of sacrifice' and 'ability to pay' were not regarded by advanced liberals as opposed principles (in contrast to the assertion of H. V. Emy, *Liberals, Radicals and Social Politics 1892–1914*, p. 192), because from the outset they interpreted 'equality of sacrifice' as implying graduation, not proportionality (Hobson, 'The Taxation of Monopolies', *IR*, vol. 9 (1906), 22; Robertson, *The Meaning of Liberalism* (1912), p. 72).

universal tax as against a universal obligation . . .'[77] The *Speaker* later explained this in its ambitious series 'Towards a Social Policy':

Publicity and directness are the safeguards of Liberal finance. A gradual removal of most of the present indirect taxes and a careful substitution of direct taxation is desirable, in order that those who bear the cost of government may know *that* they pay, *how* they pay, and *when* they pay.[78]

The accepted economic doctrine of ability to bear and equality of sacrifice was apparently clashing or better, overlapping, with an alternative doctrine, held mainly by conservatives—taxation according to benefit received. A hint of this second principle was evident in Robertson's belief in quid pro quo, though he himself later denied that the amount of benefit received was measurable.[79] This was the main reason why most liberals preferred Mill's maxim. In Samuel's words, with their implicit organicism: 'You cannot tax the various classes . . . according to the benefit they receive, for all are served by every wise expenditure, and you cannot tell what proportion of the advantage falls to the share of each.'[80] The principle of benefit received would lead again to a particularistic conception of society. But on the other hand, liberals were always ready to apply the principle of benefit received when certain groups benefited beyond what was necessary to them or to society. 'Particularism' was applied to those members of society who did not contribute their share to the functioning of the social body. The *Speaker* demanded to enforce the principle 'that those whose property benefits by public expenditure shall contribute to the public revenue. Private benefits must not be divorced from public burdens.'[81] This point was developed in 1906 by Hobson, who expressly preferred the canon of 'benefit

[77] Robertson, *The Fallacy of Saving*, p. 144.

[78] 'Towards a Social Policy. XIX. A Liberal Finance', *Speaker*, 11.3.1905. 'Towards a Social Policy', which later appeared in book form, was written by a committee consisting of C. R. Buxton, H. C. Fairfax-Cholmeley, J. L. Hammond, F. W. Hirst, L. T. Hobhouse, J. A. Hobson, C. F. G. Masterman, J. H. Morgan, and Vaughan Nash.

[79] J. M. Robertson, 'The Ethics of Taxation', *SPM*, vol. 14 (1909), 164–5.

[80] Samuel, *Liberalism*, p. 186. This did not, however, prevent Samuel from declaring, with the traditional Victorian moral concern for character, that 'Government is not called upon to tax the better members of society in order to subsidize the bad' (p. 136).

[81] 'Towards a Social Policy. VII. The Land Question in Towns', *Speaker*, 3.12.1904.

received' to that of 'equality of sacrifice'. He objected to the use of words with a negative emotional import such as 'burden' and 'sacrifice'. Hobson thus rejected out of hand the lingering feeling among liberals that all taxation was bad,[82] later to be finally dashed to the ground by the aura of permanency taxes were given by Asquith.[83] Hobson further objected to the false supposition that taxes raised on the principle of 'benefit received' should be specifically allocated by the state to finance the benefit in question. 'Benefit received', claimed Hobson, could be converted into the clearer concept of 'unearned increment'. Income was divisible into two parts: the one necessary to maintain the factors in production—a living wage, interest, profits and salaries, all of which took into account the motivation element; the other a 'surplus value' which was the result of advantages in a restricted market, and which was the product of social activity. Indeed, the unproductive surplus was a clear case of social waste and was a prime cause of under-consumption. Hence, when individuals benefited from property that was essentially social, it was capable of 'bearing taxation' without disturbing industry.[84] 'Benefit received' could, in Hobson's employ, be combined with 'ability to bear' because it did not mean that disadvantaged recipients would have to pay the full cost of what aid they received from the community. What Hobson had actually done was to change its meaning and to bring it into line with the traditional liberal attitude to monopolies. Asquith's 1907 Budget, in itself at least as important as the famous 1909 Budget, was interpreted by the *Nation* as having realized this idea of taxation. A truly constructive liberal policy would assert the right of the state to participate in property and incomes which public activities helped to create. Asquith's recognition of the distinction between earned and unearned incomes meant to the *Nation* that liberalism was now travelling along the road which eliminated Mill's 'sacrifice' and 'inconvenience' altogether.[85]

---

[82] Voiced as late as 1903 by the *Speaker* within the context of a relatively progressive article on financial reform ('How the State can Help Commerce', 5.12.1903).

[83] See below, p. 140.

[84] Hobson, 'The Taxation of Monopolies', 20–33; 'Is Socialism Plunder?', *Nation*, 19.10.1907; *The Industrial System* (1909), pp. 217–19; *The Science of Wealth*, pp. 113–16.

[85] '"Earned" and "Unearned"', *Nation*, 27.4.1907. At a later stage, the Hobsonian distinction between cost and surplus was preferred instead of 'earned' and 'unearned',

Hobson went beyond Robertson in his 'positive' attitude to taxation, but did not go as far as Robertson in insisting upon universal taxation. Taxation was to Hobson primarily a means of raising revenue for social needs and he considered the exemption of the poorer grades of workers as a 'doctrine of financial liberation'. Robertson later criticized Hobson for a scheme of taxation that was theoretically and scientifically perfect, but unethical. It was improper, thought Robertson, to tax a man up to the point where he would stop working.[86] In this he reflected the desire of most liberals to allow the individual some leeway without being strait-jacketed by the state. He was also reiterating the further guideline that the demands of social reform should be made compatible with the promotion of production. Most new liberals appreciated the implications of an almost universal application of taxation, and would have agreed with the *Independent Review* that the income tax gave citizens a keen interest in national economy and a feeling of shared responsibility.[87]

The issue really boiled down to the following: as long as there still were acute evils which had to be removed immediately, such as a high percentage of the population living below the poverty line, social reform had to be restorative. It had to be discriminatory in demanding more from those who were, unjustly, better off. Universal taxation could be practicable only after this stage of social reform had been attained and the way would be open for general social policies. In the long run Robertson's quid pro quo maxim might appear to be the more ethical one; under present circumstances 'ability to bear' excluded many who simply were not able to.[88] It was not, as the *Nation* put it, taxing one class for the benefit of the other, but 'the raising of revenues from those sources which possess ability to pay for expenditure in those ways which carry *the largest benefit to the community*'.[89] Mutual interdependence and responsibility

as a more clearly worded indicator of ability to bear taxation ('The Ability to Bear', *Nation*, 21.6.1913).

[86] Robertson, 'The Ethics of Taxation', 165. This was not Hobson's intention. See below, p. 156.

[87] Anon., 'The Reform of Taxation', *IR*, vol. 3 (1904), 5. Cf. also W. S. Churchill, *Liberalism and the Social Problem* (1909), p. 306.

[88] Robertson consequently modified his quid pro quo tenet. See below Chapter Six, p. 222.

[89] 'The Ability to Bear', *Nation*, 21.6.1913 (my italics).

was an ethical maxim that modified quid pro quo. Taxing the poor, explained the *Nation*, 'damages their personal and economic efficiency, and so cuts down the production of national wealth', again demonstrating that new liberals retained their belief in the importance of wealth along with a more solidarical conception of society.

Beyond a taxation policy there arose the further question of the compatibility of social reform with the liberal tenet of retrenchment. It was generally believed that the Boer War had impressed upon liberals that if large expenditure could be diverted to Imperial needs, it might as well be directed to an aim they were more sympathetic to—internal reform. But liberals had recognized that retrenchment was no solution to the social problems besetting the nation already some time before that. As the *Speaker* pointed out rather wistfully in 1894: 'The old electoral momentum in favour of economy has gone with the passing of our English *bourgeoisie*. The working-class elector likes to see money spent, where the middle-class elector liked to see money saved.'[90] Later, however, the *Speaker* shifted towards blaming the huge war expenditure for precluding any serious scheme of social reform.[91] And in 1902 it took the further step of virtually endorsing 'large expenditure, even at the risk of some waste, upon useful reforms and reproductive enterprises for the sake of preventing the Government from embarking upon fatal and ruinous schemes of imperial aggrandisement'.[92]

By the end of the war the old liberal watchwords of Peace, Retrenchment, and Reform (in the original electoral sense) had been 'pretty well played out'.[93] 'Retrenchment' continued to be a meaningful term mainly within the context of the growing liberal preoccupation with waste. Replying to S. Webb's accusations that liberals wanted to reduce expenditure on social reform, the *Speaker* wrote 'Mr. Webb must know that the demand for retrenchment is made in relation to expenditure which represents the waste of the national income on purposes

---

[90] 'Financial Reform', *Speaker*, 20.1.1894.
[91] 'Old Age Pensions', *Speaker*, 10.3.1900. See also 'Old Age Pensions', *Speaker*, 16.7.1898.
[92] 'The Programme of Trade Unions', *Speaker*, 6.9.1902.
[93] Hoare, op. cit. 85.

of conquest or on the aggrandisement of the rich.'[94] In its series on social policy, the weekly made it clear that retrenchment was a means, not an end, in modern liberal administration. A policy of public parsimony and a fixed level of expenditure were feasible no longer. 'Where modern conditions of industrial life produce a rapid expansion of wealth, every Government is subjected to a pressure of genuine public needs which crave satisfaction.' A Liberal Government's duty was to 'meet a slow, gradual, continuous demand for public co-operation in various fields of administrative work for the popular welfare'.[95] Many liberals were coming to believe, as Masterman claimed of social reformists in general, that money was better spent by the community than by individuals.[96] Even official Liberalism, as a perusal of Asquith's speeches shows, was coming over to the view that expenditure could not be stopped, and that it was of paramount importance to find new reservoirs, such as the income tax, upon which drafts could be made in equity and justice to meet the necessities of the community.[97]

The tracing of the development of a liberal financial policy underlines once again the increasing comprehensiveness of the liberal social outlook.[98] By 1903–4 liberals were becoming alive to the fact that a policy of taxation was both more than a means of raising revenue and more than an act of justice, or a ransom that the rich had to pay for their riches, as Chamberlain had seen it. The interconnectedness of the various issues of social reform—land, housing, poverty, unemployment, had become established in the minds of reformers. A policy of taxation was now regarded as an essential part of other reform measures, whereas formerly a discrete and piecemeal approach had been applied to them. Taxing or rating site values was now seen as a means to relieve congestion by inducing land-owners to build

---

[94] 'The Liberal Future', *Speaker*, 16.7.1904.
[95] 'Towards a Social Policy. XIX. A Liberal Finance', *Speaker*, 11.3.1905.
[96] C. F. G. Masterman, 'Liberalism and Labour', *NC*, vol. 60 (1906), 713.
[97] Asquith in a speech to a Municipal and Rating Authorities deputation, 26.2.1906. Quoted in *The Liberal Magazine*, vol. 14 (1906), pp. 64–5.
[98] Contrast this with the initial position that H. G. Wells described as typical of a young progressive: 'Finance . . . was a sealed book to us; we did not so much connect it with the broad aspects of human affairs as regard it as a sort of intrusive nuisance to be earnestly ignored by all right-minded men' (*The New Machiavelli* (1911), Penguin Books, 1966, p. 91).

houses.[99] It was thought to be the key to the housing question, to the question of the paralysis of the city community in general, and to some of the problems of the urban poor.[100] It was also conceived as the means for rejuvenating the countryside.[101] It is important to establish the change in the aim of taxation from breaking up the property and power of the rich—a theme still very central, on the emotional level, to Lloyd George's handling of the Budget issue—to financing a general policy of social organization. Connected with these phenomena was the growing importance of the Budget as a major instrument of social reform. For this the liberals must certainly get a good deal of credit even on the purely political level, as the main breakthroughs in this direction were all accomplished by Liberal governments. Harcourt's 1894 Budget had already demonstrated that liberal social policy could be relatively easily implemented by means of a financial Act. In 1904, by the time the return of the Liberals to power was imminent, advanced thinkers such as Villiers were exhorting progressives to grasp the fact that 'the beginnings of all reform are to be found in the Budget...'[102] And as it appeared, finance was the one field of reform in which official Liberalism was not lagging too far behind its theorists.[103] Asquith perceived the Budget as one of the main instruments of social planning—which by its very nature could not be piecemeal:

It is, I think, a mistake to treat the annual Budget as if it were a thing by itself, and not, as it is, or as it certainly ought to be, an integral part and a necessary link in a connected and coherent chain of policy... the country has reached a stage in which, whether we look merely at its fiscal or at its social exigencies, we cannot afford to drift

[99] 'A Plea for a Programme', *IR*, vol. 1 (1903), 16.

[100] 'The Housing Problem', *Speaker*, 27.8.1904.

[101] Masterman, 'Towards a Civilisation', 502–3. The magic of the single tax is easily explicable, but for most liberal social reformers it was only one way of dealing with social evils. See Hobhouse, 'The Contending Forces', *English Review*, vol. 4 (1909–10), 367.

[102] Villiers, *The Opportunity of Liberalism*, viii.

[103] In Hobson's words: 'The audacity of the Budget has put a new spirit into English politics. The nature and magnitude of its financial proposals have come upon our people as a surprise... To such an extent has blind, short-range opportunism become the ruling principle of English politics that any measure which, like this Budget, brings into the foreground of debate vital issues of political theory is staggering to the intelligence.' ('The Significance of the Budget', *English Review*, vol. 2 (1909), 794.)

along the stream...The Chancellor of the Exchequer...ought to budget, not for one year, but for several years.[104]

When this was strikingly carried out in the 1909 Budget one financial authority, a political opponent of liberalism, noting that to provide means for future years was unprecedented, admitted: '...no more ambitious attempt has ever been made to effect a Social Revolution by the agency of our fiscal system'.[105] Both in its details and in its general conception it was firmly based on the new liberal perception of society. As Lloyd George asked: '...should not the national resources be charged with the avoidance and prevention of unmerited poverty and distress?'[106] It was no longer a question of the rich sharing with the poor, of the obligations of property. The notion of an identifiable social entity with property of its own had come to be accepted. The resources at the disposal of the community were its own. Moreover, it was up to the community to see that its resources were well employed. The mistake made by Harcourt's 1894 Budget—in failing to allocate the revenue raised to any specific purpose—would not be repeated, Lloyd George promised.

The implementation of liberal financial policy had derived further impetus from the campaign for Tariff Reform which Chamberlain inaugurated in 1903. From the point of view of domestic politics it was clearly realized that more was at stake than the success of one fiscal system or the other. Two rival social philosophies were clashing, two alternative methods of coming to terms with the social question. The Tariff Reformers saw the expenses of social reform being met by a fiscal policy of protection, which would broaden the basis of taxation but do so by indirect taxes on some essentials in the workman's food bill. They promised, however, that in return the unemployment situation would be improved and old-age pensions would be paid. The liberals, who could not accept a 'social policy' based mainly on stimulating the productive powers of the state and executing no profound changes in the socio-economic structure of the community, had therefore to demonstrate not only that

---

[104] *Hansard*, 4th Ser. CLXXII, 1186 (13.4.1907).

[105] S. Rosenbaum (Statistician to the Tariff Commission), 'The Budget and Social Revolution', *NC*, vol. 66 (1909), 158–9.

[106] D. Lloyd George, 'The Issues of the Budget', *Nation*, 30.10.1909.

free trade would be more conducive to financing social reform, but that the economic measures they advocated were in themselves an immediate part of the process of social reform. The 1909 Budget was presented as a full vindication of this claim.

Most revolutionary of all was thought to be the Development Bill, introduced together with the Budget, which reserved a sum of £200,000 for afforestation, farming, and development of natural resources. The *Nation* wrote:

In a Budget replete with new principles, the most original and fruitful of all is the conception of the Development Grant... For the first time a definite source of income is set aside to constitute a fund available for the general development of Great Britain... the nucleus of a progressive democratic organisation of natural resources for the national use.[107]

Although the cries of 'Socialism' were mostly directed at the land taxes,[108] the principles behind them had been long established. But Robertson called the Development Grant 'the one really Socialistic proposal',[109] and Villiers agreed with him that it was the most socialistic proposal of a social-democratic Budget—the beginning of state socialism, and one that underlined that 'the vital problem is not one of mere taxation, but of social organisation'.[110]

Other liberals, however, were more touchy on the subject, not without a good deal of justification. The *Westminster Gazette* rallied to the defence of the Budget from accusations of Socialism. Its measures concerning the distribution of wealth were 'not a question of Socialism or individualism, but a question of equity and good policy between various classes of the population'.[111] As the *Nation* pointed out a few months after its first article on the subject, the Budget was not socialistic in the sense of an attack upon competitive industry. The *Nation* in

[107] 'The First Democratic Budget', *Nation*, 1.5.1909.

[108] The 1909 Budget established Land Value duties—necessitating a valuation of all land in Great Britain—and a supertax on high incomes.

[109] Robertson, 'The Ethics of Taxation', 165; Hobhouse, 'Liberalism and Social Reform', leader, *MG*, 13.12.1909—a view also endorsed by the Individualist H. Cox (*Hansard*, 5th Ser. XII 1676 (2.11.1909)).

[110] B. Villiers, *Modern Democracy. A Study in Tendencies* (1912), pp. 106–7.

[111] 'Socialism and the Budget', leader, *WG*, 3.5.1909; 'The Philosophy of the Budget', leader, *WG*, 25.10.1909.

fact grasped the very essence of the change the Development Bill was signifying in liberal social reform:

The introduction of the Development Bill marks a new stage in the realisation of Liberalism. The narrow conception of the work of Government ... has long since yielded to a fuller interpretation of the State ... But almost the whole of this enlargement of the State has hitherto been directed to the redress of grievances or the prevention of injuries ... It has always hitherto been impelled by pressure from behind, and has scarcely claimed to play a positive part in the application of national resources to the arts of industry and of social progress.[112]

This it had now begun to do, impelled by the interests of national welfare. Here was a clear statement of the regenerative function of social reform. More unconsciously than not, Liberal politicians had taken a major step in redefining the framework of social responsibilities.[113]

The 1909 Budget was generally hailed as having 'vivified Liberalism by giving it a new purpose and a new hope. It transforms the vague phrase "Social Reform" into concrete realities.'[114] Hobson was delighted with the way in which it implemented the financial measures he had been promoting for years. The cry of 'plunder' heard from its opposers was a 'class interpretation' which had 'no final validity as applied to a policy which finds its justification, not in injury to one class for the benefit of another, but in the application of public remedies to defects and diseases affecting the whole body politic...'[115] Plainly, then, it was a triumph for those holding to the organic conception of society in various degrees of conscious formulation. Hobson—with a characteristic lack of hostility towards the philosophical sense of the term—saw it as a manifestation of socialistic doctrine. But it was at the same time a bold statement of constructive liberalism, an attempt to move

---

[112] 'The Development of England', *Nation*, 4.9.1909.

[113] A comment by Samuel admirably illustrates the difference in temperament between advanced and official liberalism. Referring to the Liberal party's reaction to the Budget, he wrote: 'The general feeling on our side seems to be one of frightened satisfaction, the kind of feeling one has on being launched down an exhilarating steep and unknown toboggan run.' H. Gladstone Papers, Brit. Lib. Add. MSS. 45992, f. 219, Samuel to Gladstone, 29.4.1909.

[114] Leader, *Daily Chronicle*, 3.5.1909.

[115] Hobson, 'The Significance of the Budget', *English Review*, vol. 2 (1909), 795.

towards a rational, self-directed community marshalling its resources for social advantage while trying to ensure that all members would have the property necessary for their individual realization.

4. LIBERALISM 'PERMEATED'?

The rivalry between Liberals and Socialists as to who originated social welfare thinking or specific measures of reform was at the time very acute. In view of the fact that so many authorities attribute the promotion of such measures and ideas to people and groups within the orbit of the non-liberal British left,[116] it might be of interest to present some evidence, so often overlooked, to the contrary. There is not much doubt that the crucial financial policies were the product of liberal precepts and a liberal mind. They were in line with a gradualistic, evolutionary, ethical outlook. They hinged upon conceptions of society and social relations that differed fundamentally from conservative or Socialist ones. If indeed they resembled certain notions and ideals of British Socialists, it is because the socialism of the latter was on many points identical with social-liberalism. One cannot deduce from this, however, that the one preceded the other. Both were the creation of a similar intellectual climate which was basically a liberal one. The reasons for the rift between liberalism and other progressive bodies of thought were not ideological or philosophical, as will be claimed below. For most of the period we are concerned with social reform thinking gravitated around an advanced liberal centre— occasionally shedding an element, sometimes adding one—but drawing its basic moral and intellectual power from the liberal tradition and the liberal ideological potential.

A comparison of the social programmes advocated in the early 1890s by progressives as diverse as Dilke, S. Webb, Massingham, Atherley-Jones, and Robertson shows no basic differences of opinion. Webb may have been the most systematic of all in his detailed outlining of a social programme but

[116] See, e.g., Barker, *Political Thought in England 1848 to 1914*, pp. 190–1, 196; R. C. K. Ensor, *England 1870–1914* (Oxford, 1936), pp. 333–4; S. Hynes, *The Edwardian Turn of Mind* (Princeton, 1968), p. 57. A. M. McBriar, *Fabian Socialism and English Politics 1884–1918* (Cambridge, 1966), generally agrees that Fabian influence on Liberals cannot be unequivocally proved (pp. 238–9, 242), though he too considers the new liberalism influenced 'by Socialist doctrine of the Fabian kind' (p. 258).

there was not one proposal of his that had not been sounded by liberals far removed from Fabianism. Webb himself had accepted the Radical programme in the *Star* of 8 August 1888 as 'a statement of the current Socialist demands'.[117] It included provisions which all advanced liberals would have subscribed to, such as taxing land values, equalization and increase of death duties, differentiated and graduated income tax. An eight-hour day and a minimum wage for government and municipal employees had been accepted by a non-Fabian such as Dilke,[118] and the extension of Factory Acts and prevention of sweating were aims most civilized men had in common. Old-age pensions were advocated by Atherley-Jones and Robertson[119]—the latter a man of such forcefulness and independence of mind as to absolve him from any suspicion of having been 'permeated'. It was Robertson who moreover had advocated a gradual nationalization or socialization of one industry after another when the state had, by continuous process of democratic reform, got rid of the more easily removable conditions of social inequality.[120] Municipal socialism as—among others—a method of combating monopolies was a natural extension, as we have seen, of the liberal outlook. The new liberals were equally critical of some items on the official Liberal programme. For instance, Webb had with reason labelled plans for free land, peasant proprietorship or leasehold enfranchisement as 'survivals of the Individualistic Radicalism which is passing away'.[121] But Atherley-Jones too had stated bluntly: 'Official Liberalism is completely out of touch with the aspirations and aims of modern Liberal thought.' While less critical than Webb of Liberal land policy, he freely admitted the inadequacy of the social reform programme of the party, which was 'not calculated to kindle the enthusiasm of English artisans and labourers'.[122] Robertson, with an early hint of the emerging comprehensiveness of the liberal view, accused the Liberal

---

[117] S. Webb, 'The Basis of Socialism. Historic' in *Fabian Essays*, pp. 54–6.
[118] Dilke, op. cit. 4–5; 10–11.
[119] Atherley-Jones, 'Liberalism and Social Reform: A Warning', 629; Robertson, *Modern Humanists*, p. 272.
[120] Robertson, *Modern Humanists*, p. 270.
[121] Webb, 'The Basis of Socialism. Historic', p. 56 n.
[122] Atherley-Jones, 'The New Liberalism', 188, 192.

party of having no industrial policy, of laying least stress on democratic finance, and of preoccupation with Disestablishment and Local Veto instead of with old-age pensions and provision for the unemployed.[123] Even Massingham, at the time a member of the Fabian Society, had to admit that many members of the 1892 Liberal Parliamentary party were 'in touch with the trend of things'.[124] He also remarked that '... it is fair to remember that the Newcastle [Programme of 1891], with a little "reading in", is the skeleton even of the frankly Socialist programme of the Independent Labour Party...'[125] After all, was not the most significant fact about the 'permeation' policy in its assumption that the liberal outlook had the potential to absorb the social programme that the Fabians promoted? Whether or not the Liberal party was only to be the tool through which Fabian aims would be implemented, the measures they advocated had to be reconcilable with liberal thought, indeed, to exist within its framework.[126]

Both liberals and non-liberals were aware of the feasibility of a practical alliance on the basis of the common measures they advocated. Webb had called the young Radical an empirical Socialist of a practical type.[127] Robertson, conversely, had warned the Socialist that he had to move along the logical lines of the evolution of liberalism before he could be in sight of his truly socialistic policy.[128] By the end of the 1890s a liberal could write: '... the Socialist has announced a programme that runs roughly parallel with Radical politics'. Despite differences in ultimate aims, they could 'unite in the practical measures which, for many a day to come, will be common to both'.[129] As for their ultimate purposes, it was certainly not the Fabian philosophy that gained the upper hand in the long run. Looking at the objectives of socialism as enumerated by Webb in *Fabian Essays*, two of its widest social aims—the ultimate and gradual

---

[123] Robertson, *The Future of Liberalism*, pp. 16–17.

[124] H. W. Massingham, 'Liberalism—New Style?', *NR*, vol. 7 (1892), 459–60.

[125] Massingham, 'What Mr. Gladstone Ought to Do. III.', *FR*, vol. 53 (1893), 272.

[126] Villiers, well acquainted with the ideas of the British left, had this observation to make: 'It does not seem to me ... that the Fabians ever succeeded in making average Liberals and Radicals look at the world from a Socialistic standpoint...' (*Modern Democracy*, p. 45).

[127] Webb, 'The Moral of the Elections', *CR*, vol. 62 (1892), 275.

[128] Robertson, The *Future of Liberalism*, p. 24.

[129] Touchstone, 'Will the Liberals Repent?' op. cit. 611–12.

extinction of recipients of rent and interest, and the gradual public organization of labour for all public purposes together with the elimination of the private capitalist and middle-man— were not achieved.[130] It was the advanced liberal's formula, of rendering to society what was unto society's and to the individual what was unto him, that survived as an expression of political justice and as a fact of political practice.

That a single Progressive party was not to be seems to have been due to the tendency prevalent in Britain to equate a body of socio-political thought with a political organization. Thus liberalism was understood to be the set of ideas and beliefs held by the Liberal party.[131] The despair of Fabianism with the Liberal party appeared to underline the necessity for building up a new organizational framework when the diffusion of new ideas was desired. To this was coupled a social distance between Labour and the great bulk of the Liberal supporters, which naturally led the former to wander off in a different direction from sheer lack of *rapport*, no doubt reinforced by the liberal vacillation between the middle and the working classes. For ideologically speaking, as has repeatedly been stressed, liberalism was sufficiently equipped to supply the bulk of the working class with a programme and with ideals (if indeed that was what they wanted) that would adequately satisfy them. The social reform group within liberalism was the intellectually vital one, and once the party came to power in 1906, the social reformists—despite their numerical insignificance[132]—did virtually all the running.[133] We have already seen that during

[130] Webb, 'The Basis of Socialism. Historic', pp. 86–7.

[131] Naturally, an ideology needs the vehicle of a party to work towards its implementation, but one should not infer from this that ideology is a creation of a party. It seems a truism to state that a party cannot act as ideological vanguard for a sustained period, or that new ideas develop on its periphery. Indeed, Villiers gave substance to the contention that social reform thought originated on the periphery of the Liberal party rather than in its official centre. Witness such statements : '. . . the social reformers are by far the more numerous section among the rank and file of the [Liberal] party. . . .' *Modern Democracy* (p. 53); 'The friends of the Labour party can frankly afford to admit that the works of such writers as Messrs. J. A. Hobson, Chiozza Money, the Rowntrees, L. T. Hobhouse, and J. M. Robertson have been quite as useful in moulding modern thought as the works of the Fabians themselves' (ibid., p. 148).

[132] See, e.g. Masterman's accurate prediction in 'The Outlook for Social Reform', *IR*, vol. 7 (1905), 140.

[133] Cf. T. Wilson, *The Downfall of the Liberal Party 1914–1935* (1968), p. 19; H. Pelling, *Popular Politics and Society in Late Victorian Britain* (1968), pp. 103, 109; Emy, op. cit., p. 184.

the 1890s advanced liberals appealed to Labour to remain within their aegis.[134] Two main factors appear to be at the heart of the failure of this plea to materialize. Firstly, the majority of the Liberal party did not and could not keep up with the developments in liberal thought. Secondly, in the able words of Villiers, the split between Liberalism and Labour was not a question of creeds or programmes. There were Liberals who were avowed socialists and conservative Labour members. 'The division is upon the independence of Labour, not upon any economic or political doctrine in the ordinary sense at all...' For when it came to social and political thought, 'the line that divides advanced Radical thought from constructive Socialist writing is as blurred as that between the representatives of Labour and Liberalism in the House of Commons.'[135] The writings of J. R. MacDonald are in fact a testimony to this intellectual kinship. Despite crucial differences in his interpretation of organicism and of individualism and in his advocacy of socialization of the instruments of production, MacDonald was in full agreement with many of the issues advanced liberals were concerned with. This is evident in his assessment of the influence of biology, his appreciation of the importance of theory and ideas, his ethical conception of socialism, his stress on self-help and on many points of detail, examples of which are touched on in these pages.[136]

By the end of the period concerned, the new liberals had developed programmes with items as radical as anything that subsequent Socialist governments have been able to achieve. The reach of their programmes paralleled their broad interpretation of welfare. Hobson drew up a charter of liberty in 1909 which was in effect an operative definition of a very advanced idea of equality of opportunity. It implied a state guarantee of the following civil rights: equal access to natural resources for individual use; facility of travel by means of a national railway system; equal access to industrial power so as

---

[134] For example, pp. 124–5 above.

[135] Villiers, *Modern Democracy*, pp. 147–8. This desire for organizational independence has been corroborated in R. McKibbin's study, *The Evolution of the Labour Party 1910–1924* (Oxford, 1974). The overlapping of advanced liberal and Socialist thought is illustrated, for example, in K. O. Morgan, *Keir Hardie, Radical and Socialist* (1975).

[136] See especially J. R. MacDonald, *Socialism and Society* (1905).

to secure liberty of trade (by means of nationalizing present sources of energy and reserving to the state any future sources to be exploited); equal access to state-operated credit facilities; sickness and unemployment insurance by the state; free and equal access to public justice; and equality of access to knowledge and culture.[137] Hobson was not alone in outlining such radical proposals. The Liberal M.P. Russell Rea, for instance, envisaged a system of community aid including free heating, lighting, feeding of children, and minimum housing.[138] To claim, therefore, that liberalism underwent a transformation merely due to the borrowing of ideas consequent upon its own intellectual failure seems groundless on the basis of the above examination.

5. 'THE MASSES VERSUS THE CLASSES'—THE STRIVING FOR NON-SECTIONALISM

The rise of organized and independent Labour in the Edwardian era noticeably reversed the attitude of many new liberals to Labour and conjured up some of the old dilemmas and fears. The ambiguity of the liberal relationship to the issue of working-class versus middle-class support was exacerbated. The term 'socialism', hitherto often synonymous with a progressive conception of social relations, tended to narrow down and to be linked with distinctive political groups and purposes. The ideological expression of these changes had marked repercussions on the interpretation of social reform, and brought into prominence its exclusive 'liberalness' as opposed to Conservative or Socialist aims and policy.

The background of the aversion to organized Labour was the readiness with which liberals identified with the masses as against the classes.[139] This identification was undoubtedly an important antecedent of the emerging liberal notion of com-

---

[137] Hobson, 'The Extension of Liberalism', *English Review*, vol. 3 (1909), 673–86. Reprinted in *The Crisis of Liberalism* under the title 'Equality of Opportunity'. Though this programme falls short of the thorough social changes Hobson would ultimately have wished to see, it is a measure of the possible within the confines of a progressive liberal capitalist system. See too an earlier article by Hobson, 'The Vision of Liberalism', *Nation*, 2.5.1908—also reprinted in *The Crisis of Liberalism*.

[138] R. Rea, *Social Reform versus Socialism*, p. 11. For a similarly advanced programme see, as early as 1896, H. Dyer, 'The Future of Politics', op. cit. 8–11.

[139] See above, section 1.

munity. Hitherto directed against privileges at the upper end of the social scale, it now became the ultimate rebuke of an independent Labour policy.[140] Hence it serves as a further example of a mechanism by which liberalism met new demands while preserving its continuity. A slogan directed at liberating the *bourgeoisie* from the trammels of the old social order could now contain the new universalistic perspective made necessary by the extension of the franchise. But the old confusion still reigned. In their quest for a national policy, liberals could not agree among themselves whether Labour was the sectional interest or whether Labour itself represented the masses whose welfare liberals had at heart. This was now aggravated by the dual identification of Labour with the working class on the one hand and with a political creed and organization on the other. Official Liberalism tended to see Labour as 'the greatest of all interests' and objected to Labour's independence:

The one [liberalism] presumably denotes a set of principles; the other [Labour], so far as it has any meaning, suggests thoughts of industry or occupation . . . The fact that a person *labours* does not surely, *ipso facto*, carry with it as a consequence that he embraces or opposes 'Liberalism'.[141]

The slogan 'masses v. classes' implied the rejection both of a sectional middle-class party and of a sectional working-class party, the ideal of an organization of all progressive forces in the country, able by persuasion and by numbers to pursue a national policy, becoming prominent in the new liberal mind as well.[142] The *Independent Review* thought in 1903 that 'the formation of a progressive organisation separate from, and in competition with, the Liberal party, will confuse the counsels and divide the forces of progress . . .' More dangerous from the liberal point of view, 'it would proclaim and stereotype the monstrous idea that there is any future for a Liberalism not continually concerned with the welfare of the masses of the people'.[143] Atherley-Jones claimed that the extension of the

[140] See, e.g., Robertson, *The Mission of Liberalism*, pp. 7–8.

[141] 'Liberalism and Labour. Some Opinions', *Speaker*, 12.9.1903. This was J. E. Ellis's opinion, in a symposium that also included A. Birrell and E. Robertson.

[142] See, e.g., J. A. Rees, *Our Aims and Objects*, Young Liberal Pamphlets (1903), who saw the new liberalism as a new political force which would regard national rather than party interests as its first care (p. 2).

[143] 'A Plea for a Programme', *IR*, op. cit. 9–10.

Liberal party to include not only Whigs and the wealthy middle class but 'young men who dream dreams' had rendered any antagonism between the aims of Labour and Liberalism obsolete.[144] The most energetic theoretical statement of this approach to independent Labour was Hobson's, propelled by his abhorrence of particularism. For him even à federation of all trade unions in a nation, displaying the most powerful solidarity of Labour, could still only offer a class solution to the problems of industrial life, as he wrote in 1899: 'As a present factor, the labour movement, even in its widest significance, is distinctively a class movement . . . and, as such, must simply be regarded as the largest form of individualism.'[145] Furthermore, the scope of the labour question could not cover the whole of the social question and the solutions Labour offered could therefore not apply to social problems *in toto*.

In face of the rise of organized Labour, the emerging pattern among new liberals became a retreat into what was essentially liberal in their views. This by no means meant the abandonment of the working class but rather a resurgence of interest in the traditional liberal bastion, the middle class, which advanced liberals had given up as lost to their cause. The eclipse of the middle class had of course paralleled the wooing of the working class. In 1888, Haldane had still advocated a policy designed to attract 'the more radical members' of the middle class, upon whom the Liberal party was dependent for a permanent majority.[146] Others had given up the middle class, maintaining that 'now . . . for the first time in the history of English politics, we find Liberalism almost exclusively identified with the particular interests of the working class'.[147] This was no doubt an exaggeration, but it seemed to many observers to be the tendency, whether they were in sympathy with it or not. Concurrently, advanced liberals repudiated the typical middle-class issues of education, temperance, and disestablishment[148] —all of which had no appeal for the public at large. Haldane, who apparently was moving to the left, with the Webbs proudly

[144] Atherley-Jones, 'Liberal Prospects: Mr. Chamberlain's Proposals', *New Liberal Review* (1903–4), 488, 493.
[145] Hobson, 'Of Labour', in J. E. Hand (ed.), *Good Citizenship* (1899), p. 105.
[146] Haldane, 'The Liberal Party and its Prospects', *CR*, vol. 53 (1888), 148.
[147] Atherley-Jones, 'The New Liberalism', 187.
[148] See below, Chapter Six, p. 197.

taking the credit, could write in 1896 that the extension of the franchise had ushered liberals into a new period in which middle-class grievances were no longer central. The adoption of a social policy was for Haldane, as for many other liberals, the automatic consequence of the new reliance on the working class, or as Haldane put it, the 'sense of dependence, not so much on sections as on the people as a whole'.[149] Still, new liberals definitely rejected the identification of a social reform policy with a working-class policy, because that would imply either of the following inadequate assumptions: that the working class was equivalent to the people at large—a majoritarian notion of society—or that social policy, being for the benefit of the working class, was particularistic.

The partisanship of organized Labour and the search for an inclusive perspective changed the trend among liberals. It was now understood that the role the middle class could play in the reorientation of advanced liberalism was dual: as the traditional group associated with liberalism it could serve as a bulwark of inherently liberal values; and side by side with the working class it could testify to the comprehensiveness and universalistic tendencies in liberalism. What Haldane had written on the middle classes in 1888 received a new significance: 'Their importance is of more consequence than their numbers; their function is to rescue us from the stigma of being a class party.'[150] The disillusionment of the new liberalism with the middle class was now transformed into a new appreciation of its value and importance. The spirit of the new social liberalism was perceived as appealing to the common interest of the middle class and the working population.[151] Parallel to this trend was an extension in the scope of social reform thought, a process to which Masterman contributed. It was not only the very poor and the very rich who deserved to be in the public limelight. 'The town life is manifesting its influence not only upon these two extreme types, but also upon the great bulk of its inhabitants—the labourers the artisans, the clerks—the "average" men of the coming century.'[152] The plight of the urban

[149] Haldane, 'The New Liberalism', 135.
[150] Haldane, 'The Liberal Creed', CR, vol. 54 (1888), 465.
[151] 'Notes on Current Events', IR, vol. 7 (1905), 365.
[152] Masterman, Preface, The Heart of the Empire, vi.

dweller was the price people in general had to pay for an industrialized civilization. Welfare thought was making its first steps towards dealing with the predicament of modern man. A complication was however introduced into the situation. The middle class incorporated after all two very different elements—on the one hand the capitalists, industrialists, and well-to-do—a key factor in the production of wealth and the finance of social reform, and, not unimportant, in defraying the costs of the Liberal party. On the other hand was the lower middle class, the 'backbone of England' which was clamouring for a share of the national cake now being offered at its expense to the working class. These two were often mistakenly lumped together as plain 'middle class'. Masterman, for instance, still sometimes thought in terms of the old image of the middle class, as when he wrote of the 'extraordinary prosperity and the extraordinary contentment of the middle classes'.[153] This was the reason, he thought, for their apathy and disinterestedness in social reform. But others interpreted the middle-class attitude to social reform less as an expression of complacency than of acute hostility. 'The bitter cry of the middle classes' was raised in 1906 in a series of articles in the *Tribune* by G. R. Sims, who described them as being hard pressed both by capitalists and by Socialists. The series provoked a discussion that went on for weeks. The *Speaker*, commenting, admitted that the middle classes 'have little sympathy with new ideas of social reform', and moreover 'the class they most despise is the class from which they have climbed . . .' Their characteristic desire to attain more for themselves made them resent carrying the main burden of social reform on their shoulders. It was precisely this lack of a sense of solidarity that made their aims run counter to the new developments in liberalism. This was evident, claimed the weekly, in their rejection of democracy, equality, and communal institutions. Two important courses of action were necessary, in the *Speaker's* opinion. The one was to recognize the justice of the grievances of the lower middle class, 'that most deserving and most long-suffering section of the community'. The addition of the lower middle class to the working class as beneficiaries from Liberal financial policy was a further step in

---

[153] Masterman, 'The Outlook for Social Reform', 136.

conceiving of social reform as catering to national social needs, as implying the responsibility of the community to the citizen *qua* citizen. The other course of action was to indulge in active propaganda among the middle class in the work of social reform, to bring about a change in social outlook, so essential to the ethical character of social reform.[154]

From 1906 onwards the increasing efforts of liberals to appeal to the help of the middle class were reflected also in liberal thought.[155] By 1908 even the *Nation* was regarding middle-class liberalism as the only scientific instrument of social and political change.[156] But at the same time Masterman was accurately defining the Liberal dilemma:

Can [the Liberal party] retain, for example, its few men of wealth, without losing those adherents who demand direct taxation of that wealth in the interests of social reform? Can it continue to bridge over that wide chasm of interest which exists to-day between the lower middle class and the working class, which leads the former always to associate itself in interest with the classes above, and alternately to fear and to despise the classes below; which is causing in that middle class a violent revolt to-day at the pampering of the working man and a vague fear of an advancing social revolution.[157]

With regard to the men of wealth, the answer depended on success in educating them that their real interest was in an efficient British worker,[158] quite apart from moral considerations. They were also less likely to feel personally the pinch of higher taxation. If this might appear to be far-fetched optimism, one must remember the existence within the liberal ranks of such men as Brunner, Mond and Cadbury. With regard to the lower middle class, not much could be done via state machinery to cure a deep-rooted psychological anxiety. But a more impartial approach to social reform was deemed possible.

[154] 'The Bitter Cry of the Middle Classes', *Speaker*, 11.8.1906. By 1908 Masterman too was speaking in similar terms of the confrontation between the middle and lower classes, a major theme of his *The Condition of England* (1909).

[155] 'The Month', *WR*, vol. 166 (1906), 489.

[156] 'A Lesson from Haggerston', *Nation*, 8.8.1908.

[157] Masterman, 'Politics in Transition', *NC*, vol. 63 (1908), 12.

[158] Samuel, *Liberalism*, p. 181, and below, p. 234.

Two lines were consequently pursued by liberal theorists. The one was to oppose too heavy burdens on industry. Even beyond the simple need for capital, the point was, as Massingham admitted in 1912, that 'Liberalism is not a revolutionary force, and it cannot dispense with middle-class brains and management.'[159] This was related to the liberal attitude to incentives, an attitude ultimately rooted in the belief that the individual will was the mainspring of social progress. Here too Hobson's exposition tackled the issue squarely. In one of a series of illuminating articles which appeared in the *Nation* in 1907 and 1908 he reminded Socialists that the individual still had an important role to play in the production of wealth. Although production and consumption were to a large extent determined by social co-operation, and although not all producers were creative individuals, Hobson believed that a realistic social reformer could not ignore the questions of individual incentive and personal remuneration when designing social improvements. Hence his definition: "Social reform, whether applied through politics or not, consists in a thoughtful endeavour to discover and apply the minimum incentive for maximum personal efficiency.'[160] This could entail both levelling up and down, connected as it was to an adequate relation between payment and services. In the larger context, this was a novel and unorthodox interpretation of social reform. It implied social and economic reorganization in line with individual psychological characteristics. It was an ultimate expression of a 'utile' society. It was a constructive approach to social questions, based not on a negative elimination of ills, but moving beyond what was imperative to correct, to what was ultimately desirable to attain. And not least important, it regarded social reform from a new angle, not one of aiding underprivileged groups, but one of changing the essence of socio-industrial life, stressing the universal aim of reforming human social behaviour as such, no matter in which segment of society an individual was positioned.

The other line pursued by liberal thinkers was an attempt to alleviate the condition of the smaller rate-paying and shop-keeping classes. Liberals turned to these groups once the major

---

[159] Massingham, 'Mr. Churchill's Career', *Nation*, 13.1.1912.
[160] Hobson, 'Are Riches the Wages of Efficiency?', *Nation*, 9.11.1907.

Acts of liberal social policy had been passed by the Liberal administration. Of great interest in this connection is a memorandum to a Committee of the Cabinet on the unrest in the labour world entitled 'Labour Unrest and Liberal Social Policy', compiled in 1912. Its significance lies not only in its contents but in its signatories, who seem to have come straight from one of the famous *Nation* dinners and included many of the key liberals considered here: Massingham, Joseph Rowntree, Hobson, Hobhouse, P. Alden, B. Seebohm Rowntree, E. R. Cross, and A. S. Rowntree. The document made the point, among others, that no additional burdens could be placed upon the middle class, especially the retail trade. Raising the issue to the level of liberal principles, the group wrote: 'Indeed, we are of opinion that *progressive Liberalism* ought to find some measure of relief for these classes.'[161] The remedy suggested was one that dealt a blow to some cherished liberal precepts. The memorandum demanded Government action to readjust Imperial and local taxation, and relief for the poorer municipalities from the cost of such social services as could really be considered national—education, health, the Poor Law, and main roads. Liberals had opposed the system of Grants in Aid for a long time,[162] one of the reasons being that they interfered with the direct responsibility and controllability of a local authority *vis-à-vis* its ratepayers. But here was not only a reversal of a democratic tenet, but a tacit admission that municipal socialism, so much praised by some liberals as the only acceptable form of 'practical' socialism, was not always an unqualified success—mainly because it functioned in isolation from the rest of the community. To the contrary, wrote the group, the burden of local taxation came close to paralysing the efficiency of municipal administration. This was no longer a question of social justice, maintained the *Nation*, but a condition of social progress.[163] As to liberal-democratic fundamentals, the memorandum attested that direct democracy and responsibility were making way for an indirect network of responsibility, where each unit was dependent on a centre

[161] Lloyd George Papers, C/21/1/17, 'Labour Unrest and Liberal Social Policy' (my italics).

[162] See, e.g., 'Financial Reform', *Speaker*, 20.1.1894.

[163] 'The New Liberalism at Hanley', *Nation*, 20.7.1912.

which regarded the unit within the framework of national needs. Was this not the triumph of the organic conception of society?[164]

Having second thoughts about the middle class did not mean that liberals were returning to their original social base to the exclusion of a wider one. The movement towards a universalistic and comprehensive conception of society was crystallizing in liberal thought. The crucial point, thought the *Nation* in 1910, was that modern British liberalism was no class movement and therefore its goals belonged to 'a high form of statecraft'. The pursuit of national interests was exemplified in 'the conception of a higher standard of living achieved for the whole people, largely by the regulative and persuasive action of the State' and in 'the adaptation of the common knowledge and the common funds to finer, more humane, more skilfully directed ends'.[165] The organic perspective, which insisted on the merits of the variegated parts as well as the whole, was leaving its mark. This was a long step forward even from the relatively advanced opinions of G. F. Millin, who in 1892 still saw the solution to problems of social reform through making 'that prosperous, comfortable middle-class as large as you can by absorbing into it as rapidly as you are able all the best of the sad and suffering section beneath it'.[166] Liberal social reform had transcended the faith in comfort, prosperity and a particular life-style as the cure-all for the evils of the time.

6. THE CONSTANCY OF LIBERAL ESSENTIALS

The growing liberal desire to construct their own concept of social reform was reflected in the aspiration of new liberals both to extend the range of services a society could offer its members and to maximize—beginning from the base—the number of people whose welfare they would actively pursue and whose interests they could represent. At the same time they made every effort to emphasize the uniqueness of their notions on social reform and especially—why they merited the epithet 'liberal'. The mutual recriminations between the Liberal and

[164] These proposals were largely realized in the Budget of 1914. See H. Samuel, *Hansard*, 5th Ser. LXIII 1575–81 (22.6.1914).
[165] 'From Old to New Liberalism', *Nation*, 20.8.1910.
[166] [G. F. Millin], *The Social Horizon* (1892), p. 76.

Labour parties of 'dishing' each other's aims and programmes made this all the more necessary. Such delimitation was not usually undertaken by the liberal intellectual *avant-garde*, still bent upon a unification of all progressive forces, and thus more apt to stress the common than the exclusive. But the fact remains that the essential characteristics of liberalism were meticulously preserved by the diverse subscribers to that faith and were the central focus of the liberal consciousness, even though their ideas on social reform often differed. Hence new liberals would have assented to the opinion of a disciple of Kidd:

...the Liberal has begun to see that social legislation and Socialism are different things. The idea—partly confusion of thought, and partly a fretful prejudice—that social legislation was merely a truckling to Socialism...is, happily for the fortunes of the Liberal Party, tending to extinction...[167]

Detailed versions of the differences between liberal social reform and Socialism became increasingly frequent after 1906, despite the common meeting ground of *practical* social reform. It is however important to stress that 'practical' did not mean 'pragmatic'. The pragmatic aspect of social reform, which was sometimes regarded as singularly liberal,[168] was diametrically opposed to the views of most new liberals. As one writer complained, epitomizing the changing liberal attitude to social policy: 'Nor will it pass muster to say, as Mr. Asquith did, that each case must be judged on its merits...it is no credit to Liberalism that it has no "abstract formula" on the subject.'[169]

More central to the liberal viewpoint was the retention of competition in one form or another, as has already been observed. Believers in the rationality of the individual will could, on a superficial level, join forces on this issue with supporters of a natural cosmic order to which the individual had to succumb. Many liberals echoed the distinction drawn by

[167] Touchstone, 'Will the Liberals Repent?', op. cit. 611.

[168] 'It is a question of degree, to be determined in each particular case and by demonstration of a measure's specific injustice, not by a loose and question-begging epithet, how far a restriction of a man's "right to do as he will with his own" is or is not a contribution to true liberty, and how far a financial arrangement is a just or an unjust penalization of certain classes for the benefit of others.' (Leader, *Tribune*, 21.10.1907.)

[169] 'A Radical of '85', op. cit. 141. See Chapter Seven for an elaboration of this point.

Arnold Toynbee between desirable competition in production
and undesirable competition in distribution.[170] As a moderate
liberal wrote, social legislation which would minimize social
inequalities—by free education, the maintenance of poor
children, a Shop Hours Act, the use of the Poor Law modernized in the form of a comprehensive social scheme administered by the state—would bring out the advantages of competition.

It is possible, then, to regard social legislation on the lines just
mentioned as a safeguard against the more extreme form of collectivist
Socialism, inasmuch as it enables us to retain the competitive
organisation of society, while excluding those features which are by
common consent regarded as dangerous, or revolting, such as the
actual extermination of the unsuccessful.[171]

Instead of being coterminous with *laissez-faire*, competition was
combined with a moderate state interventionism.

A key participant in this debate was W. S. Churchill. It is, of
course, quite incorrect to depict him—as is often the case—as
one of the architects of the welfare state.[172] This might be true
only in the limited sense that advanced liberals were lucky to
have a forceful and energetic sympathizer in a position of power
to push through some important reforms. Churchill was a
bright young man with a penchant for picking up and hurriedly
digesting such ideas as appealed to his fancy. Far from having a
philosophical bent of mind, let alone an original one, his main
service to liberal theory was the imaginative eloquence in which
he could clothe the questions of the day. Two of his speeches
have become classics of the new liberalism and it is worthwhile
looking at them to locate the elements in new liberal thought
which were now becoming part of the national heritage by
means of Churchill's heroic amplification. In the first speech,

[170] A. Toynbee, *Lectures on the Industrial Revolution of the Eighteenth Century in England* (1884), p. 87.
[171] W. M. Lightbody, 'Socialism and Social Reform', *WR*, vol. 167 (1907), 291.
[172] See, e.g., K. de Schweinitz, *England's Road to Social Security* (Univ. of Pennsylvania, 1943), pp. 200–1. A similar tendency is to see Churchill and other Liberal Ministers as leaders or formulators of the new liberalism, rather than its mouthpieces. This is a failure to distinguish between originators of social thought and policy in the wide sense and instrumental executors of policy. The political élite is not necessarily the ideological one. See T. H. Marshall, *Social Policy* (2nd edn. 1967), p. 28, and A. M. McBriar, *Fabian Socialism and English Politics 1884–1918*, who indiscriminately lumps together Churchill, Hobhouse, Hobson, and Massingham (p. 257).

delivered on 11 October 1906 and reprinted as 'Liberalism and Socialism' in 1909, Churchill recognized that liberalism had become irrevocably collectivist. This was incumbent upon the nature of man and of society. In his words:

It is not possible to draw a hard-and-fast line between individualism and collectivism . . . That is where the Socialist makes a mistake . . . No man can be a collectivist alone or an individualist alone. He must be both an individualist and a collectivist. The nature of man is a dual nature. The character of the organisation of human society is dual.[173]

Liberalism was thus presented as unique in having the advantage of a superior viewpoint. It alone realized the complexity of society by encompassing within its scope both collective organization and individual incentive. Churchill went on to give a very good definition of the relationship between a minimum standard of life and competition, as most liberals now understood it. It was still a far cry from the creative, artistic, and to a large extent spiritual competition as construed by Hobson and others. But it did not have the calculating and ruthless efficiency of Kidd's version either. Churchill himself, not very clear on the theory behind his words, started off by saying: 'The existing organisation of society is driven by one mainspring—competitive selection.' The Social Darwinist conclusion did not follow, however. Instead came an unconscious acknowledgement that liberalism had now added to the idea of competition a humane and responsible regard for all members of society—considered by new liberals to be a second mainspring of social strength. Churchill, unaware of this, formulated the end-result admirably:

I do not want to see impaired the vigour of competition, but we can do much to mitigate the consequences of failure. We want to draw a line below which we will not allow persons to live and labour, yet above which they may compete with all the strength of their manhood. We want to have free competition upwards; we decline to allow free competition to run downwards.[174]

No doubt Churchill was thinking of straightforward, material competition over tangibles. But he had also recognized the basic unity of social interests.

[173] Churchill, *Liberalism and the Social Problem*, p. 79.
[174] Churchill, op cit., p. 82.

In a second speech on 14 May 1908, Churchill juxtaposed liberalism and Socialism. He saw liberalism as levelling up, not levelling down; as reconciling private interests with public right; as rescuing enterprise from the trammels of privilege and preference. Once more he stressed that, though abhorring complete collectivism, he desired a greater collective element in state and municipality. Practically, this meant for him not much more than socializing services which were in the nature of monopolies,[175] apart from spreading a net over the abyss. But he was keenly aware of the 'immense differences of principle and of political philosophy' between liberalism and doctrinaire Socialism and was convinced that the liberal road to social reform, preserving individual enterprise within the framework of responsibility towards the masses, was the only one. The *Nation*, in reviewing Churchill's volume, assessed the specific liberal attitude to reform:

This moving equilibrium of the forces of collectivism and individualism, not a contradiction or a compromise, but a harmony, is of the very essence of that social progress to which Liberalism commits itself with fresh faith and with growing courage, as the nature of her task becomes clearer to consciousness, and draws its inspiration from a firmer grasp upon the principles of social justice.[176]

Massingham, who was at that time enthusiastically giving Churchill his wholehearted support, detected the essential point about Churchill's presentation of liberal ideas. They were '"interdependent" parts of a large and fruitful plan of Liberal statesmanship'; they displayed 'a unity and sincerity of thought', 'a wide and eager outlook on the future of our social order'. This was 'new territory ... as a clearly seen vision and a connected plan of British statesmanship; not new as actual experiment in legislation, and as theory held by progressive thinkers of many schools, including some of the fathers of modern Liberal doctrine, and most of our economists.'[177] A general theory of social reform had finally penetrated the field of party politics. It was not merely the legislation itself that counted, but the spirit and the context in which it was

[175] Ibid., pp. 155–6.
[176] 'The Social Policy of Liberalism', *Nation*, 27.11.1909.
[177] Massingham, introduction to Churchill, *Liberalism and the Social Problem*, xiii–xvi.

conducted. From the perspective of liberal social reform thought the national minimum was 'not a problem of "relief", it is a method of humanity, and its aim is not merely to increase the mechanical force of the State, but to raise the average of character, of *morale*, in its citizens'.[178] In this sense, at the very least, liberal social reform had departed from a materialistic and quantifiable attitude to social improvement.

The retention of competition in conjunction with collectivism was related to the concept of the national minimum, which had of course its most ardent advocate in Webb. But in this case, too, it was a logical concomitant of the social ideas of progressives and radicals in general. Robertson had declared in 1891 that the fixing of an income below which none were taxed 'is an admission that a certain minimum of comfort should be allowed for before a citizen is asked to make any special sacrifice in the name of public action'.[179] Hobson, too, had repeatedly advocated a minimum wage and objected to treating labour as a commodity.[180] The *Daily Chronicle*, in taking up the demand of the Fabians, wrote:

The 'living wage' means more than house and home, than food and fire; it means the development of the personal character of the workers, and the reflection of their character in what they produce, in what they desire, in what they do ... It represents more clearly than anything else that has yet happened, that permeation of economics by humanity which will be seen to be the most striking characteristic of the intellectual development of the present age ... If Mill should be against the principle of the 'living wage', so much the worse for Mill, or rather, so much the better for us.[181]

Thus, although the living wage, in its rejection of the wage-fund theory, was in a sense a departure from the old liberalism, it still aimed at achieving the same ends. Many years later, the *Nation* was prompted to remark, in terms that will be clarified in the next chapter: 'The practical proposals of the "minimum" policy sweep aside the vapid and paralysing discussions between the rival schools of reformers who laid primary stress,

[178] Ibid. xx.
[179] Robertson, *Modern Humanists*, p. 265.
[180] See, e.g., Hobson, 'The Industrial Situation and the Principle of a Minimum Wage', *South Place Monthly List* (April, May, 1912).
[181] Leader, *Daily Chronicle*, 21.11.1893.

respectively, upon character and environment.' Child nurture, health, housing, regular income, and employment were essential both to a sound character and to a healthy environment. This was a meeting place between moderate individualists and socialists.[182] Hobhouse too regarded the living wage as a matter of justice and an inherent feature of the social system simply because a man was a working member of the community— whose welfare was the ultimate aim.[183] And Villiers saw it as part of the emerging trend towards 'Guarantism'—the securing by the state of immediate but moderate and gradualist improvements in the conditions of living.[184]

Webb's ideas on the subject fitted well into advanced liberal thought because he too had envisaged a minimum of efficiency combined with open-ended stimulation to upward initiative.[185] This is precisely what was wholeheartedly accepted by a very wide range of liberals. In 1908 the Select Committee on Home Work saw the minimum rate of payment as a new departure in legislation but also as the development of an agreed principle: '... your Committee are of opinion that it is quite as legitimate to establish by legislation a minimum standard of remuneration as it is to establish such a standard of sanitation, cleanliness, ventilation, air space, and hours of work.'[186] The national mimimum appealed to the new liberals because it constituted an important juncture between the sciences of biology and psychology, and the ethics of liberalism. On the obvious level it enabled a 'beneficial' competition between individuals commensurate both with communal responsibility and with individual excellence. It fitted into the division of labour between machinery and art which Hobson, Villiers, and others had postulated. But furthermore, in its scientific approach towards physical efficiency—to which even advanced liberals did not object—it was an expression of the

---

[182] 'The Real Enemy', *Nation*, 19.10.1912.

[183] Hobhouse, 'The Right to a Living Wage', in *The Industrial Unrest and the Living Wage*, pp. 67–8.

[184] Villiers, *Modern Democracy*, pp. 31–4 and *passim*. Cf. '"Guarantism"', leader, *MG*, 7.6.1912.

[185] S. Webb, 'The Policy of the National Minimum', *IR*, vol. 3 (1904), 172–4.

[186] Quoted in T. P. Whittaker, 'A Minimum Wage for Home Workers', *NC*, vol. 64 (1908), 520. Cf. *Parl. Papers* 1908, VIII (246), p. xiv. Cf. also *Hansard*, 5th Ser. II 2113–14 (26.3.1909).

new role the biological understanding of man was coming to play in social policy.[187] The notion of physical efficiency was not less vital to the earning power and hence to the individual welfare of the worker and his family than to the productivity of the nation at large, a fact that all liberals concerned with social reform had come to appreciate. This was combined with an enhanced understanding of the psychological element in work—mainly that of motivation, to which Hobson had substantially contributed. The securing of adequate production became a question of an intricate balance which operated on two levels. On the one hand the satisfaction of the worker's needs had to be countered with incentives to induce him to work rather than to immerse himself in the pursuit of his private welfare. On the other hand, the remuneration of employees had to be balanced against the readiness of the employer to continue his entrepreneurial activities.[188] Liberals never made light of the centrality of the profit motive as fundamental to the functioning of the industrial system. It not only had to be satisfied but even, in its absence, manufactured. This was a social policy based upon what appeared to be immutable principles of human nature. But ethical considerations of welfare, reinforced by considerations of social utility and gain, became themselves integral parts of this policy. The concept of a minimum thus progressed from what was necessary to keep human work-power going (and this is where the Marxist critique of capitalism applied) to what was commensurate with both individual and social health.[189]

A lively and intelligent assessment of the uniqueness of liberal social reform came from the Liberal M.P. Russell Rea—a politician close to progressive circles,[190] yet loyal to the traditional frameworks of liberalism. The terminology Rea used in differentiating liberal social reform from Socialism once

[187] See, e.g., C. Money, *Hansard*, 5th Ser. L 508–9 (13.3.1913); P. Alden, *Hansard*, 5th Ser. LI 1308 (9.4.1913).

[188] See Sir E. Grey, *Hansard*, 5th Ser. XXXV 2181 (21.3.1912); Lloyd George Papers, 'Labour Unrest and Liberal Social Policy'.

[189] D. Lloyd George, *The Insurance of the People* (Liberal Publication Dept., 1911), pp. 3–4; P. Alden, *Democratic England* (1912), p. 65; 'The Policy of the Minimum Wage', *Nation*, 20.12.1912. For a further discussion see Chapter Six, p. 240 ff.

[190] He was active both in the Rainbow Circle (see below, Chapter Seven) and in the Ethical Movement. See Hobson, *Confessions of an Economic Heretic*, p. 95; G. Spiller, *The Ethical Movement in Great Britain* (1934).

again clearly demonstrates that the former had gone a long way towards answering the basic needs of the time—a sense of community, a concept of society, a planned social re-organization, a qualitative appreciation of individual and social life—and that awareness of this transformation was now common knowledge. Progress under liberalism, said Rea, was towards 'a high type of national life'. In the language of classical liberalism he saw the achievement of liberal social reform in that 'all the poor and the working classes have acquired a new and a vast stake in the country'.[191] This term is most significant, for it implied a real integration of the outcast into the system, forged by the dual bonds of interest and right. The substitution of common for individual action, Rea believed, was the general principle underlying the development of civilization, and was not peculiar to liberalism. Yet the difference between the (liberal) social reformer and the Socialist, between the social state and the Socialist state, was one of kind, not degree. 'The Social Reformer is governed by a different principle and a higher principle . . . the great principle of Liberty.' The central issue for the liberal was how to avoid sacrificing liberty for equality:

The questions the Social Reformer would ask are not one, but two. Has it tended to equality? Then it is *so far* good. And, more important still, has this surrender of liberty secured a larger liberty for the individual? Has it given him a better and a freer life? *This is the test.*[192]

And this was also, maintained Rea, the actual achievement of liberal social legislation.

To this interpretation of social reform Rea now added an important insight. To the Socialist contention that social reforms were mere palliatives, he replied:

I say there is no final limit to the application of Social Reform; there is only one limit, and that is not fixed, but infinitely elastic. It cannot advance at any particular time and place beyond the moral development of the people. It can only proceed on one principle, viz., that as the higher activities of a people develop so their lower needs may be Socialised.[193]

Apart from an acceptance of the Hobsonian formula concerning the relation between individual and social activity, Rea

[191] R. Rea, op. cit., p. 4.   [192] Ibid., p. 8.   [193] Ibid., p. 10.

realized two things: first, social reform was an ethical process as much as a socio-political one. It was the concomitant of ethical evolution, but it obviously could not anticipate it.[194] Second—an inevitable conclusion once social reform was linked to evolution—it was a dynamic approach to social questions, a ceaseless improvement of conceptions and of facts. Rea's opinions endorsed the philosophical and scientific contributions Ritchie and Hobhouse had made to liberal theory. His views were in direct contradistinction to the old, static, attitude to social reform as concerned with repairing social defects—an approach that sometimes lingered on in the Bismarckian and conservative outlooks. Social reform was no longer a means to a political end external to itself, such as social stability. It itself had become an end, an expression of social progress, a permanent feature of social life.

...given a universal, perpetual, never-satisfied desire for something better than anything that is ever realised, always striving for a better standard of life—more comforts, more leisure, more interests; given this moral atmosphere, then it may be safe to go farther and farther on the same path of Social Reform.[195]

Rea had a further sharp observation to make about the nature of the social reform state. '...equality of condition, though never enforced, will always be aimed at, always be more and more nearly approached, and never quite reached'.[196] This epitomized the ambiguity of advanced liberals towards social equality. They preferred it as an ideal rather than as reality, as directing framework rather than achieved situation. In the liberal-democratic tradition it tended to be a normative rather than a descriptive concept, a recognition of the equality of intangibles such as human worth, dignity and rationality, rather than equality of condition which was in the main an economic concept. Ultimately liberals saw a tension if not a contradiction between these two equalities. The nearest they got to equality of condition was in formulations such as 'a more complete equalisation of economic possibility in the social apparatus of ordinary existence'.[197] This equalization enabled

[194] Hobhouse had made a similar point. See Chapter Two, p. 47.
[195] Rea, op. cit., p. 11.
[196] Ibid., p. 12.
[197] Masterman, *Youth and Liberalism*, Young Liberal Pamphlets (1911), p. 8.

individuals to employ their energies 'more actively than ever in a competitive struggle for higher and better things'[198]—a viewpoint strongly indebted to the ethical tradition in liberalism[199] for which equality of condition was basically a facet of materialism. Moreover, natural inequalities in creative behaviour could be reinforced by certain inequalities in condition (such as pecuniary incentives) and would in turn cause new inequalities. Hence absolute equality of income (a scheme which G. B. Shaw put forward at the National Liberal Club) was unacceptable to liberals, as the *Nation* explained. If it were converted into tangible goods, 'there would be a maximum alike of waste and want, and the widest inequality in the amount of good got out of the different units . . .'. If it remained in the form of money income, 'the fact that different persons cannot make an equally good use of the same money income in terms of personal satisfaction means that an equal distribution of money income would involve inequalities of waste . . .' This would only substitute one form of inequality for another.[200] Liberalism, as has been noted, could logically extend its preferred term 'equality of opportunity' so as to make it identical with another interpretation of equality, generally accepted by radicals and revolutionaries alike. 'From each according to his powers, to each according to his needs', as an ethical ideal, did not after all imply equality of condition. It was, thought the *Nation*, 'in conformity with the general law of organic distribution . . . the ability of cells, organs, or other cooperative units of an organic whole, to utilise, in healthy vital activities, the food which comes to them.' The organic equality of use was far better than Shaw's mechanical equality. The *Nation*, while recognizing the large measure of equality in common humanity, requested at the same time to heed the 'elements of inequality which mark one man from another and constitute his individuality'.[201]

It was precisely the infiniteness of social reform and social progress that negated a finite term such as equality of condition. The field of common, primary necessities became in new liberal

[198] Rea, op. cit., p. 12.
[199] See quotation from J. Rae in Chapter Two, p. 55.
[200] 'Equality of Income', *Nation*, 10.5.1913.
[201] Ibid.

thought a residual category, growing only through a process which concurrently produced new qualitative inequalities. Equality of condition *had* to be an elusive goal in a concept of society that was based on striving, not attaining. An ideal once attained would be transformed into a static conservatism, a 'rule of routine', in Rea's words. To guarantee built-in dynamism was to prevent this.

By 1914 liberalism had been enriched by the emergence of a notion of community, and issues of social reform were approached within that frame of reference. Hobson's position, as analysed by Hobhouse, had become, even if on a lower level of sophistication, an apt description of the new liberal in general. It was a social philosophy attained by

a higher synthesis wherein the truth of the old gospel, with its doctrine of liberty, equality, and full opportunity for the individual should be brought into harmony with the later view of the collective responsibility of the State for the well-being of its members.

The social problem was one, Hobhouse continued—what do we mean by society and in what lies the value of social life? Hobson had not sought a panacea in any single political social reform, but had rather sought to promote the ascendancy of a higher social conception which would gradually reorganize the economic basis of society in accordance with the Ruskinian principle: wealth is life.[202] This social conception was now guiding a large number of progressive liberals in their practical efforts to break down the prejudices and conventions of an old order and establish social life on a new basis both just and true to human nature.

[202] Hobhouse, 'Towards a Social Philosophy', review of Hobson's *John Ruskin Social Reformer* and *The Social Problem*, MG, 2.12.1904.

V

Social Reform and Human Improvement

I. THE ENVIRONMENT OF CHARACTER

ALTHOUGH the main implications of social reform concerned the fabric of society, the ethical ends of the community and the quality of social relations, there was another aspect to social reform which even the most avowed collectivist would not deny. This was the development of a 'better' human being—for, after all, the condition of the basic social unit was the key to the social condition. This question was indissolubly connected with the ethical and scientific modes of thinking of the period. Basically, there were two facets to human improvement—physical and moral-spiritual. As with the field of social study, the relevance of physical factors to total individual development had only lately been recognized. The recent advances in biology had now drawn attention to a new set of preconditions not only for a healthy society, but for a healthy individual. The connection between physical normalcy and intellectual and moral progress was until then far from being evident. The traditional concern of liberalism, and not of liberalism alone, had been the fostering, as independent categories, of the moral and intellectual capacities of individuals, and these, especially the former, were generally described by the word 'character'. Character, of course, did not cease to be a prime aim of the new liberalism as well, although the connotations of that word were, as will be seen, rather unfortunate. But moral improvement was no longer regarded as a consequence solely of exercising individual and autonomous will power. Here again, the self-contained individual was challenged by a new understanding of his dependence on his environment in the widest sense of the term—human and non-human. Moral improvement became thus a question of reforming the framework in which the individual functioned. In part this meant changes in social relations. But it also called for a further expansion of the concrete concerns of social reform. Under present social circumstances, the free, conscious, and voluntary action believed essential to the practice of morality became chimerical. And inasmuch as moral improvement depended on the manipulation of factors beyond individual control—the material and physical determinants of human behaviour—social reform had to assume responsibility over a new domain. The new issues of social reform were best expressed in two themes that dominated the period. The one became known as the character versus environment issue, the other revolved round the breeding of better human stock. This last issue was of special interest as regards liberal theory because of its very close impingement on questions of human individuality, freedom, and ethical self-determination.

For J. S. Mill, character was essential to happiness and progress. In his definition, 'a person whose desires and impulses are his own—are the expression of his own nature, as it has been developed and modified by his own culture—is said to have a character'.[1] It is important to note that later liberal theorists did not essentially reject this idea of character, not did they assess differently the consequences of character to society. Indeed, progressive social reformers continued almost universally to regard the cultivation of character as one of the ends of humanity.[2] Even Sidney Ball, demonstrating the tenuous delimitation of left-liberalism and some varieties of socialism could write, whilst endorsing competition: 'The State can have no end which is not an end of individuals; its end can be realized only in the free wills of individuals: its end is, in fact, the development of character.'[3] But with the aroused interest in the condition of the people a note of confusion crept in. The importance of character was stressed by conservatives and progressives alike, but with different aims in mind. The one school held that character, being an expression of individual will, could only be developed by exercising that will autonomously. For these people, best typified by the Charity Organisation Society, the virtues of self-reliance and self-help

[1] J. S. Mill, *On Liberty*, pp. 115, 118.
[2] S. A. Barnett, 'Sensationalism in Social Reform', *NC*, vol. 19 (1886), 289.
[3] S. Ball, 'A Plea for Liberty: A Criticism', *ER*, vol. 8 (1898), 337, 338.

became the sole means to character-building as well as the central components of character. And as, from this perspective, social improvement was attainable only through every man improving himself, 'character' became known as *the* method of social reform even more than its end. Progressive social reformers, conversely, interpreted character as denoting more than mere structural independence of individual actors from outside influence and assistance. Moral excellency could not be summed up by qualities such as the strength, independence, and spontaneity of individual will and behaviour, though these were obviously conditions of such excellence. Moreover, when, on the C.O.S. view, all improvement was ultimately to be generated within the individual and applied to himself, one could hardly speak of *social* reform. Only with the advent of the new theories of social life was character understood to be geared to the claims of the environment—social and physical—in which it existed, rather than based on an independent entity. Hence the misleading juxtaposition of character versus environment made way for the improvement of environment *and* will power as means to character.

The basic dogma of the C.O.S. was already under attack in the 1880s. Originally the opposition to excessive reliance on self-help was connected with the 'removal of hindrances' school, for as Green had urged, it was necessary to endow every man with the power to make the best of himself, and the state could supply certain conditions for this end without interfering with individual independence.[4] The ideological struggle was not, however, over Green's principle, but over the priority and relative weight of environmental factors in individual and social life, and over the limits—as unclear as ever despite Mill and Green—of state action regarding the environment. After all, even Barnett—the former C.O.S. supporter—acknowledged that besides teaching the people, conditions had to be changed.[5] Charity was only a temporary remedy. Society had to cure the evils at the root of human misery.

Both the element of competition and the rational mastery of the human mind over impediments to its dominance appealed

---

[4] Green, *Liberal Legislation and Freedom of Contract*, p. 13.
[5] Barnett, 'Sensationalism in Social Reform', op. cit. 290.

to the liberal mentality. J. A. M. Macdonald, a Liberal active in the left wing of his party, admitted:

... we allow, of course, the truth of the general proposition that strength of character is the result of struggle with circumstance. And we further admit that, as a general proposition, it is true that any attempt to interfere with the free action of circumstance is a mistake. But ... it is not ... true as to every circumstance of our life ... before circumstances can operate as a real discipline in life, before they can become the means of evoking the reason in us, they must themselves be in their nature reasonable.[6]

Samuel characteristically tried to combine the different viewpoints. True, he maintained, improvement was to be found in the continuous toil of individual men, and self-reliance and thrift were virtues that should not be damaged by state action. Moreover, he was—together with many other progressively minded people of the time—curiously insensible to the problems of the idle, drunk, and incapable, for whom moral opprobrium was still predominant. Yet at the same time he realized that low surroundings bred low character. One could give a stimulus to self-improvement by making it easy for men to rise. Education, moral influences, better surroundings, these were the 'most powerful means for raising the standard of life and character'.[7]

There was however a growing tendency among liberals to upgrade the role physical environment played in moulding character. The importance of environment was also the outcome of the acceptance of Weismann's biological theories, for a good environment would secure the development of potentially gifted individuals at the foot of the social scale.[8] The obsession with environment—as key to the immediate manipulation of desirable human traits—was rather a characteristic of Socialists, especially of the Fabian type,[9] though one of them, R. A. Bray, may serve as an example of a careful and balanced, basically liberal, approach. Following the ethical perspective, Bray granted that one could not directly influence the moral character of individuals. But the reformer could create new

[6] J. A. M. Macdonald, 'The Problem of the Unemployed', *NR*, vol. 9 (1893), 575–6.
[7] Samuel, *Liberalism*, pp. 16, 19–20.
[8] See above, Chapter Three, pp. 88–9.
[9] S. Webb, 'The Policy of the National Minimum', *IR*, vol. 3 (1904), 163.

needs and interests. A wide field was open to the reformer in the improvement of environment, for 'if you are anxious to eradicate a habit, which is fostered by the environment, change the environment or alter the conditions in such a direction as will encourage the growth of a counter habit'.[10]

Bray also touched upon a related subject of great importance in the liberal tradition, concerning the belief in individual autonomous character and in self-help. The advocators of this belief were prepared at the most to recommend some sort of aid in strengthening character, which by its nature could only be based on personal contact between two wills—the one educating the other to self-expression. Impersonal forms of aid, unlike—ostensibly—charity, would not be felt by the recipient to concern the needs of his specific character directly. This fitted well into the liberal faith in voluntary association and co-operation (collective self-help) as the primary means of social organization. Bray restricted the role of individual enterprise in the domain of personal influence to an experimental or pioneering one. Once it had explored a certain field and established its needs, it was time for the state to move in with its vast resources.[11] This underlined the division of labour which new liberals were coming to accept between individual and state action. The automatic connection between individuality and voluntarism was now open to doubt. This point had been made by Ritchie as early as 1887, when he voiced the 'heresy' that voluntary associations had a tendency to stiffen into rigid bodies whereas the state—being the outward expression of the national spirit—was more flexible. He too wanted voluntary associations merely to lead the way in social experiments.[12]

But it must be made clear that nowhere in liberal thought was there a reversal of faith in the importance of the individual virtues of self-reliance, personal exertion, and the like. Rather, serious inroads were made into the absolute assertions about the attainability of these virtues and their sufficiency for social progress. This was apparent on such questions as the scientific validity of thrift, and the increasingly common distinction between poverty and pauperism—the first reflecting an econ-

---

[10] R. A. Bray, *The Town Child* (1907), p. 65. Cf. Chapter Three, p. 91.
[11] Ibid., pp. 70–80.
[12] Ritchie, *The Moral Function of the State*, p. 10.

omic condition and the second a type of character.[13] In general, liberals were being persuaded that 'The principle and policy of social self-help are as essential to wholesome life under modern conditions as the principle and policy of individual self-help.'[14] Yet the faith in self-help, which, as will be seen in some political issues examined in the next chapter, retained its central importance as a liberal end, posed a problem for the thoughtful liberal as far as the environment and character issue was concerned. The old tension between mind and matter was aroused in new form. It revolved round both the feasibility of differentiating mind from matter, now that man was seen to be not only part of society but part of nature, and the independence of mind as against mind. On the basis of the new political and scientific theories, a collective effort to control environment was no longer contrary to the essence of human nature. And by collective effort the rational control of mind over matter, of the human spirit over its material environment, could yet be attained. Whereas on the one hand the new tendency in political thinking was seen to be: 'Create a good physical environment, and all the products of that environment will tend to be satisfactory',[15] many new liberals retained their faith in individual character and attitude of mind.

A further important issue concerned the question of social environment. The undermining of the 'monadic myth' caused a setback to the liberal belief in the autonomous creative individual. A number of new liberals were particularly incensed by the C.O.S. approach because, as Ritchie put it, 'it is supposed that there is a complete severance between morals and politics'.[16] Morality, consigned to the realm of personal help, ignored the organic structure of society. As Ritchie pointed out, the deplorable behaviour of some members of society who were unable to follow the maxim of self-help was produced by social organization and social opinions. For those people, and for the conditions in which they lived, all were responsible as a community.

[13] The separation of poverty from pauperism was deemed by the *Nation* to be 'a more liberal and humane conception of public assistance for the poor' ('True Conceptions of State Help', 6.3.1909). See Chapter Six, p. 206 ff.

[14] 'The Prevention of Destitution', *Nation*, 9.4.1910.

[15] R. G. Davis, 'New Tendencies in Political Thinking', *WR*, vol. 173 (1910), 507.

[16] Ritchie, *The Moral Function of the State*, p. 2.

By the denial of individualism and of the supposed arbitrary and absolute freedom of the individual will, it must not be imagined that our responsibility is diminished : it is enormously increased. Because of the *solidarité* of mankind, no man can escape from being 'his brother's keeper'.[17]

The organic viewpoint also rendered obsolete the 'removal of hindrances' school which not only postulated an independent individual will but was predominantly concerned with material dependence instead of social environment. This argument was developed by Hobson, whose opinions followed directly from his ideas on the social organism and the general will. He called for 'a recognition of the interdependence and interaction of individual character and social character as expressed in social environment'.[18] He too severely condemned the C.O.S. approach which gave no allowance for an organic connection among separate wills, and could 'block the work of practical reformers upon political and economic planes, by an insistence that the moral elevation of the masses must precede in point of time all successful reforms of environment'.[19] The improvement of material circumstances, though prior to the direct moral reform of individuals, was directed in turn by the general will and the spiritual solidarity of the community. Central to Hobson's argument was his assertion that character never was entirely a question of individual will, because the latter concept was an abstraction.[20] This opinion was not typical of the liberal mainstream. Most other liberals would have agreed that the individual was not free to exercise his own will—but merely because there were material environmental impediments in the way of such an exercising, not because of its theoretical impossibility. It is important to note that for Hobson, as well as for Hobhouse, the most significant environment was social, not material, and this is what Hobhouse had referred to when he claimed that 'the conditions of social life were found to be the prime means of accelerating or retarding development'.[21] But whereas for Hobhouse the interdependence of humans was the

[17] Ibid., p. 5.

[18] Hobson, *The Crisis of Liberalism*, p. 207.

[19] Ibid., pp. 206–7.

[20] Contrast this approach with T. H. Green, *Prolegomena to Ethics*, pp. 120–2.

[21] Hobhouse, *Democracy and Reaction*, p. 117. In general usage, though, the expression 'social conditions' signified physical environment.

prime environmental factor in individual behaviour, for Hobson this was hardly 'environment' at all, but rather part of one's individuality. Still, the common conclusion was that character should be cultivated in line with the social nature of human life by concentrating on the socially-oriented attributes of personality. As Ritchie had remarked, morality was the conscious and deliberate adoption of feelings and acts which were advantageous to the welfare of the community. Perfection of character was a concept dependent on reference to the well-being of mankind.[22] Hobhouse summarized the issue as follows: 'Now, self-reliance and endurance are very good qualities, and we must not depreciate them, but a view of human nature which centers on these to the omission of the other side of character is a view which has got out of focus.'[23]

None of the three theorists would, however, have denied that the human personality was the motive power of social action. For Hobson, indeed, self-expression was the highest function of personality within the context of the social organism theory. By 1912 he was already cautioning against the new trends in social thought: '... we are tempted to neglect the end for the means: to strive after an improved environment, material, political, intellectual, moral, ignoring the direct care of the self, the human personality who is to be the tenant of this improved environment.'[24] The automatism of manipulating man via his environment was thus countered by liberals with the freedom and power of the individual to manipulate his environment for human, ethical ends.

2. DEFICIENCY AND EFFICIENCY: A TWILIGHT-ZONE OF LIBERALISM

Nowhere were the dilemmas posed for liberals by the above issues more clearly defined than in the question of the unfit. The common belief of the times was that much of the misery, many of the vices, which constituted the social problem were due to categories of physically and mentally deficient incurables. The

---

[22] See above, Chapter Three, pp. 99, 112–3.
[23] Hobhouse, *Social Evolution and Political Theory* (1911), p. 48. Cf. also Hobson, Character and Society', in P. L. Parker (ed.), *Character and Life* (1912), p. 78.
[24] Hobson, 'Character and Society', p. 53. Cf. also Kirkup, *A History of Socialism*, p. 293.

perceived danger from such people increased several-fold because of the conviction that such qualities were hereditary and transmittable. In the 1890s the standard approach to the problem had been to advocate the sterilization of the unfit and the prevention of the propagation of chronically diseased, mentally defective, and criminal people.[25] The surprising thing about those proposals lies not only in the scientific unsoundness of the facts on which they were based, but in the virtual absence of any protest on liberal and humanitarian grounds about possible infringements of liberty and about the irreversibility of the 'remedy'. Even Hobson, for example, was at the turn of the century a strong advocate of race improvement—the given reason for the elimination of the unfit, and recommended 'sternly repressing the anti-social conduct which produces the physically unfit ... society ... would certainly claim to say what marriages should not take place',[26] although this could be achieved by the force of public opinion, not necessarily legislation. In 1901 Hobson elaborated on the rationale of communal intervention:

Selection of the fittest, or at least, rejection of the unfittest, is essential to all progress in life and character ... To abandon the production of children to unrestricted private enterprise is the most dangerous abnegation of its functions which any Government can practise.[27]

One must be very careful, in judging these statements, not to rely too heavily on the benefits of hindsight which can trace the ultimate inhumanity that emerged out of race-thinking. In an era when the stunted products of slum-life were let loose upon a world that was incapable of leaving any mark of civilization on them, it was easy to assume that their removal might afford a glimpse of light in the abyss. The production of a better type of human did not involve for these liberals any *a priori* discrimination between groups. It was to be controlled purely on the outcome of empirical findings. The flaw was to a great extent in theories of natural science rather than in social philosophies. After all, the question could also be seen from a different angle, as a positive departure on the part of the state from previous

[25] See H. Dyer, 'The Future of Politics', *WR*, vol. 145 (1896), 10.
[26] Hobson, 'Mr. Kidd's "Social Evolution"', 308–9.
[27] Hobson, *The Social Problem*, p. 214.

disinterestedness in the life of its citizens, [28] or rather in aspects of their private lives which were now seen to be relevant to the public interest such as birth control, communal responsibility towards children, and the endowment of motherhood. To maintain the physical, mental, and moral standard of its citizens society claimed the right to veto the production of bad lives. Strictly speaking, this was not race thinking, inasmuch as it did not extol the virtues of one race as against another. 'Race' was really society in its physical aspects, those concerning the health of its units.

But all said and done, there was yet a strong illiberal trend on the question of physical fitness, in so far as it involved unparalleled restrictions on individuals who did not always visibly harm their fellow citizens or who were often arbitrarily judged as defective or irrational. The basic difficulty was that a scientific opinion was often indiscernible from a moral valuation. The economist Pigou, for example, could recommend 'violent interference' with individual liberty when dealing with the 'wreckage of society'. [29] But many progressive thinkers were becoming alive to the dangers besetting the problem of the unfit, and this instigated a lively intellectual ferment. Whereas Social Darwinists objected to hygienic improvements as racially suicidal, the contrary position, as expressed by Mona Caird in a contribution to the South Place Ethical Society's journal was that 'only the very "fittest" have a chance to survive, and therefore our slums ought to produce a race of gods and goddesses'. Conversely, 'that which preserves the existence of the unfit, must, *a fortiori*, favour the increase and preserve the well-being of the fit, as well as conduce to the production of more and more fit individuals ...' [30] In this case, environmentalism was combined with the liberal assertion of individuality, for the retention only of the fittest would lead to monotony of type and to stagnation.

Caird realized that the essentially illiberal point was 'the growing readiness on the part of even the thinking public to approve of the coercion of the individual on account of his

[28] Ibid.
[29] A. C. Pigou, 'Some Aspects of the Problem of Charity' in Masterman (ed.), *The Heart of the Empire*, p. 246.
[30] M. Caird, 'The Survival of the Fittest. I.', *SPM*, vol. 4 (1899), 98, 100.

misfortune, for the supposed good of the race'. A definite evil
was being committed in the name of a conjectured good. Even if
the community suffered as a consequence of respecting the
liberties of unfit members, there was no reason why it should not
suffer. 'Why, after all, should the community shirk the consequences of having produced its invalids by its laws, sentiments, habits and methods of education?'[31] Hobson himself
had elsewhere laid down a similar rule,[32] but in his treatment of
race-improvement it seems to have eluded him. Caird, on the
other hand, expressed an important principle of liberal social
welfare which the rediscovery of community sometimes obscured: 'Unless a State is ready to stand by its individual
members, and to protect their liberties through thick and
thin—even at sòme little cost on occasion—how can it hope for
that vitality and inward unity which alone can make it really
invincible?'[33]

At this stage of his intellectual development Hobson—despite
his keen sense for the interconnectedness of aspects of human
existence—was strangely unaware that social and racial fitness
demanded a cultivation not only of physical but of moral
health—understood as free development of personality, and that
concentration on the one to the exclusion of the other would
result in social imbalance. This is no more evident than in an
article Hobson wrote in 1897, where he made the astonishing
statement for a liberal: 'The sanctity which modern feeling has
attached to human life as such, irrespective of the quality or
social uses of that life, is fraught with the gravest risks to
national physique and character.' He was convinced that
morality was proportionate to the soundness of the body, and
that to pronounce matters of procreation as private was
perverse and anti-social.[34] His article elicited an immediate
response from Scott Holland, the editor, who warned against
'the impression that the increasing tendency of society to save
the unfit from perishing under the law of natural selection is
itself at fault'.[35] This was of course not Hobson's intention, but
he was guilty of ignoring the moral damage that direct selection

[31] Ibid., 114, 115.
[32] See above Chapter Three, p. 112.
[33] Caird, op. cit., 114–15.
[34] J. A. Hobson, 'The Population Question. II.', Commonwealth, vol. 2 (1897), 170–1.
[35] H. S. Holland, ibid.

could cause. Holland brought in Huxley to support him in asserting that planned, rational extirpation of the weak was morally stultifying and suppressed the virtues of natural affection and sympathy. The result was 'the calculation of self-interest, the balancing of certain present gratifications against doubtful future pains',[36] which often was, indeed, the approach of 'old' liberals whose belief in individual rights and self-help masqueraded as a paramount concern for the interest of the community.[37]

On another, connected, level, the problem of the unfit raised the issue of the attitude towards future generations. As already noted, Kidd and Hobson came out in favour of determining the conduct of each generation by the good of future generations. Hobson, it is true, had seen no contradiction between the interests of the living and the unborn but Kidd's theory had demonstrated quite clearly that a tension existed which could damage liberal maxims. Caird had opted firmly for the interests of present generations. Their welfare could not be bought at the expense of the betrayal of the few by the many, for this would mean not so much the physical transmission of deficiencies as the social transmission of a weaker moral bond. This was an important point to make in an era that was dominated by questions of biological rather than social inheritance. In Hobhouse's words, 'tradition is, in the development of society, what heredity is in the physical growth of the stock'.[38] The trend among progressive thinkers was not, however, always in this direction. They were often too absorbed in the discovery that social responsibility could extend through time, not only through space,[39] to notice that they were partially deserting the empirical, liberal-democratic tenet of catering to him whom the shoe pinches. Severe statements to the effect that hardness to one generation may turn out to be kindness to the race[40] added weight to an illiberal collectivism in an age of 'national

[36] Ibid., quoted from T. H. Huxley, *Prolegomena to Evolution and Ethics* (reprinted in T. H. Huxley and J. Huxley, *Evolution and Ethics* (1947), p. 55).

[37] W. M. Lightbody, 'The State and Parental Responsibility', *WR*, vol. 163 (1905), 289, 293.

[38] Hobhouse, *Social Evolution and Political Theory*, p. 34.

[39] Review of Kidd's *Principles of Western Civilisation* (1902) in *WR*, vol. 157 (1902), 576–7.

[40] Pigou, op. cit., p. 246.

efficiency'. On the other hand, Samuel's summary of contemporary liberal thought formulated the issue in terms more
acceptable to the liberal mainstream: 'The nation would not be
induced by the distant promises of the theorists to allow further
generations to be sacrificed in the attempt to cure these [social]
maladies by leaving them alone.'[41] Indeed, as far as responsibility towards the future went, a completely different liberal
attitude demanded of liberals 'to educate, to agitate, and to
organise on such lines as hold out the best hope that the present
generation may hand on to the next a better heritage than it
received from its predecessors. We do not require to theorise as
to a remote future.'[42] Here heritage was conserved in legislative
achievements and the future referred to was the foreseeable one
in contradistinction to Socialist utopias.

The treatment of the unfit has also to be seen in the light of the
widespread preoccupation with efficiency. That fashionable
term was used in a variety of contexts. Efficiency could be
physical, moral, mental, industrial, communal, and national.
In general it signified optimal functioning of the unit in
question and implied a tendency to evaluate an individual or
social activity by its output (preferably quantifiable) and by its
smooth and undisrupted performance. That such an attitude to
human actions did not usually go down well with new liberals is
no surprise, although it must be stressed that the term was in
almost universal circulation. But, as is wont to be the case, it
meant different things to different men. It was Kidd who had
contributed much towards the illiberal connotation of social
efficiency, because his concept meant simply the success or
survival of the species measured quantitatively. This was
illiberal not only because an efficiency used solely in conjunction with rivalry and stress was a reversal of the ideas of
social reformers but because efficiency as such was not an
ultimate value for liberals, and at most was acceptable as a
means to attaining other ends. Thus when Hobson was
discussing the living wage he noted that although it had to
contain an element of economic efficiency—by which he meant
to keep the worker going—it had to consist of more than that,

[41] Samuel, *Liberalism*, p. 26.
[42] A. Hoare, 'Liberalism in the Twentieth Century', *World's Work*, vol. I (1902–3), 86.

for the worker could not be regarded merely as a productive machine.[43] In its narrow and uncontroversial sense, efficiency was physical or industrial and related directly to productivity.[44] The difficulty obviously arose when it became unquantifiable— such as when referring to intellectual or moral capacities—and when it was applied on the grand scale to national behaviour in general. 'National efficiency' was not only quite unmeasurable and thus operatively meaningless, but conjured up an image of a society whose *raison d'être* was to be mobilized in some sort of *Gleichschaltung* towards attaining policies decided upon by expert managers. It was of course Webb who had floated that concept at a time when the Boer War had caused Englishmen to reflect on the alarming shortcomings in what was believed to be a crucial test of a nation's vitality, or as Webb put it, virility.[45] Performance, not participation, was the criterion of a healthy political system. On this Webb was in agreement with Asquith, who actually defined positive liberty as making 'the best use of faculty, opportunity, energy, life ... everything, in short, that tends to national, communal, and personal efficiency'.[46]

Most liberal theorists would have objected to the automatic equation of liberty and efficiency. Foremost among them was Hobhouse, for whom the doctrine of efficiency implied expediency. An exclusive stress on good administration and adequate power for expert officials, cautioned Hobhouse, resulted in a mechanical notion of government that paid little consideration to methods. The dangers were twofold: it promoted '"efficiency" as opposed to principle, and ... the expert as opposed to the responsible ruler'—that is, it might supersede responsible government, popular rights, and free discussion. Secondly, 'perfection of machinery is not life, and may be so used as to destroy life'. Spontaneity and civic spirit could be repressed. Ethical evolution, though also couched in terms of collective progress, did not lead to 'efficiency'.[47] This blended

---

[43] Hobson, 'A Living Wage', *Commonwealth*, vol. 1 (1896). See below Chapter Six, the discussion on property, section 3, C.

[44] See, e.g., Dyer, 'The Future of Politics'; Rae, 'State Socialism and Popular Right', *CR*, vol. 58 (1890).

[45] Webb, 'Lord Rosebery's Escape from Houndsditch', *NC*, vol. 50 (1901), 385.

[46] Asquith, introduction to Samuel's *Liberalism*, x.

[47] Hobhouse, *Democracy and Reaction*, pp. 119–24.

into the syndrome of liberal distrust of bureaucracy, as Buxton noted.[48]

New liberals tended on the whole to restrict their use of efficiency to the physical and, occasionally, mental performance of the individual. An important aspect for those liberals, but admittedly only an aspect, of the improvement of the condition of the working classes was to augment the power of the workman to work and consequently to consume. This would benefit not only himself but, on the organic analogy, the entire community. In this sense Samuel, Masterman, and the *Nation* were concerned with efficiency and even Hobhouse talked of physical efficiency.[49] Only Hobson regularly used the term 'social efficiency', though he meant by it behaviour in accordance with the strictures of the social organism model.[50]

Yet the idea of efficiency gave rise to some rather startling remarks, even among reform-minded liberals. No better example can be given both of the high-handed moral attitude still retained when dealing with questions of poverty, and of the essential illiberality of 'efficiency', than the following passages from an article by Beveridge, hardly compatible with his work a few decades later. Reviewing the problem of unemployment, he wrote: 'The ideal should not be an industrial system arranged with a view of finding room in it for everyone who desired to enter, but an industrial system in which everyone who did find a place at all should obtain average earnings ...' To secure that

The line between independence and dependence, between the efficient and the unemployable, has to be made clearer and broader. Every place in free industry, carrying with it the rights of citizenship— civil liberty, political power, fatherhood, conduct of one's own life and government of a family—should be, so to speak, a 'whole' place ... Those men who through general defects are unable to fill such a 'whole' place ... must become the acknowledged dependents of the state ... with the complete and permanent loss of all citizen rights— including not only the franchise but civil freedom and fatherhood. To those, moreover, if any, who may be born personally efficient, but in excess of the number for whom the country can provide, a clear choice

[48] Buxton, 'A Vision of England', *IR*, vol. 7 (1905), 153.
[49] Hobhouse, *The Labour Movement*, pp. 21–2; Samuel, *Liberalism*, pp. 37–8, 181; Masterman, 'The Problem of the Unemployed', *IR*, vol. 4 (1905), 560; 'The Nation and the Insurance Act', *Nation*, 29.6.1912.
[50] See Chapter Three, p. 108.

will be offered: loss of independence by entering a public institution, emigration, or immediate starvation. The slow starvation of the casual labourer [in form of temporary work], like that of the 'sweated' worker, must become impossible.[51]

The utter callousness of this plan, coming from the pen of a liberal social reformer—a product of Toynbee Hall and future architect of the welfare state—is inexplicable. The state was to abrogate its responsibility, and preferably destroy, those who could not meet its test of industrial efficiency. Efficiency in such extreme form completely ruled out the liberal concepts of welfare.

3. EUGENICS—A REJECTED ALTERNATIVE

The mental climate concerning efficiency has to be borne in mind when examining the issue of the unfit. The immediate outcome of the crisis that British society was passing through, hammered in by the Report on Physical Deterioration,[52] was a resurgence of interest in the possibilities of artificially improving the quality of the newborn. This interest received a scientific aegis under the name of eugenics, probably the most controversial branch of study that grew out of awareness of the social problem. As Robertson remarked: 'The aim of Eugenics is to promote such calculation or choice in marriage as shall maximise the number of efficient individuals.'[53] Raising the issues of stock and race improvement to the level of a planned science, evaluating physical soundness as an end of human development, might have deterred the liberal-minded observer. Yet in the first great enthusiasm for eugenics liberals were prominently to the fore, simply because what appealed to them was the rationality of the science, the possibility that man could now control a new aspect of his 'environment'—his own body.

---

[51] W. H. Beveridge, 'The Problem of the Unemployed. Report of a Conference held by the Sociological Society on 4.4.1906', *Sociological Papers* (1906), 327. Elsewhere Beveridge saw his proposed unemployment policies as corresponding exactly to the aim of the C.O.S.—giving support with reference to permanent needs. That these needs were not determined by the recipient but were attendant upon a certain concept of character did not detract from his advocacy of the method. (See W. H. Beveridge, *Unemployment. A Problem of Industry* (1909), p. 207.)

[52] Inter-Departmental Committee on Physical Deterioration 1904 (Cd 2175).

[53] J. M. Robertson in Symposium on 'Eugenics: Its Definition, Scope and Aims', *Sociological Papers* (1905), 72.

After all, the multiplication of healthy bodies enabled good stock to be preserved. Hobhouse, the most sceptical of the progressive liberals on anything connected with biology and non-spiritual approaches to human behaviour, commented: 'The bare conception of a conscious selection as a way in which educated society would deal with stock is infinitely higher than that of natural selection with which biologists have confronted every proposal of sociology.'[54] Hobson, who was of course more susceptible to this type of thinking, gave eugenics a sanguine welcome when reviewing the symposium:

... the meeting of biology and psychology under the cover of the term 'eugenics' is destined to play a great part in the future, as soon as a sufficient body of trustworthy facts is collected and co-ordinated. Though 'stock' and 'race' are not everything in national life and the world struggle, they are most necessary starting-points of profitable study, especially for those who hold that the evolution of mind enables civilised man to economise energy by substituting rational for 'natural' selection and rejection as modes of progress.[55]

For Hobson here was a unified 'life science', a means of preventing human waste, as the final triumph of rational, spiritual evolution.

Eugenics could also be seen as an alternative approach to the subject of population control, which was a source of concern to all Malthusian disciples. Many liberals had adopted that cause for their own. Mill had advocated 'provident habits of conduct'—as social reformers remembered—and it was considered a necessary corollary to social reform.[56] Robertson repeatedly recommended the limiting of the birth-rate, which he thought could be attained by state propaganda.[57] Parental prudence sometimes seemed the only way to ensure a permanent amelioration of the condition of the working classes.[58] For the free-thinkers it was basically a question of the need to

[54] Hobhouse in *Sociological Papers*, op. cit. 63.
[55] Hobson, review of *Sociological Papers*, *MG*, 25.4.1905. Cf. also Dyer, *The Evolution of Industry* (1895), pp. 31–2.
[56] J. S. Mill, *Principles of Political Economy*, ed. by D. Winch (1970), p. 125; F. Dolman, 'Political Economy and Social Reform: A Protest', *WR*, vol. 133 (1890), 640.
[57] See Robertson, *Modern Humanists*, pp. 269–70; *The Fallacy of Saving*, p. 122; *The Future of Liberalism*, p. 22; etc.
[58] Columbine, 'Social Problems', *WR*, vol. 151 (1899), 377.

rationalize all aspects of man's behaviour.[59] Eugenics, as Hobson pointed out, merely extended the question of population to include qualitative and not only quantitative considerations. In effect, though, the connection between eugenics and Malthusianism was tenuous for, as Robertson was quick to grasp, while restricting the propagation of the unfit, eugenics encouraged the multiplication of better types of families.[60]

The defects of the new science soon became a matter of increasing liberal concern. Robertson, in the course of the symposium, had already warned that high physical stamina was not probably a condition of high brain power. Moreover, it was mistaken to separate eugenics from politics, as the bad physical and moral conditions set up by poverty were a cause of 'kakogenics'. Regulating individual conduct in matters of procreation obscured the real way to social regeneration, by means of environmental reform.[61] The environment and character controversy emerged in new form. Eugenics was taken to support the view that heredity was a prime factor in social improvement and that, moreover, it was the main determinant of character. Physical unfitness seemed to eugenists to be correlated with a 'moral' inability to abstain from bringing children into the world. Educating the individual—appealing to the character of those endowed with a strong one—was one way of disseminating eugenic views. But as education was not of much use to the degenerate, only force could prevent them from multiplying. Thus character was something you either had or did not have, and it was in the interest of the community to prevent the birth of more 'characterless' people. This was connected to a curious interpretation of Weismannism. The eugenists opposed environmental reform because

Acquired characters are not inherited, and the improved environment of one generation does not either raise or lower the inherent qualities of the next...You can only alter the average quality of each generation by altering the proportion between 'fit' and 'unfit' children.[62]

[59] C. H. Seyler, 'The Shallows of Rationalism', *SPM*, vol. 5 (1900), 134.
[60] Robertson, *Sociological Papers*, (1905), 73.
[61] Ibid. 73–4.
[62] 'Eugenics and Social Reform', *Nation*, 27.8.1910.

But as Paley had pointed out, the average quality of each generation could also be raised by improving the environment of people who were naturally vigorous.[63] After all, as Blease observed, 'It is only when all have a chance of survival that we can distinguish the naturally inefficient from the accidentally inefficient.'[64] Environment and heredity, like environment and character, could then be seen as complementary rather than opposing terms—yet another synthesis which accommodated the ethical base of the new liberalism to scientific developments. Hobson understood it as a further clarification of the existing loose conception of 'character': 'The modern science of eugenics bids fair to afford a reconciliation between the two schools of reform, by giving a more exact and intelligible meaning to character and by showing more clearly the nature of the interplay between character and environment.'[65] Nevertheless, a major failing of the eugenist in the eyes of liberals was that he automatically assumed, just as the C.O.S. did, that the poorer classes were the weaker ones, and were therefore basically anti-progressive. As the *Nation* realized:

His doctrine provides those who, from whatever reason, shrink from any interference with the existing economic and social system, with a convenient excuse for taking no part in politics . . . The eugenist tends to become an aristocrat, morbidly afraid of the 'uneducated'.[66]

Nevertheless, even if they were not explicitly Conservatives, many eugenists added weight to that trend in liberalism which regarded with concern manifestations of an increased sense of community. The central thesis of one of the leading eugenists, A. F. Tredgold, was that modern legislation eased parental and social responsibilities and destroyed positive national characteristics. Race progress was thwarted by sentiment, whereas '. . . even where these poor creatures are relatively harmless, we have to protect society from the burden due to their non-productiveness'.[67] Once more, the notion of social responsi-

[63] See Chapter Three, p. 89. See also Hobhouse, *Social Evolution and Political Theory*, p. 62, who maintained that Weismann did not rule out the possibility of environment influencing the organism and thus the germ-cell.

[64] W. L. Blease, *A Short History of English Liberalism* (1913), p. 340.

[65] Hobson, 'Race-Regeneration', *MG*, 10.10.1911.

[66] 'Eugenics and Social Reform', *Nation*, op. cit.

[67] Address in May 1909. P.R.O., Cabinet Papers, Cab. 37/108, 109.

bility was stood on its head by interpreting it as the duty of the individual to remain socially isolated in his needs and wants. The *Nation* cynically observed that such voices had 'the cunning to dress up their old individualism in the new finery of eugenics'.[68] Yet Churchill circulated Tredgold's address as a Cabinet paper, merely remarking that he was informed it was not an exaggerated statement, so overwhelming did the eugenic arguments seem at the time.[69]

The most outspoken critic of eugenics in the name of liberalism was Hobhouse, despite his theoretical acceptance of rational selection. His counter-argument was that eugenists asserted certain knowledge on questions that were open to doubt and lacked a social philosophy. It did not follow from their emphasis on unfitness in certain qualities such as self-reliance and endurance that other qualities were deficient as well. Hobhouse thus issued a handy reminder to all those— eugenists or C.O.S. adherents—who identified their scheme of human improvement with a particular one-sided moral stance. He questioned whether it could be scientifically proved that a process of physical degeneration was already in operation and whether weak stock always reproduced itself, or, conversely, was not in some way essential to produce good stock. He did not deny the reasonableness of forbidding parenthood to a person of vitiated stock. But the main thesis that he wanted to substitute for the eugenic one was that individual and social progress were a function of ethical development. The elimination of individuals possessed of high ethical qualities usually led to national deterioration. For Hobhouse, social development depended on ensuring success to the *socially* fit.

... if the more social qualities are to have their chance, it is on political and social institutions that that chance must depend. Freedom of thought and action, freedom of choice by women, the repression of violence and fraud, these are all eugenic agencies which tend to diminish the contrast between the successful and the fit.[70]

---

[68] 'The Claim for a Share in Life', *Nation*, 28.9.1912.

[69] See also Asquith Papers, MS. 12, fos. 224–8, Churchill to Asquith, December 1910, where he described the growth of the feeble-minded coupled with a 'restriction of progeny among all the thrifty, energetic and superior stocks' as a 'very terrible danger to the race'.

[70] Hobhouse, *Social Evolution and Political Theory*, p. 54.

This was the liberal doctrine of according maximum scope to the development of superiorly qualified individuals, by whose talents society at large would benefit. Indeed, Hobhouse developed Mill's belief in the encouragement of eccentricity and gave it a biological foundation.

... it may be said that the most fundamental necessity from the point of view of racial progress is to maintain an environment in which any new mutation of promise socially considered may thrive and grow, and by this line of argument we arrive once more at the conclusion that liberty, equality of opportunity, and the social atmosphere of justice and considerateness are the most eugenic of agencies.[71]

Equality of opportunity was an indispensable element in ascertaining the truly fit.

The problems raised by eugenics were usually confined to discussions on a theoretical level, but on one notable occasion they occupied the public stage and brought the opposing ideological positions into a direct clash. This was the case of the Mental Deficiency Bill of 1912 which proposed machinery and means of dealing with the mentally unfit.[72] The crux of the issue was compulsory detention of the mentally deficient in special homes at the decision of a Court of Summary Jurisdiction, after a medical certificate had been obtained. One of the most interesting aspects of the Parliamentary debates on this Bill was that only one Liberal M.P.—Josiah Wedgwood, a slightly eccentric single taxer—saw grounds for actively opposing it from the very start in the name of liberty. The general opinion of the House was that the community had to be protected from the probability of increased racial degeneracy if the unfit were allowed to reproduce. But it appeared that the liberal mind, especially as expressed in the press, was still very much alive to questions of individual versus state action, despite the new definitions of the public interest.

In defining the issue Wedgwood posed dichotomies that seemed more reminiscent of the old liberalism:

Either you must rely on what you believe to be the benefit of society and the good of the human race, or you must base yourself on

---

[71] Ibid., p. 71. Cf. Hobson in Chapter Three, p.112.
[72] This was also the gist of a Private Member's Bill (Feeble Minded Persons (control) Bill) which was debated concurrently.

something which I do not know how to describe, but which I think is something like the individual conscience ... We believe that justice is the important thing, and that the welfare of the State must come second, not first.[73]

Not even arch-Individualists would have recognized their vocabulary in Wedgwood's speech. Was not the cultivation of individual conscience for the benefit of society? Was welfare to be excluded from the idea of justice? But the actual points Wedgwood made carried weight. It was really the old question of balance between individual and social claims that was again at stake and that Wedgwood had in mind. He, too, accused the community of merely wanting to save money. This was a doctrine of expediency. But improving the race in future was also, he thought, expediency. Justice and fair play ran contrary to compelling people to be locked up on what appeared to him to be insufficient evidence. Such Bills were in the spirit of the

horrible Eugenic Society which is setting out to breed up the working classes as though they were cattle. The one object in life of the society seems to be to make mankind as perfect as poultry ... all this form of school Eugenics seems to me to be the most gross materialism that has ever been imported into human society.[74]

Two things were obviously at cross purposes with liberal principles. Firstly, the reduction of human improvement to the 'technical' terms of betterment of stock; secondly, communal tampering with individual liberty when there was even a shadow of a doubt as to its unavoidability or relevance to the social good.

The liberal press was quick to take up the issue. The *Nation* conjured up visions of a ruthless machine with a totalitarian aura, hounding out the unfit. The definition of a defective was 'sufficiently wide and sufficiently elastic, and empowers any enthusiastic eugenist, who rises to office, to make what experiments he pleases upon the community'.[75] Amazing indeed was the clause that defined the feeble-minded as incapable 'of competing on equal terms with their normal fellows' or 'of

---

[73] *Hansard*, 5th Ser. XXXVIII 1468–9 (17.5.1912).
[74] *Hansard*, 5th Ser. XXXVIII 1474 (17.5.1912).
[75] 'The Crime of being Inefficient', *Nation*, 25.5.1912.

managing themselves and their affairs with ordinary prudence'.[76] 'The modern efficient community' was now coming to
regard old age and infirmity as a crime, warned the *Nation*,
correctly detecting a dangerous trend:

Under the whole eugenic theory lies an assumption which we believe
to be as unscientific as it is menacing to liberty. We have just escaped
from the school which diagnosed incompetence and degeneracy as a
form of moral evil, and traced unemployment and failure merely to
faults of character. The modern cant which has replaced it insists
rather on bad heredity.[77]

Hobhouse, writing in the *Manchester Guardian*, cautioned against
making the vague knowledge of eugenics the basis of compulsory legislation. He preferred dealing with the feeble-
minded on a voluntary basis.[78]

But there were also other liberal voices, which lend weight to
the conclusion that the appeal of eugenics was as much in the
hope that it held out for a rational reconstruction of society as its
stress on personal morality. The social reform oriented *Economic
Review*, organ of the Christian Social Union, came out with an
editorial supporting the Bill as a means to 'clean up the littered
débris of society'. The editorial expressed sympathy with 'that
intellectual wing of the Liberal party which flies the flag of
freedom and pleads the cause of all the little poor people', but
was of the opinion that control infringed upon fewer rights than
freedom and that the state had to assume the responsibility of
controlling the feeble-minded.[79] The *Westminster Gazette* wrote
of the mentally deficient: 'It would, indeed, be the last crime in
the name of liberty if we were prevented, by some fanciful or
superstitious regard for our own personal freedom, from
applying a rational treatment to these unfortunate beings.'[80]
Such a plea could well explain the trepidations of some other
liberals, for, after all, rationality as an imposed criterion had
been known in the liberal tradition to assume ugly manifestations. On the occasion of the final reading of the amended Bill
a year later the *Westminster Gazette* saw it as 'overcoming a small

[76] *Parl. Papers* 1912–13 iii 993 (Mental Deficiency Bill [2 and 3 Geo. 5], 17 (2) (C)).
[77] 'The Crime of being Inefficient', *Nation*, 25.5.1912.
[78] Hobhouse, leader, 'The Mental Deficiency Bill', *MG*, 14.10.1912.
[79] Editorial Note, *ER*, vol. 22 (1912), 242–4.
[80] Leader, 'The Liberty of the Subject,' *WG*, 4.6.1913.

but stubborn opposition, pleading individual liberty against the scientific treatment of an irresponsible class'.[81] Liberalism had indeed gone some way in the preceding twenty years if a liberal newspaper could give priority to science over the essential liberal precept of liberty.

But the outcry against the Bill had to a large extent mitigated its worst aspects. Hobhouse welcomed the disappearance of any reference to the eugenic idea in the final version of the Bill, eugenics being not a science but a propaganda. The 'competing on equal terms' clause was also eliminated.[82] Hobhouse perceptively pointed out that the opponents of the Bill who had secured its improvement were a 'little band of liberty men— which in these days does not necessarily mean Liberals'. He complained that many liberals could not distinguish between compulsion necessary for liberty—that which prevents one man from injuring another, and compulsion which restricts liberty— 'that which coerces A for his alleged good and orders his life for him in the name of philanthropy'.[83]

Hobson alone among the major liberal theorists continued to be an admirer of eugenics, though even he considerably modified his original stand. The concern and responsibility for future generations remained a key item in his advocacy of eugenics. But by 1909 he had realized that

there is a limit to this, as the individual must be presumed to know what is good for his comfort and pleasure, but cannot know so well what is good for the next generation, and still less for remoter generations. There is a limit to the duty due to posterity... Each generation must lead its own life.[84]

He further claimed that there were more effective means than control of parenthood by the state—better environment, education, and economic opportunities.[85] Health, knowledge, and security were themselves important factors in rational selection

[81] Leader, *WG*, 30.7.1913.

[82] Hobhouse, leader, 'The Guardianship of the Feeble-Minded', *MG*, 3.1.1913.

[83] Hobhouse, leader, 'Coercive Philanthropy', *MG*, 31.7.1913. See also speech by L. A. Atherley-Jones, *Hansard*, 5th Ser. LIII 289–94 (28.3.1913), who saw the Bill as a monstrous interference with public liberty.

[84] Hobson, 'Eugenics as an Art of Social Progress', *SPM*, vol. 14 (1909), 170.

[85] Ibid.

of prospective parents.[86] But while he could not accept the eugenist contention that the individual was a mere transient vehicle of the life of the race, he warned against the contrary doctrine. The regulation of population was too important a matter to be left to a 'new calculus of individual self-interest'. Devoting all energy to the enrichment of personal character and life, an ideal to which many liberals would have subscribed as the end of social reform, overlooked the organic linkage of generations and left too much to individual short range 'reason'.[87] Hobson's attempt to balance individual and racial factors was not less liberal, because it aspired to a wider rationality and was motivated by a desire to forestall any decrease in the pace of human progress. It was the expression of a scientific urge to bring the factors of human life under control and a reaction to those aspects of welfare which always gravitated towards materialism and complacency.

The cross-currents which liberalism was subjected to, from the natural sciences and biology in particular, and from conflicting conceptions of individual morality, were a powerful agent in the reformulation of liberalism. The insights into human nature which they afforded gave rise to new ideas about desirable individual qualities. These were now evaluated from the perspective of social needs. The deeper appreciation of the total nature of man extended the area of interest for the reformer from moral and mental to physical attributes as well. But a total outlook did not become a totalitarian one. Despite a fascination with the new vistas opened up by the biological sciences and an eagerness to support the claims of the social body, liberals were sufficiently aware of the need to safeguard liberal essentials even when the trends of the time pulled in the opposite direction. If the issues dealt with occasionally obscured basic liberal tenets, they more often than not initiated debates which helped to keep liberalism alive, *au fait* and capable of responding to crucial issues of social life and policy.

[86] This last point was made by G. A. Paley, 'Biology and Politics', *New Quarterly*, vol. 1 (1907), 133–4. The birth-rate, he noted, was controlled by economic conditions and by controlling these conditions the state could ensure increased multiplication of the fit.
[87] Hobson, 'The Cant of Decadence', *Nation*, 14.5.1910.

VI

The Social Policy of the
New Liberalism

I. THE ISSUE DEFINED

THOUGH the legislative achievements of the Liberal Adminis-
trations of 1905–14 have been much trumpeted, the gulf
between the ideas and policies of official Liberalism and the new
liberals was often immense. Because of the marked gap between
the floating of new liberal proposals and their translation into
social action, the method followed in this chapter is to focus on
some key issues of Liberal social legislation as treated and
discussed by the new liberals, rather than by those immediately
responsible for them. The intriguing question is, after all, what
was specifically liberal in the nature of the measures introduced? The answers to this query are more readily inferred
from the statements of the new liberals, whether from their
newly attained seats in Parliament or by means of their
conventional modes of expression, as authors and journalists.
Through the progressive liberal debate, new light is shed upon
the ideological complexities involved in the Liberal legislation,
complexities not always voiced but omnipresent in every move
of the policy planners and executors. Through it, too, one can
evaluate the extent to which the legislative end-product
reflected or met the current liberal demands for social justice. It
will further be seen that the issues examined below were vital to
the working out and testing of the liberal theories discussed in
this study. Concurrently, although it is usually difficult, if not
futile, to establish clear-cut proof of ideological influence, a
reasoned exercise of judgement is bound to lead to the
conclusion that the new liberalism was a pervasive set of ideas
that, moreover, flourished during a period of English history in
which ideology was unusually significant. That the new liberals
were the ideological 'activists' and innovators of liberalism

seems indisputable. In fact, they succeeded in having many of their central ideas and thought-patterns adopted in current political argument, if not indeed made public property.

One further observation concerns the influence of other left-wing ideologies on the new liberalism. Though obviously not all items of social reform originated with liberalism, many of them, habitually associated with English Socialism, were—as we have seen—developed independently by new liberals or assimilated into their outlook. The point is that an ideology is judged not only by its originality but by the construction it puts on the facts and ideas it is confronted with. Ideologies are often distinguishable by the different ways they employ to process a common fund of ideas.

No better example of some of the ambiguities reigning at the time—and consequently today—can be found than by comparing what two progressive liberals had to say in 1906 on the relation between Liberal and Labour programmes. Masterman thought the two parties had entirely different notions of social reform. He admitted that 'it would be quite easy to draw up two programmes, every item of which would be endorsed by both parties'. But then he continued:

... the attitude of determination and choice in the realisation of these programmes would make a profound chasm in actual political energies. The one might consist of these: the Education Bill, Temperance Reform, One Man One Vote, Reform of the House of Lords, Disestablishment of the Welsh Church, Retrenchment on Naval and Military Expenditure. And for the other we might have the following: Feeding of School Children, Old Age Pensions, Graduation of Income Tax, National Work for the Unemployed, Land Nationalisation.[1]

Each party, thought Masterman, would generally endorse the programme of the other, while the Tories would resist both. Atherley-Jones, on the other hand, remarked after an examination of declared Labour policy that with the exception of the nationlization issue,[2]

[1] C. F. G. Masterman, 'Liberalism and Labour', NC, vol. 60 (1906), 712.

[2] As to liberals in general, an anti-Socialist theorist such as Robertson was prepared on this point to advocate railway nationalization and more (see above Chapter Four), and an anti-Socialist journal such as the Westminster Review campaigned for railway, canal, and telephone nationalization (vol. 166 (1906), 487). See below, p. 221.

there is nothing . . . that differentiates the policy of the Labour from that of the Liberal party. Old-age pensions, educational reform, adjustment of taxation, feeding of schoolchildren, workmen's compensation, support of the unemployed, international arbitration—all these are accepted items of the Liberal programme, and some of them are already in course of legislative treatment. Upon programme, therefore, the Labour party is unable to claim any advantage over Liberalism, or, indeed, in respect of many of the items, Conservatism.[3]

Even official Liberals had a keener sense for the necessity of real social reform than Masterman tried to suggest by the time the article was written towards the end of 1906. Moreover, the first four items specified by Masterman as part of the Labour programme had multiple origins and had for some time been adopted by the new liberals as expressing fundamental liberal aims. The tendency among British politicians and scholars to judge the validity, indeed existence, of a social or political policy on the basis of its practical results and effectiveness has always been a source of confusion. The fact that Liberalism failed to implement its advanced theories for reasons unconnected with the adequacy of its philosophy cannot justify an attempt to attribute its ideas, measures, and programmes to future successful completers of the task, or an attempt to deny the 'liberalness' of these notions.

It is also important to realize that many new liberals had discarded most of the items that Masterman had put at the top of the Liberal programme. After all, Masterman himself had done so and had warned that the traditional concern with education and temperance was with 'middle-class measures for which working men as a whole care nothing at all'.[4] Hobson had voiced a similar opinion when speaking of 'the discord and unreality disclosed in what we may term the typical middle-class issues of education, temperance, and disestablishment . . .'[5] Robertson, as already mentioned, had accused the Liberal party of an undue deference to the demands of the mass of the Nonconformist clergy—disestablishment and local veto.[6]

[3] L. A. Atherley-Jones, 'The Story of the Labour Party', NC, vol. 60 (1906), 585.
[4] Masterman, 'Liberalism and Labour', 715.
[5] J. A. Hobson, A Modern Outlook (1910), p. 304.
[6] J. M. Robertson, The Future of Liberalism (1895), p. 17.

The fact that advanced liberals spent a great deal of their energies in criticizing the Liberal party during the 1890s should in itself demolish the identification of the theory with the organization, an identification which Socialist critics of Liberal performance were for tactical reasons eager to maintain. Most vehement on this issue was Atherley-Jones, who claimed that official Liberalism was completely detached from the aims of liberal thought.[7] During the short period the Liberals were in power in the 1890s Atherley-Jones did not become more hopeful. The prospects of social reform, he wrote, were not encouraging because the Liberal leaders were imbued with the traditions of the Manchester School.[8] Robertson labelled the Liberal politicians helpless empiricists whose views were not advanced enough for many progressives. He complained bitterly about the failure of the leadership, Gladstone and Rosebery in particular, to formulate a coherent set of political principles concerning social inequality.[9] And in 1906 Graham Wallas expressed the general concern of advanced liberals that the progressive backbenchers would not be utilized by the Liberal Administration.[10] The list is endless. The flood of criticism directed by liberals against their own party should have toned down the claims of the Socialists to have forced collectivism on the Liberals or to have provided the only constructive alternatives to Liberal party policies. The pressure from within was widespread and consistent and must surely have had at least as significant a role as that originating in external groups.

It is important to stress that new liberals believed that the unity of perspective imposed on social problems by liberal theory had its counterpart in the interconnectedness of the concrete issues of social reform. Many historians of Liberal

---

[7] Atherley-Jones, 'The New Liberalism', NC, vol. 26 (1889), 188. An anonymous writer, 'Socialist Radical', speaking from the position of one who desired the electoral triumph of the Liberals, expressed concern about the lack of a truly progressive spirit in the leaders and the vagueness of the official programme: 'I confess I cannot see that some Liberal leaders are doing anything but stopping development within the ranks of their own followers.' (A Socialist Radical, 'Mr. Morley and the New Radicalism', NR, vol. 1 (1889), 611.)

[8] Atherley-Jones, 'Liberalism and Social Reform: A Warning', NR, vol. 9 (1893), 633.

[9] Robertson, The Fallacy of Saving, p. 128; The Future of Liberalism, pp. 3–15.

[10] G. Wallas, '"Remember 1880"', Speaker, 27.1.1906.

legislation have argued that the Liberal approach to social policy was piecemeal and experimental. But even on the official level Liberals were aiming at a planned, concerted attack on social evils. A tactician such as the Master of Elibank, Chief Liberal Whip, when commenting on the Government record after the introduction of the Insurance Bill, felt the need for claiming that

... all these measures of social reform are not to be regarded simply as so many scattered attempts to cure this or that evil. They are to be taken as developing together a deliberate, strenuous attack all along the line on our social and industrial ills ... The Social Reform policy of the Government is a consistent policy, carefully planned and prepared for, and persistently and consistently carried through.[11]

This consistency was to a certain extent ensured by the deeper understanding of the facts, for as the *Tribune* remarked: 'One of the characteristics of the social reform problems now to the fore is the manner in which they all link up with each other.'[12] The ties between the various fields of social reform had been highlighted, as we have seen, in the development of a liberal financial policy. But the unity of the social question was powerfully brought home on issues of housing and land reform as well. As the *Speaker* remarked, a true housing policy could not be formulated without concurrently dealing with the land question, the locomotion question, and the local taxation question.[13] The land question as the key to the solution of social evils was of course the argument of the single taxers.[14] But even those who refused to see it as the only problem of social reform agreed that rural depopulation, housing, and local taxation[15] were inseparable: 'Start from what point you wish in the discussion of any one of these questions, and you find yourself led eventually, by the logic of the facts, to the examination of the other two.'[16] Ultimately, with a growing comprehension of the organic nature of reform, advanced liberals saw agreement

[11] The Master of Elibank, speech in Edinburgh, 18.11.1911 (*The Liberal Magazine*, vol. 19 (1911), 700).
[12] Leader, *Tribune*, 11.9.1907.
[13] 'The Progress of the Housing Question', *Speaker*, 22.3.1902. Cf. Masterman, 'Towards a Civilisation', *IR*, vol. 2 (1904).
[14] The *Westminster Review* continuously supported this line.
[15] And sweating as well. See 'The Cost of Old-Age Pensions', *Nation*, 27.7.1907.
[16] 'Vital Aspects of the Land Question', *Nation*, 27.4.1907.

on the essentials of national well-being converging along a number of paths—health, leisure, education, insurance, housing, improved transport, utilization of natural resources, and a minimum income.[17] In the specific measures which will now be examined, the underlying trend to regard them as parts of a comprehensive social reconstruction cannot be ignored.

But a note of caution must be sounded. The awareness of the connections between various social defects operated on two levels. On the simpler level the interconnectedness was that of the social defects themselves, which had to be removed to reveal the true character of man. This interlinkage merely reflected the influence any one sphere of human activity had on the others and was related to the 'removal of hindrances' school. For the new liberals, on the more complex level, society was organic in the sense that its members constituted one body and one will. This had to entail a change of mentality beyond what legislation could achieve. Social legislation was therefore a necessary but not sufficient condition for social regeneration, though if expressive of the deeper organicism of society it could be conducive to such regeneration.

2. OLD-AGE PENSIONS: THE RECOGNITION OF SOCIAL SERVICE

Old-age pensions were first and foremost among the advanced measures of social reform recommended by liberals. Progressives from all walks of political life were agreed on this question and many schemes were circulated in the hope of providing a morally and financially acceptable solution. The background to the rise of old-age pensions has been amply described.[18] It was one in which disillusionment with the methods and pauperization of the Poor Law, vested interests of friendly societies, insurance companies and trade unions, the impact of the findings of Charles Booth and other researchers, the desire of the two major parties to pass an impressive piece of social reform legislation, all combined in the working out of a plan. One of the first new liberal theorists to advocate old-age pensions consistently was Robertson. It was a development of

---

[17] 'The Claim for a Share in Life', *Nation*, 28.9.1912.
[18] M. Bruce, *The Coming of the Welfare State*, 4th ed. (1968), pp. 173–81; B. B. Gilbert, *The Evolution of National Insurance in Great Britain* (1966), pp. 159–232.

his 'quid pro quo' philosophy,[19] a concept of social relations that turned up in various forms in liberal social theory. Robertson attacked the C.O.S. standpoint, in particular C. Loch's opposition to a pension scheme, on the grounds that it was an extension of poor relief and would manufacture pauperism:

> Mr Loch is wrong in implying as he unavoidably does that the man who works while he can, and then draws from the public treasury, has deserved ill of society... let us be just to those workers who do unquestionably render service to the community before they idly consume services.[20]

Apart from the humanitarian question of the 'utter penury' and 'unjust degradation' of the aged poor, it was a question of justice: '... if pensions are justly payable to State servants so-called—soldiers and sailors, and postmen and policemen—they are equally due to all workers whatever who render lawful services.'[21] Robertson's theory of fair exchange was based on the recognition of the social element in all individual behaviour, on the mutual dependence and interconnectedness which characterized human societies. The securing of old-age pensions would establish what from the new liberal point of view was the heart of the matter: they were 'a new and wider recognition of the membership of all in the community'. Robertson thought it the one modern measure in the state treatment of poverty which savoured distinctly of conscious socialism.[22] On a parallel level, old-age pensions were also a means of tackling underconsumption, increasing spending, and stimulating production. Echoing Hobson, Robertson noted: 'Humanity and economic science here join hands.'[23] This was one of the important points new liberals were trying to make— social arrangements, to be just and efficacious, had to reflect what science had discovered about the structure and workings of society.

The question of thrift had usually been interpreted as a

[19] See Chapter Four, p. 135. See below, pp. 222–3.
[20] Robertson, *The Fallacy of Saving*, pp. 133–4.
[21] Robertson, *The Future of Liberalism*, p. 20. Cf. J. F. Wilkinson, *Pensions and Pauperism* (1892), p. 88, quoted in Bruce, op. cit. 176. This phrasing became very common.
[22] Robertson, *The Meaning of Liberalism*, pp. 60, 140.
[23] Ibid., p. 63.

moral, rather than an economic issue, not only by Conservatives or the C.O.S. but by old liberals as well.[24] Another
opinion was, however, emerging which, while still evaluating
pensions from the perspective of character, drew contrary
conclusions. As Samuel remarked: '... the proposal is advocated on this very ground among others, that it would promote
thrift by removing that feeling of despair which is thrift's
greatest enemy'.[25] Thrift, under such living conditions as
typified the aged poor, was accepted as an impossibility. This
point was also made in the *Speaker*'s series on social policy,
employing the usual mixture of ethical and financial arguments
on the subject. It reiterated the claim that much of the money
needed for pensions would be saved by reductions in Poor Law
expenses. This type of argument was always of greater interest
to liberals than to Socialists as the middle class had to bear the
brunt of any new welfare costs. But the weekly also mentioned
the duty the nation had to its old and the incentive to personal
and social thrift that would accrue from pensions.[26]

The assumption of office by the Liberal government brought
a resurgence of interest in the subject from 1906 onwards. With
the usual tendency of the age, old-age pensions—like so many
other reforms—were elevated almost to the degree of a panacea.
Furthermore, as the 'Lib-Lab' M.P. F. Maddison realized, old-
age pensions would help to draw the line between liberalism
and Socialism:

A civilised State must recognise its social obligations, of which old age

[24] L. Stephen, 'The Good Old Cause', *NC*, vol. 51 (1902), 17; Pigou, 'Some Aspects
of the Problem of Charity', in Masterman (ed.), *The Heart of the Empire*, p. 247; H. Cox,
Hansard, 4th Ser. CLXIX 230–3 (13.2.1907). Addressing himself to another M. P. Cox
said, in direct contradistinction to the new liberal position: '... there was no obligation
between them, except he hoped the obligation of friendliness, and there never had been
any obligation between them to entitle him to go to his hon. friend and ask him to
support him in his old age' (col. 232). Of course, Cox missed the point by arguing the
case between private people on the same terms as that between the state and its citizens.

[25] Samuel, *Liberalism*, p. 138. This point was repeatedly made to forestall criticism
during the final shaping of the old-age pensions Bill. In explaining its principles,
Hobhouse reinforced the view that saw socialism v. individualism as a false dichotomy:
'Essentially they contemplate an extension of individual or private rights as against the
community, which is the same thing, viewed from the other end, as an extension of the
responsibility of the State towards its individual members.' Social action would
stimulate individual development by strengthening independence of character and
incentives to industry (Hobhouse, 'Old-Age Pensions: The Principle', *MG*, 29.2.1908).

[26] 'Towards a Social Policy. XIV. The Aged Poor', *Speaker*, 28.1.1905.

is a characteristic one, and its ability to do so is an effective answer to the shallow thinkers who are always predicting the breakdown of a society resting on private property, but which is really better able to bear these social burdens than one based on their theories.[27]

The strength of the liberal approach to the problem lay in the combination of questions of social justice and communal responsibility with a realistic approach both to the financing of old-age pensions and to the economic importance of the aged. The *Nation* was typical of new liberal opinion in its enthusiastic welcome for universal pensions. It was, for the paper, a notable move away from the spirit of the Poor Law:

Poor relief is a State recognition of the duty of succouring those who fall by the wayside of life. It is a legal organisation of charity . . . Its concern is with men and women who at the best are failures . . . The proposal of old-age pensions starts from a totally different principle. It is a recognition at once of the *solidarity of society*, and of the actual economic situation produced by the play of industrial forces in the modern world.[28]

No measure, to the mind of liberals, expressed more successfully the sense of community they were trying to develop and reflected more clearly the new concern of social reform with the essential principles of social life and structure. Social reform proceeded from patching eyesores or at the best alleviating the condition of the underprivileged, to the incorporation of all classes who had merited it[29] 'as a right conferred by citizenship, rather than . . . a boon conferred on poverty alone'.[30] In the words of Chiozza Money, who described the organic implications of old-age pensions:

[27] F. Maddison, 'Old-Age Pensions', *Speaker*, 19.1.1907.
[28] 'Pensions and the Poor Law', *Nation*, 16.3.1907, (my italics).
[29] Hobhouse often expressed the hope that the result of old-age pensions would be methods more humane to the deserving and less indulgent to the thriftless (see, e.g., 'The Old-Age Pension Scheme', leader, *MG*, 30.5.1908). Though traces of moral stigma for social failures still remained throughout the Edwardian age, there was a significant shift in moral condemnation. It was those who had failed to do their duty by society, as well as by religious or social notions of individual propriety, who were subject to public opprobrium.
[30] 'Pensions and the Poor Law', *Nation*, 16.3.1907. Compare this to J. Burns's complete and for him not atypical misrepresentation of the social philosophy involved: 'It is the boon of the benevolent State at the cost of the bounteous rich for the benefit of the aged poor . . .' ('The Liberal Government and the Condition of the People', speech at Bradford, 11.11.1912 (Liberal Publication Dept., 1912), 9).

... a labourer, whether he worked mentally or physically, worked not only for his employer, but for the nation at large, and ... the nation as a conscious entity was coming increasingly to regard itself as an organisation. When that was once realised it was seen that the worker ... was in a very real sense a contributor to the greatness and wealth of his country, and, therefore, it became the duty of the State to assert itself consciously on his behalf.[31]

The method of payment—via the state and not through intermediary associations—was particularly important for new liberals and overruled any sympathy they might have felt for payment of pensions by employers. In line with Robertson's insistence on universal taxation as against universal state obligation as the correct method of financing and paying pensions, H. Spender advised that '... a wise Chancellor of the Exchequer ... will probably strenuously avoid connecting Old Age Pensions with any idea of a special burden either on rich or poor'. Instead of that, he 'will throw the burden broadly over the whole of society'.[32]

An important shift had occurred here within liberalism itself. In the early 1890s most liberals who advocated old-age pensions had not yet advanced much towards a philosophy of society. J. A. Spender, for instance, in a typical and oft-quoted book was prepared to recognize that the misfortunes of old age were not due to the failings of the poor, but did not attribute them to a fault in the social system. Rather, they were due to unavoidable misfortunes which occurred despite thrift.[33] Another liberal, J. Fletcher Moulton, said of state pensions: 'I would rather that the money should be spent in rendering the life of the poor successful than in palliating its failure.' But on the other hand he moved towards a determination of the basic problem when he realized that all plans for pensions were an attempt

to endow the poor, or to aid the poor to endow themselves, with *an income which is beyond the reach of misfortune* ... For the first time we have put before us the conception of the members of the poorer classes becoming possessed of property sufficient to give them the decencies of

---

[31] *Hansard*, 4th Ser. CLXIX 242–3 (13.2.1907).

[32] H. Spender, 'The Government and Old Age Pensions', *CR*, vol. 93 (1908), 106. Cf. also W. H. Lever, Liberal M.P. and industrialist, *Hansard*, 4th Ser. CLXXIV 474 (10.5.1907).

[33] J. A. Spender, *The State and Pensions in Old Age* (1892), p. 21.

existence, which cannot be taken from them and of which they cannot divest themselves.[34]

However, this view did not derive from an appreciation of mutual obligations of members of a community, but from a desire to preserve inalienable individual liberty. Hobhouse, though, continued the above line of development to its advanced liberal conclusion when he wrote: 'The first point to be observed is that pauperism among the aged . . . is the *normal* fate of the poorer class . . . It is not due to exceptional shiftlessness and improvidence; it is due to insufficiency and irregularity of earnings.'[35] Old-age pensions were thus a contribution towards the attainment of a minimum standard of life. Its absence was a defect of the social system society had to correct by adopting a new concept of social relations.

The fact that in their final version old-age pensions were not universal, in that they were not granted to high-income groups and retained some sort of character test, does not detract from their implicit idea of universality. The restriction of pensions was accepted by new liberals on grounds of expense.[36] Hobhouse argued that it was only a temporary limitation of the universal rule and that, ideally, pensions should be universal after the capacity for work was over.[37] The *Nation* accepted the need for excluding certain classes of people, but objected to any discrimination that was reminiscent of the Poor Law.[38] Later it wrote:

. . . every exception to the universality of the scheme threatens to impair the principle underlying it. This principle is that to the old support is due rather as a right than as a charity . . . an instalment of economic justice, a redressing of the balance of industrial fortune . . .[39]

For similar reasons most liberals objected to a contributory scheme. As Lloyd George, with a good grasp of the philosophy of taxation, maintained: '. . . when a scheme is financed out of public funds it is as much a contributory scheme as a scheme

[34] J. Fletcher Moulton, 'Old-Age Pensions', *FR*, vol. 51 (1892), 471–2.
[35] Hobhouse, 'Old-Age Pensions: The Principle', *MG*, 29.2.1908 (my italics).
[36] J. M. Robertson, *Hansard*, 4th Ser. CLXXIV 509 (10.5.1907).
[37] Hobhouse, 'Old-Age Pensions: The Principle', *MG*, 29.2.1908.
[38] 'The Cost of Old-Age Pensions', *Nation*, 27.7.1907.
[39] 'The Programme for 1908', *Nation*, 16.11.1907.

which is financed directly by means of contributions...'[40] A contributory system, apart from its technical difficulties, was considered unequal in its treatment of the working class. Hobson saw it as a false conception of state expenditure: it would either exclude the very poor, in which case the whole purpose of the pension scheme would have been missed, or it would force them to pay at the expense of the comfort and efficiency of their families. But a state pension could not be based upon eleemosynary principles either. Hobson, as was often his wont, stressed the social interest in pensions rather than the mutual exchange of responsibilities between individual and state by which most advanced liberals described the principles involved.[41] This was after all a forceful way of presenting an argument at the time, especially when considerations of efficiency were supplemented by assertions of ethical duty.

3. UNEMPLOYMENT

A. From Personal Vice to Social Malady

The question of unemployment, always a major issue of social reform, was a particularly complicated one, there being no single simple solution visible. The periodical 'crises' and depressions were traditionally dealt with on an *ad hoc* basis, such as the famous Mansion House relief fund. Reformers in general came to accept, as part of the breakdown of faith in the rationale of the Poor Law, that many of the unemployed were out of work owing to factors beyond their control. Although the Poor Law distinction between pauperism and poverty remained, it was realized that the poor as well as the paupers had to be helped. In Barnett's words, the unemployed were formed of two classes—those unable, and those unwilling, to work. 'Each class must be attacked by a different method. Those unable to work must be relieved; those who are unwilling to work must be disciplined.'[42] This attitude to unemployment in particular remained very marked among liberals.[43] But it was not a mere question of

---

[40] *Hansard*, 4th Ser. CXC 565 (15.6.1908).
[41] Hobson, 'Old Age Pensions. II. The Responsibility of the State to the Aged Poor', *SR*, vol. 1 (1908), 295.
[42] S. A. Barnett, 'The Unemployed', *FR*, vol. 54 (1893), 743.
[43] 'Poverty and Pauperism', *Nation*, 16.5.1908.

affording help and relief without the stigma of the Poor Law, of tiding men over in certain industries, and of coping with emergencies as they arose. Many advanced liberals were among those who took a broader view. J. A. M. Macdonald summarized the new approach thus:

The evil is not local. Nor is it limited to a single trade, or group of trades. It is the result of a cause that is essentially connected with the course which the development of our industrial system as a whole has taken, and it is therefore general in its operation. . . . It is essentially a subject which calls for the consideration and action of the whole community.[44]

This was the theme adopted in the main by new liberals, whose terminology is unmistakable in these words. It was for them a national question not only because it was evident everywhere but because it was caused by defects in social organization and social responsibility. It could therefore only be cured by a reorganization of society as such, by communal action. Significantly, the notion of the community as an identifiable, responsible, and active entity was on this problem of social reform as well as on other issues the starting point—and, indeed, the path towards solution.

The question of relief or reorganization is once more that of the restorative versus the regenerative concept of social reform. In the case of unemployment the boundaries between the two were not very clearly defined. Consequently, this field was particularly resistant to the penetration of advanced liberal ideas. It was widely appreciated that unemployment could be dealt with indirectly, for example through labour colonies or afforestation. In a sense, this was relief—as such measures tackled the symptoms, not the causes. But they were intended to be more than that: productive and economically beneficial works, a possible means of retraining workers, and they were often interlinked with other measures of reform, such as the return to the land,[45] a fact that strengthened the scientific awareness that many reform issues hinged together and could only be coped with *en bloc*. As P. Alden, Liberal M.P. and Fabian, wrote, unemployment called for treatment

[44] J. A. M. Macdonald, 'The Problem of the Unemployed', *NR*, vol. 9 (1893), 575.
[45] See, e.g., Samuel, speech to Liberal meeting at Henley, 27.3.1895 (election pamphlet).

as a serious economic disease which afflicts the body politic. We have long since surrendered what may be called the 'monadist' view of society, and in theory if not in practice we recognise the responsibility of the State towards these unfortunate victims of our modern industrial system.[46]

Consequently Alden and other new liberals repeatedly pointed out the interlinkage of the social problem. In a book written in 1905, Alden adopted Hobson's theory that unemployment was due to underconsumption and that the ultimate remedy was redistribution of consuming power,[47] which would concurrently cope with the problems of poverty and old age. From this perspective redistribution was a mechanism by which the scientific cohesion of society could be expressed, though, as Alden later wrote, there was no hope for a final solution of the unemployment problem without reducing the evil of the land monopoly.[48] But the immediate solutions Alden had to offer were not, any more than those of other progressive reformers, fundamental to the problem. He recommended labour employment offices and registries to increase the mobility of labour and the continuance of temporary relief. Even in 1912 he was still thinking in terms of detention colonies for those unwilling to work and free colonies for those unable to.

In fact, relief works continued for a long time to be the only practical solution contemplated by progressive liberals. Samuel regarded the strengthening of character consequent upon relief as a question of national expediency.[49] The four guidelines he stipulated were typical: discrimination between deserving and undeserving by means of a labour test; work for wages instead of charity; temporary work so as not to deprive industry of labour; and lower wages than those prevailing in the ordinary labour market. The remnants of the 'stigma' of the Poor Law are still discernible. Unemployment was considered an abnormal and unavoidable phenomenon, and therefore society could not be

[46] P. Alden, 'The Unemployed Problem', *Speaker*, 3.1.1903. This is strongly reminiscent of Hobsonian terminology. Elsewhere Alden wrote: 'The community is responsible for the unemployed problem so far as a community may be said to be responsible for anything.' (P. Alden, *The Unemployed: A National Question* (1905), p. 44.)
[47] Hobson, *The Problem of the Unemployed* (1896); P. Alden, *The Unemployed: A National Question*, p. 37.
[48] P. Alden, *Democratic England* (1912), pp. 118, 92.
[49] *Hansard*, 4th Ser. CXVIII 315 (19.2.1903).

held responsible for its occurrence. But society was responsible for the welfare of its members and the basis of its economic prosperity. At the most, the unemployed, 'the helpless victims of an industrial system faulty in its working, have a claim on the Society, which maintains and profits by that system, for opportunities to labour'.[50] Nevertheless, society did not have a duty to give the unemployed equal standing with those who had, in due conformity with accepted liberal doctrine, employed their energies and showed resourcefulness and enterprise within the existing industrial system. Therefore, insisted Samuel, relief works were not to be competitive so as not to injure the trade of private employers and to throw other men out of work, nor should they throw an excessive charge upon the tax-payer.[51] This was a very shadowy version of the notion of community.

Similar attitudes prevailed among other progressive liberals. Masterman, as many others, regarded—rightly or wrongly[52]— the 1905 Unemployment Act as a move towards the acceptance of national responsibility for a national disease.[53] In 1904 Masterman could think of nothing better than endorsing Barnett's scheme—the dual system of labour and penal colonies which had also been adopted by Samuel. Yet the point for him was not that England was directly responsible for unemployment but that England, 'in face of such abundance of resource and wasteful prodigality' could afford to do something about it.[54] In an article written slightly later, Masterman elaborated on possible solutions. The direct approach remained the construction of a labour reservoir, the crucial point being that the work had to be remunerative and to present some return to the community.[55] This was the other aspect of the reaction to charity—not only was it degrading but it failed to grasp the mutuality, the element of exchange by which the community was tied together. Social reform had ceased to be merely a question of gratis transference of wealth from one sector to

[50] Samuel, *Liberalism*, p. 126.
[51] Ibid., p. 127.
[52] See B. B. Gilbert, op. cit., p. 238; M. Bruce, op. cit., pp. 188–9.
[53] Masterman, 'The Unemployed. A Hopeful Outlook', *Commonwealth*, vol. 10 (1905), 361.
[54] Masterman, 'Towards a Civilisation', *IR*, vol. 2 (1904), 508–11.
[55] Masterman, 'The Problem of the Unemployed', *IR*, vol. 4 (1905), 564.

another. Contribution towards the general wealth was a positive act of citizenship.

The indirect approach Masterman advocated was the draining of the abyss. Again, this problem concerned 'a population which gives to the community less than it gets from it; in consequence, forms a continual burden upon productive industry'.[56] Here Masterman was referring to a deeper issue—the causes of the creation of a class more or less unemployable, from which the army of unemployed was constantly being recruited. This theme was further developed at the end of 1905, when Masterman realized that no reforms or relief work were tenable unless coupled with measures for countering the increased misery and disorganization of the classes at the base of society—classes squeezed out after select individuals from their midst had been given work. Solutions to the problem of the unemployed had therefore to include not only a legislative minimum wage, but a series of social policies encompassing assistance and subsidies for the residue. As in the case of old-age pensions, what was necessary in the long run was a readjustment of the national income, a more equal distribution of the national wealth.[57]

In the light of the opinions of advanced liberals such as Hobson, Alden, and Masterman, it appears that to regard Beveridge as the representative of the new liberal attitude to unemployment[58] is a view which has to be seriously qualified. The mainstream of advanced liberalism became consistently more comprehensive both in its approach to social evils and in the range of people to be affected by its proposals. Beveridge, on the contrary, dealt with the problem of unemployment very much in detachment from other crucial issues of social reform, with little consideration for the totality of human needs. It was for him more a question of organizing a specific sub-system than one of the individual welfare of all members of society. The problem of unemployment was after all only one aspect of the 'condition of the people' issue, but Beveridge did not take into account that the reorganization of industry should primarily be

[56] Ibid. 567.
[57] Masterman, 'The Unemployed. A Hopeful Outlook', 362–3. Cf. also Masterman, 'The Unemployed', *CR*, vol. 89 (1906), 106–20.
[58] See, e.g., G. Stedman Jones, *Outcast London* (Oxford, 1971), p. 334. Once again, it would be more correct to think of Beveridge as the liberal who most influenced the Liberal Cabinet.

dictated by considerations of general welfare beyond it. The main feature missing in Beveridge's analysis is the element of redistribution. He displayed aversion to Hobson's theory of underconsumption which was gaining ground among new liberals, and accused him of advocating taxation for its own sake. Beveridge was only prepared to condone taxation in so far as the money was needed for public purposes.[59] He had no conception of taxation as an instrument of social justice, as a means of reapportioning the product to the producers, and could not see his way to any indirect method of radically improving people's living conditions, such as giving them more power to consume and thus keeping labour busy.

Beveridge's attitude to unemployment as a problem of industrial reorganization was not a new one either. This had been the standard approach of advanced social reformers for quite some time. His main service was perhaps in bringing to public attention the problem of underemployment and casual labour. But here too he deviated from the general new liberal line. The industrial system was a closed shop for Beveridge, one which catered only for those who managed to succeed within it, as has already been illustrated in the previous chapter. The illiberality of Beveridge's viewpoint is underlined in his abrogation of communal responsibility for citizens who could not be absorbed into the industrial system simply because there were no places for them:

... the state guarantee of work pledges the community as a whole to accept all up to any number who are born into it and to find room for them as citizens. Ignorance as to probable or possible course of population in the future makes this a pledge given absolutely in the dark. The interest of the state is not to make room for an indefinite number of citizens, but to see that all the citizens *it admits* are healthy and happy.[60]

---

[59] W. H. Beveridge, *Unemployment. A Problem of Industry* (1909), p. 63, n. 1. The fact that Beveridge accepted higher wages and shorter hours as 'excellent things *in themselves*' (my italics) only accentuates his lack of a general concept of social policy. See also J. Harris, *Unemployment and Politics. A Study in English Social Policy 1886–1914* (Oxford, 1972), pp. 21–4.

[60] Beveridge, 'The Problem of the Unemployed', *Sociological Papers* (1906), 327 (my italics). Interestingly enough, even Hobhouse, in an early article supporting unionized work, suggested regarding unorganized workers as objects for the workhouse or of charity (L. T. Hobhouse, review, *ER*, vol. 1 (1891), 142).

This was far more extreme than the new liberal tendency to prefer future to present interests, because it was not combined with any theory of responsibility towards future generations.

B. 'The Right to Work'

The clash of approaches on the unemployment issue was never more evident than on the 'right to work' principle. Though that principle did not originate within the liberal camp, new liberals had much to say on this issue and the controversy surrounding it illustrates the new direction liberal thought was willing and able to take, as well as attesting to the strong ideological element that pervaded British politics at the time. The traditional liberal attitude to the right to work defined it as 'the right of the unemployed to get labour in their own trades and at good or current rates of wages'.[61] This, as Rae claimed, was economically wrong as it increased depression and turned out of work men who were still employed. Rae was also concerned with the attractiveness of public aid and its effect on character. As an alternative he suggested relief for the industrious poor—a limited right to labour in order to prevent degradation and facilitate self-recovery. This constituted, Rae thought, the line between state socialism and sound social politics. In fact, though, the interpretation of the right to work as the right to receive relief was a main source of the future antagonism towards the idea.

The question arose again in full force because of the repeated attempts of the Labour party to pass a Right to Work Bill. The *Manchester Guardian* wrote in 1905 that the right to work was 'the simplest expression for the least objectionable mode of relieving a distress which the State does not and cannot ignore'. If the unemployed were paid from taxes and rates to which they themselves contributed when in prosperity, declared the newspaper, relief would become a mutual insurance against distress rather than mere charity.[62] A few months later it pointed out that there was an immense significance involved in the principle of the right to work. If a universal right to work was admitted, the question became a national one and the state had in that

---

[61] J. Rae, 'State Socialism and Popular Right', *CR*, vol. 58 (1890), 880.

[62] Leader, *MG*, 21.11.1905. This was a misinterpretation of the principle of insurance. See below.

event to intervene. The *Guardian* considered this to be wise public policy.[63] But the consensus among most liberals was that the right to work, understood as relief works, dealt only with the symptoms and was a mere palliative. Many regarded it as a Socialist scheme.[64] Burns, taking the extreme view, repeatedly argued that it was pauperizing and demoralizing.[65] In the Cabinet he opposed the right to work principle because it required the rate- or taxpayers to provide employment and because it created an artificial system of industry 'in which labour is to claim as its right that work is to be executed at the public cost, not because it is wanted or will be remunerative, but as an excuse for paying wages...'[66] This, as will presently be shown, was contrary to the opinions of new liberals, who came very close to seeing the right to work precisely as such an 'excuse', or rather as the manifestation of the right of each man to a minimum income.

Among the new liberals one pattern was clearly emerging. Unemployment was not merely a problem of industry, as Beveridge had made it out to be. Chiozza Money put the matter in a nutshell when he said: 'We can never hope by any legislative scheme to make the industrial work go with perfect smoothness. Such work is naturally irregular.' Unemployment was a many-sided problem which had to be approached from different angles. Among the various methods of tackling it, Money realized that one central principle was salient:

That principle which we apply to ourselves whenever we can, and which we apply in large part to the working population already, that principle in time to come will have to be extended to the whole population. That undoubtedly will be the final solution—the recognition that work is irregular, *but pay must be regular*.[67]

Money rejected Beveridge's one-sided approach, namely, his plan deliberately to decasualize labour and to create through

---

[63] 'Municipalities and the Unemployed', leader, *MG*, 17.3.1906.

[64] Leader, *Daily Chronicle*, 14.3.1908; leader, 'The Corrector of Socialism', *WG*, 13.3.1908; 'A Test Case', *WG*, 14.3.1908; *Hansard*, 4th Ser. CLXXXVI 35 (13.3.1908).

[65] See, e.g., *Hansard*, 4th Ser. CLXIX 952–62 (20.2.1907); *Hansard*, 4th Ser. CLXXXVI 65–74 (13.3.1908).

[66] P.R.O., Cabinet Papers, 37/91, 33 (J.B., The Unemployed Workmen Bill, 9.3.1908).

[67] *Hansard*, 5th Ser. XXI 611–13 (10.2.1911) (my italics).

the Labour Exchanges an unemployed residuum.[68] But even Churchill, for whom Beveridge had been working, had already realized the danger:

To establish a system of compulsory labour exchanges, to eliminate casual labour, to divide among a certain proportion of workers all available employment would absolutely and totally cast out a surplus of unemployed, before you have made preparation for dealing with that surplus, would be to cause an administrative breakdown, and could not fail to be attended with the gravest possible disaster.[69]

Hence Churchill decided on voluntary exchanges, to be complemented by unemployment insurance. Owing to the restricted nature of that insurance, this was an inadequate approach to the question of the minimum level of subsistence, which had become for new liberals a central component of their concept of citizenship.[70] Though strictly within a competitive framework, the minimum—to which Churchill had been won over—was understood to entail a decent standard of re-muneration for the unemployed by guaranteeing work for those willing and able. The *Nation* saw this as the liberal answer to the challenge of Protection on the one hand and of full economic Socialism on the other.[71] But as the mouthpiece of the new liberals, the *Nation* continued to display their ambivalence on unemployment. The principle of the minimum came into conflict not only with the realities of the situation but with other principles that were gaining in importance. True, 'the obli-gation of the State to provide public work or public mainten-ance for unemployed workers ... is no new or revolutionary principle. It has been embodied in the Poor Laws of this country for several centuries ...' But what the *Nation* objected to was to offer the unemployed the current conditions of employment in their trade—'offering a preferable employment to the less effective workers'. The notion of 'less eligibility' arose here in an entirely new context and with a completely different meaning. It was no longer a question of moral stigma, but a concession made to the prevailing ideas on efficiency, a warning against

[68] *Hansard*, 5th Ser. XXI 610 (10.2.1911).
[69] *Hansard*, 5th Ser. V 506 (19.5.1909).
[70] Beveridge had recommended unemployment insurance, but mainly for workers temporarily laid off, and had virtually ignored the surplus (*Unemployment*, pp. 228–30).
[71] 'The Policy of the Minimum Standard', *Nation*, 15.2.1908.

'the most illicit form of Socialism, which would seek to build up the new industrial order with the least efficient human material, in the worst organised industries, under the most difficult conditions'.[72] This attitude, to be prominently expressed by Lloyd George, was made more palatable—and, indeed, was entirely justified in the minds of the liberals concerned—by an appeal not to efficiency but to community. Even Hobhouse, who so detested the doctrine of efficiency, could write in 1911 '. . . the function of the State is to secure conditions upon which its citizens are able to win by their own efforts all that is necessary to a full civic efficiency'. But this had to be read within the context of the following sentence: 'The "right to work" and the right to a "living wage" are just as valid as the rights of person or property. That is to say, they are integral conditions of a good social order.' For Hobhouse it was simply a question of an enhanced sense of common responsibility which, vindicated by the teachings of experience, recognized individual claims of justice.[73]

Future articles in the *Nation* tended to stress that a right to work was a matter of plain public interest and if the state could not fulfil this obligation (the only justification for waiving the right), it would have to find ways to do so.[74] Most of the time the *Nation* avoided advancing beyond the pace set by Churchill and Lloyd George, so much admired by its editor, Massingham. It was only in 1911 that the weekly gave full scope to the principles underlying the new liberal view on unemployment. Commenting on a Labour Amendment to the Address, it asked: '. . . the question persists whether the "right" which Labor thus boldly claims does not express a genuine truth . . .' namely, '. . . that every normal man should have the power of earning an adequate living by useful work is one of the fundamental conditions of social welfare, and that is the proper meaning of a "right"'.[75]

C. *The Social Determinants of Rights: Utility and Reciprocity*

From the perspective of liberal theory the debates over old-age pensions and the 'right to work' played a crucial role in the

---

[72] 'The State and Unemployment', *Nation*, 14.3.1908.
[73] Hobhouse, *Liberalism*, pp. 83–4. See below, p. 240 ff.
[74] 'The Right to Work', *Nation*, 31.10.1908.
[75] 'The State and the Right to Work', *Nation*, 18.2.1911.

reformulation of liberal fundamentals. They brought to a head the implicit principles involved in these issues and emphasized the problems of political theory immanent in their treatment. The concepts of community, responsibility, and obligation were clarified concurrently with a redefinition of the notion of right. The abandonment of the 'natural right' dogmas had, of course, been going on for some time. Bentham had already dealt them a crushing blow by maintaining that all 'rights' were only a question of expediency and had no natural, abstract, or absolute basis. This was often the starting-point taken by the critics in our period, though with different aims in mind and varying conclusions as to the nature of rights. In the meantime, however, Mill had offered a modified version of absolute individual rights so that a new break had to be made with tradition. This was undertaken most thoroughly by Ritchie in his book *Natural Rights*. He sharply re-emphasized the negation of natural rights from a perspective very much in line with the modified utilitarianism of new liberal thought. This was part of what he called the transition from Individualist to Evolutionist Utilitarianism—in other words, the influence of evolutionary theory upon the construction of more scientific conceptions of human society. Individual rights were not to be comprehended apart from society because moral action was social action.[76] The result, as we have seen, was a new utilitarianism which limited state action not by an entrenched sphere of natural rights or individual freedom but by reference to the welfare of the social organism.[77]

Special attention is due to Hobson's original and penetrating treatment of the subject. Like Ritchie, Hobson quickly disposed of Mill's *a priori* delimitation of fields. He also went along with the opinion that rights were created by society for its own protection and gain, as was the case with old-age pensions.[78] But in a novel interpretation of the term he redefined the meaning of 'natural'. True to his deep concern with the biological aspects of human behaviour, Hobson discarded 'natural' in the sense of 'innate' or 'self-evident' and adopted it instead in the sense of physiologically and psychologically

[76] Ritchie, *Natural Rights*, pp. 101–2.

[77] Ritchie, *The Principles of State Interference*, *passim*, esp. pp. 167, 169.

[78] Hobson, 'Old-Age Pensions. II. The Responsibility of the State to the Aged Poor', *SR*, vol. 1 (1908), 295.

necessary to the adequate functioning of the human being. Witness his discussion on the rights of property. The sweating system was condemned because it denied to a worker 'the natural property' in the results of his labour, and thus the capacity of production. In a manner not far removed from Marxist analysis, Hobson stated:

> This natural right of property . . . may be summed up by saying that, out of the current production of wealth, whatever portion is required to maintain the productive power of workers is their natural property—*i.e.* a property which considerations of social utility will secure as a right in accordance with natural laws.[79]

The individual right of property extended beyond the bare subsistence wage, in accordance with Hobson's understanding of the ever-expanding nature of welfare. Here the translation of theory into practical injunctions was impressively illustrated. The total, unified perspective on human behaviour had directed Hobson to a joint consideration of biology and psychology. The rejection of the philosophical dualism between man and nature meant that 'the human will is a part of nature and the motives which operate through it conform to "natural" laws'.[80] If the satisfaction of the human will was part of the 'need-complex' of the individual, a full conception of welfare would have to cater to human motivation as well. At this point the concept of incentive which Hobson had endorsed as part of a competitive social system, and which thus coincided with maxims appealing to all shades of liberals, became grounded in the fundamentals of human behaviour. To the notion of the minimum subsistence wage Hobson thus linked as an inseparable part something that was more in the nature of an 'optimum' wage. It was not merely a question of working efficiency but of stimulating the worker to give his best. The right to such a wage was natural 'in the sense that, unless it is conceded, human nature will refuse the effort that is asked of it'.[81] Wealth and welfare were linked in a twofold bond. Not only, as was generally accepted, was human welfare dependent upon the production of wealth, but the reverse was true as well.

[79] Hobson, The *Social Problem*, p. 103.
[80] Ibid.
[81] Ibid., p. 105.

A respectable wage, a respectable part of the individual's produce, was necessary to a just and orderly functioning of the industrial and social systems and was a cornerstone in any policy of social welfare. Moreover, this concept of 'right' also fitted into the pattern of qualitative welfare Hobson hoped would ultimately prevail. The physiological determinants were the static facet of the right, whereas those pertaining to the will were the source of human progress, putting forward new wants necessitated and adjusted by considerations of social utility.

Hobson's granting of the right of subsistence to individuals was justified by the 'feedback' nature of the social organism by which such 'rights' benefited individual welfare in order to benefit social welfare. Typically, he was disturbed by the fact that this 'socialist' justification of right was often motivated by the recognition of an 'Individualist' right. He suspected the dominant motive behind the 'right to work' slogan to be 'the immediate relief of the material or economic needs of a section of the people'. Furthermore, the unemployed consisted of those people whom the public could least effectively and least profitably support—for, after all, the good of the community had first claim and that would be 'Socialism at the wrong end'. But the other side of the coin was that the right to work, although no absolute individual claim, was one 'which a well-ordered State will recognize as an individual right, endorsed by public expediency'.[82] In terms of more traditional liberal thought, it was simply the extension of the right to live. Hobson was impressed by the argument of a German scholar[83] who wrote: '. . . there is a moral duty incumbent on the State to make "the right to live" a corollary of the "legal compulsion to be born".[84] "This right to live" implies a "State guarantee of a minimum standard of life".' Hobson commented that, 'since work is alike a physical and a moral necessity for a healthy life, this admission of a public guarantee of life involves, *a fortiori*, the provision of public work for those who require it'.[85] This differed considerably from the Poor Law, he asserted, in that it was not a purely eleemosynary provision.

[82] Ibid., pp. 198, 200.
[83] Stein, *Die sociale Frage im Lichte der Philosophie* (Stuttgart, 1897). Reviewed by Hobson in the *Economic Journal*, vol. 8 (1898), 378–81.
[84] Referring to the prohibition of abortion and the starvation of children.
[85] Hobson, *The Social Problem*, p. 201.

Hobson, too, equated the right to work with public relief works, although—as he explained in a later article—he refused to attach a stigma to what, after all, people considered as part of the cost of industrial and social progress. As much unemployment was unavoidable,

> organised society should make provision for those who incur ... losses in its service. They have a clear claim upon the State, as representative of society, to be kept, and not in idleness, which obviously impairs their efficiency and corrupts their character, but in work.[86]

A strange mixture, if not ambiguity, evolved: Hobson reiterated the common insistence on the uncompetitiveness of public works and on paying out lower wages than in the outside trades. Any other course would be a socialism fatal to the task of organic reconstruction, he thought. On the other hand, the wages had to be sufficient to keep the workmen and their families in industrial and social efficiency. In effect, this reflected the constant tension in new liberal thought between the demands of society, the claims of individuals as individuals, and the claims of individuals as members of society. The delimitation and balancing of these sometimes conflicting, oft-overlapping, claims which had always been the concern of liberalism continued to present themselves on a more sophisticated level in a host of practical social problems.

Nevertheless, Hobson's treatment of rights was the most elaborate of the liberal attempts to reconcile them with the new understanding of society. What was common to all such attempts was the interpretation of right as a benefit conferred by society for the mutual advantage of the recipient and the conceder. What they were not prepared to accept was the idea of an unconditional right, irrespective of whether it was either feasible or merited—which is what an absolute right is. The question of feasibility reflected the ubiquitous liberal practical-mindedness. As Maddison remarked of the right to work: 'It is not rights, it is opportunities to work, the ability to work, we have to talk about.'[87] Or as Robertson formulated it, 'that which is impossible to society as at present constituted cannot rationally be claimed by any man as a right'.[88] The new liberal

---

[86] Hobson, 'The Right to Labour', *Nation*, 8.2.1908.

[87] *Hansard*, 5th Ser. IV 652 (30.4.1909).

[88] Robertson, *The Meaning of Liberalism*, pp. 53–4.

attitude to rights did not arise out of any wavering in their belief in individuality or liberty. Rather, it was caused by the intervention of two new factors: the one was the realization that the state was the tool of society, not its enemy, and a boundless optimistic faith in human co-operation which supplanted the previous liberal attitude. The other was the appreciation that to confer a right meant creating an obligation, that each benefit was balanced by a liability. In sum, granted the solidarity or at least interdependence of society, there was no gain to be achieved by removing from the sphere of public concern and control those aspects of human behaviour which were ultimately conditional on the existence and action of society.

The special bearing of the reinterpretation of rights on the subject of property deserves further comment. Already in the 1880s the absoluteness of property rights, as one of the fundamental conditions and manifestations of individuality according to classical liberalism, was being questioned by a growing number of liberals. Property was seen as relative or conditional—the test being national or collective expediency.[89] The theory of unearned increment was no doubt the main agent in redefining property as the outcome of social effort as much as individual exertions, although the concept of property as the expression of individuality was, as we have seen, retained by Hobson on the social level as well.[90] H. Scott Holland elaborated on the connection between this redefinition of property and the new understanding of character and personality that advanced liberals had attained.[91] Personality meant a capacity for intercommunion and was always collective in basis. 'Fellowship and Individuality are correlative terms.' The right of an individual to hold property was an expression of his membership in the community and its justification was to be found in the welfare and will of the community. If, moreover, personality was collective, it could be realized through collective ownership.[92] The development of the idea of a separate social entity entailed the realization that

[89] Anon., 'Liberalism Philosophically Considered', *WR*, vol. 132 (1889), 342; Jevons, *The State in Relation to Labour*, p. 8.

[90] See Chapter Two, pp. 45–6.

[91] See Chapter Five, p. 177.

[92] H. Scott Holland, 'Property and Personality', in C. Gore (ed.), *Property: Its Duties and Rights* (1913), pp. 186–8.

property could be social in its production and value (and not merely in the sense that organized society was a necessary condition for the preservation of property rights),[93] and furthermore that its apportionment should be collectively regulated.[94]

The securing of an equitable proportion for each man of the fruits of his own labour was judged by new liberals not only to be an act of justice but one essential for the adequate functioning of society. This, after all, was the main justification of the minimum wage. Here was also a precondition of social stability, as Churchill was quick to grasp, for private property would only be respected if associated with ideas of justice and reason, 'with the idea of reward for services rendered'.[95] Yet it is no surprise to find many new liberals advocating not only socialization of municipal services, but the nationalization of mines and railways. As one liberal maintained, there was nothing in nationalization to endanger a single principle vital to liberty.[96] Railway nationalization in particular was taken up by liberals not only, as Hobhouse remarked, because '... every railway... owes its existence to a series of private and public Acts of Parliament...'[97] but because it was seen as an integral part of extending programmes of social reform into new fields. As new liberals saw it, here was a concrete example of the interlinking of various facets of social reform, which would work for the benefit of the community as a whole, would ease the way to treating agriculture and trade within the context of a broad national policy, would enable socially beneficial experiments, secure reasonable conditions for railway workers, reduce town rents by enlarging the choice of residence, contribute to mobility of labour, and minimize the hardship of unemployment.[98] Once again, the discovery of the 'social organism' as a workable and realistic theory of society is overwhelmingly evident in this optimistic prediction. No wonder that under

[93] Hobhouse, *Liberalism*, pp. 97–9.
[94] Hobhouse, 'The Historical Evolution of Property, in Fact and in Idea', in C. Gore, op. cit., p. 29.
[95] Churchill, *Liberalism and the Social Problem*, pp. 318–19.
[96] F. V. Fisher, 'Social Democracy and Liberty', op. cit. 648.
[97] Hobhouse, 'The Railways and the State', *MG*, 19.8.1911.
[98] 'Labour Unrest and Liberal Social Policy', Lloyd George Papers, op. cit., pp. 2–3.

such circumstances nationalization was also the best business the nation could undertake.[99]

Out of the analysis of rights there emerged a central explanatory concept for the nexus of human relations: the notion of reciprocity, as developed by Robertson. Reciprocity, of which old-age pensions were an excellent example, was an improvement upon his original notion of quid pro quo in that it was not a mere tit for tat, a relationship conditional upon actual exchange, a handout in return for something received, but an ethical precept, an 'ought'. It was a universal moral law, 'the generally avowed duty of doing as we would be done by'.[100] The significance of this formulation can be appreciated in the light of the prevailing justifications of social responsibility. On the one hand, it could be based on humanitarianism and social justice. This tradition was a prominent one in its desire to represent individual welfare either as a man's birthright or deriving, as was often the case in Hobhouse's presentation,[101] from his moral essence. Most new liberals, however, preferred more concrete and factual arguments and consequently inclined towards a second theme which grew in importance during the Edwardian era, namely, that social benefits should be granted in return for individual services. Robertson's concept of reciprocity in effect brought both themes together. It did not in any way imply a return to the narrow contractual type of relationship by which earlier liberals preferred to describe the web of society. Rather, Robertson considered it as a more useful and precise way of conceiving of human conduct in society than through the use of the concept of rights.[102] This was the element of utilitarianism he was prepared to accept. As

---

[99] C. Money, *Hansard*, 5th Ser. L 512 (13.3.1913). See below for a further discussion of business principles.

[100] Robertson, *The Meaning of Liberalism*, pp. 46–7. Cf. Chapter Four, pp. 135–6, 138.

[101] See Chapter Two, p. 66. In his practical proposals Hobhouse was as progressive as the most forward-looking of liberals. The fact that his working concepts were those of Green, and often reminiscent of Mill, testifies to the flexibility and viability of the liberal tradition. But, as we have seen, Hobhouse stopped short of a scientific concept of a social entity to buttress his belief in the supremacy of social welfare. He was also, more than his colleagues, on the defensive as far as human rights were concerned and thus more likely to gravitate towards the conventional liberal emphasis on their fundamental importance for the individual, in an atmosphere of theorists who were sometimes bending backwards to highlight newer truths.

[102] Robertson, 'The Right to Work', *SPM*, vol. 14 (1909), 52.

a general ethical precept it incorporated an advanced notion of social welfare—because it did not insist on actual quantifiable services as claims to citizenship, when such services could for some reason or other not be rendered. But it also had a particular concept of human nature attached to it, namely 'contributors...working, wealth-creating, service-rendering units'.[103] This was the new understanding of a wholesome human personality—a definition of the individual as creator of values for the benefit of the group. Granted that conception of a human being, the retention of an 'unofficial' moral stigma for those who would not participate (not for those who would not perform their duty to themselves) becomes clear.[104] Such people were not honouring their obligations, as social creatures, in the exchange system of which they were part. They were thus false to their own 'scientifically established' nature rather than to injunctions concerning what was *a priori* right or good. Obviously the question of social interest loomed large side by side with that of social justice. Organicism had indeed made them identical. This is what appealed to the practically minded among the liberals and to those for whom commercial, business. and economic values in a broad sense entered their philosophy of how to run a nation.

But Robertson, differing from the standpoint Hobson would have adopted, did not think reciprocity was identical to 'public utility'. Reciprocity had in it an element of uncalculating altruism which was beyond the scope of economic and industrial considerations.[105] This separation of moral duty from public utility set Robertson apart from the new liberal mainstream, as will be seen below, although it must be pointed out that it was contrary to his own assertions about Benthamite theory, when he recognized the utilitarian element of reciprocity. It would have been more correct, even by his own standards, to see public utility as a partial component of the reciprocity principle. But whether he did so or not, reciprocity

---

[103] Robertson, *The Meaning of Liberalism*, pp. 47–8. Compare this with Hobhouse's 'rights of citizenship conditioned by fulfilment of responsibilities', which was his understanding of the reciprocal relationship, and which supplemented his primary appeal to inherent rights in the social system (Hobhouse, 'The Right to A Living Wage', in *The Industrial Unrest and the Living Wage*, p. 70).

[104] See above, p. 203 n. 29.

[105] Robertson, *The Meaning of Liberalism*, pp. 63–4.

in the latter sense is a convenient description of the new liberal attitude to social relations.

From the perspective of reciprocity Robertson would not accept the 'right to work' because it was presented as a one-sided claim. Instead,

What the unemployed have a 'right' to claim is an earnest consideration of their case, and an earnest effort by the legislature to find the best way of succouring them. To refuse to make this effort is, on the part of any citizen, a repudiation of the law of reciprocity, and a negation of the real membership of the unemployed in the community.[106]

This last clause is what counted so crucially in the new liberal mentality. The definition of man as a communal being tinted the spectacles through which the phenomena of human behaviour were observed. The requisite of participation was the modern counterpart of the 'stake in the country'. Individuality was invested in the community, and the right to consideration resulted therefrom. That is why old-age pensions, in the words of the *Nation*, were 'a right conferred by citizenship'[107]—in the active sense of the word. As the liberal analyses of old-age pensions and the 'right to work' demonstrate, the redefinition of the complex of rights and obligations entailed at the very least a new appreciation of the totality of human welfare and needs, if not the practical expression of a concept of society in which catering to those needs was dictated by the public interest.

4. THE FEEDING OF SCHOOLCHILDREN : THE ASSUMPTION OF COMMUNAL RESPONSIBILITY

A third field of social reform in which strong ideological differences arose, and in which the issue of communal duties was thoroughly aired, was the feeding of schoolchildren. A number of commentators have hailed the Education (Provision of Meals) Act of 1906 as the opening of a new era of social legislation[108] and it seems worthwhile, by inquiring into the ideological genesis of the Act, to see why this is so. Despite the

---

[106] Ibid., p. 54.

[107] 'Pensions and the Poor Law', *Nation*, 16.3.1907.

[108] See C. W. Pipkin, *Social Politics and Modern Democracies*, vol. I (New York, 1931), pp. 72–3, who called the Act a revolutionary principle; and B. B. Gilbert, op. cit., p. 112, who sees it as the beginning of the welfare state.

enforcement of public education, the relation of the state towards children still remained a touchy one. The sanctity of the family unit and the inviolability of the relations between its members were still jealously guarded. Any interference from the outside had to be subtle and indirect to be tolerated. Indeed, Mill's discussion on education had set the pattern for a long time to come. Arguing the case for compulsory education, he wrote:

Hardly any one indeed will deny that it is one of the most sacred duties of the parents . . . to give to [their child] an education fitting him to perform his part well in life towards others and towards himself. But while this is unanimously declared to be the father's duty, scarcely anybody, in this country, will bear to hear of obliging him to perform it.[109]

But Mill contemplated enforcement of what was considered a *parental* obligation, at the parent's expense. The question was one of the duty of one individual towards another. The state was not considered entitled to any independent action on behalf of the child and could only insist on respect for the latter's rights. This attitude persisted among liberals until after the Boer War,[110] when the question of feeding schoolchildren became a national issue, although it had already been raised in municipal contexts long before. Faced with the problems of the unfit and the unemployable, liberals had not only queried the feasibility of parents carrying out their obligations under certain conditions, but allowed for direct state intervention on behalf of the children in specific cases. The *Speaker* thought that the vicious circle of social distress could best be broken in the life of the child. 'More and more society is coming to the position that at any cost this child shall be placed in the world equipped with the possibilities of intelligent and desirable life.' This would necessitate vesting the state with the right to insist that every child in elementary school should have the physical sustenance required for its development, 'that the parent either shall supply this, or in the case of refusal or inability, it shall be supplied from outside—by voluntary means or by municipal

[109] Mill, *On Liberty* (1910), p. 160.
[110] See for example the attitude of the *Speaker* in 1893, which held up to ridicule working-class demands for the feeding of schoolchildren as illiberal and endangering national interests. ('Liberalism and the Working-Man', *Speaker*, 25.2.1893.)

contributions'.[111] This was an important step towards extending social responsibility for children beyond merely prosecuting the parents. Municipal action was after all for liberals the logical and practical preliminary to national communal action. Moreover, it was another *de facto* enlargement of 'equal opportunity'—to include not only intellectual but physical provisions, thus again demonstrating the comprehensiveness of welfare.

The justifications of communal state feeding were varied and usually not based on a single argument. Broadly, one can differentiate between the general progressive case for feeding schoolchildren, directed against those opposing it, and the diverse arguments in favour within the liberal camp. An article in the *Monthly Review* can serve as introduction to the general case. The author, F. H. Barrow, commenting on the lack of a unified plan of action, enumerated three schools of thought: state maintenance of all children (the Labour party position), free meals only to the underfed, and feeding children only through their family (the C.O.S. position). Barrow rejected the latter as totally inadequate and as unable to locate all real cases of need. He believed that regular outside feeding would often raise and civilize rather than lower and pauperize. Here again there was a need for co-operation between the state and private charity, as many of the practical liberal social reformers were advocating. The state would supply authority and guarantee continuity and funds, while charity would supply the personal interest.[112] Behind such practical propositions lay the inferred notion that collective action was necessary and desirable, but as the final social unit was the unique individual, all methods of social reform had to be tailored to individual needs in their ultimate application. Barrow was making the point Barnett, Bray, and Buxton had also upheld—the need for combining the organized power of the collective and personal, voluntary mutual aid between men.[113] Many advanced liberals, while agreeing with the principle, tended to overlook or ignore the personal touch in the machinery of reform. Partly, though, this

[111] 'Towards a Social Policy. X. The "Unemployable"', *Speaker*, 24.12.1904.

[112] F. H. Barrow, 'Free Meals for Underfed Children: A Means to an End', *Monthly Review*, vol. 19 (1905), 1–2, 5–7.

[113] S. A. Barnett, 'Public Feeding of Children', *IR*, vol. 6 (1905), 154–62.

was due to the failure of private charity itself to supply the personal element.[114]

Barrow dismissed the idea of feeding all children as more socialistic than free education and as involving enormous expense. There remained the scheme of feeding destitute children. As against those who saw in it the thin edge of the wedge, Barrow countered that the chief aim of every society should be to make justice the first consideration, and that free meals were only a starting-point for drastic measures which were clearly to the benefit of the community. The main issue for him was a stricter enforcement of social morality and responsibility, to which state intervention could contribute by 'importing more "authority" into our social system'.[115] The emphasis on 'character' remained, with the state functioning as the principal educator.

The new liberal motives for advocating free meals were mixed, and mirror admirably the intertwining of arguments for social reform among liberals in general. Although justice and humanitarianism ranked first on the scale of justifications, other important reasons were stressed. A Fabian Medical Officer of Health described the demand for state intervention in favour of children as springing from two sources—the development of a communal conscience combined with a growing sense of social solidarity, 'which regards the welfare of the community as depending upon the welfare of the children so intimately that any injury inflicted upon the children is transmitted to the whole community'.[116] This was an echo of organic ideas clearly acceptable to new liberals. Here also lay a further justification for 'the gradual assumption by the State of certain definite duties in relation to the child, of certain functions which may fairly be described as parental'. This was the interest of the community in pursuing measures conducive to national self-preservation.[117] In organic theory these justifications were always interlinked. As the *Nation* remarked in 1908:

By punishing the parents through the child the State is guilty of a confusion of ideas, and it practises a short-sighted economy... To

[114] See, e.g., Masterman, 'The Outlook for Social Reform', *IR*, vol. 7 (1905), 147.
[115] Barrow, op. cit. 14–16.
[116] G. F. McCleary, 'The State as Over-Parent', *Albany Review*, vol. 2 (1907), 47.
[117] Ibid. 46–7.

secure the proper nurture for children is a matter of the highest importance, not merely from the point of view of the suffering child, but of the society into which the child is born.[118]

There was also a third justification. The school dinner itself was an education in citizenship by which the child absorbed the knowledge of its own dependence on and place in social life.[119] The significance of the shift in ideas was that the state often assumed direct and always ultimate responsibility for the welfare of children. Its assistance could indeed be interpreted as of prime educational value in demonstrating to the parents their duties. The concept of welfare had once more been expanded under the impact of a new appreciation of the 'natural resources' indispensable to the well-being of the community. Children had become too valuable to be left entirely to the responsiblity of individuals, though they be the parents themselves.

T. J. Macnamara, Liberal M.P. from 1906 and one of the main supporters of school meals, elaborated on the *raison d'état* argument. Commenting on the idea of daily feeding without pauperizing the parents he wrote: 'All this sounds terribly like rank Socialism. I'm afraid it is; but I am not in the least dismayed. Because I know it also to be first-class Imperialism. Because I know Empire cannot be built on rickety and flat-chested citizens.'[120] This kind of argument would not have had much appeal among new liberals but could make it more acceptable to many sworn enemies of social legislation. Another type of justification derived from the eugenic point of view—not merely interest of state but interest of race. One commentator, W. M. Lightbody, concerned that the 'industrious section of the community' was footing a very heavy bill in the form of poor relief and charity, suggested that 'it might prove greater economy in the long run to undertake the entire support of many of the poorer children, and to place them in the way of becoming useful and self-supporting citizens'.[121] But the combination of these last two qualifying adjectives is symptomatic of an attitude far removed from the organic approach to

---

[118] 'Poverty and the State', *Nation*, 4.7.1908.

[119] B. Kirkman Gray, *Philanthropy and the State, or Social Politics* (1908), pp. 294–5.

[120] T. J. Macnamara, 'In Corpore Sano', *CR*, vol. 87 (1905), 248. See also *Hansard*, 4th Ser. CLII 1425 (2.3.1906).

[121] W. M. Lightbody, 'The State and the Children', *ER*, vol. 17 (1907), 436.

social reform of the new liberals. Lightbody perceived the ultimate responsibility for the family as residing in the parents, whether or not they were actually capable of discharging it.[122] Thus any plan for feeding children would have to be linked with more severe measures for dealing with idlers. Beyond this loomed the spectre of 'race suicide' and the question of keeping the state in existence. A parent who produced a large family, thought Lightbody, should receive encouragement and support from the state, 'so long as the youthful citizens he provides are of a desirable type, and likely to prove useful members of society'.[123]

The philosophy of self-support to which many eugenists subscribed was to leave the bulk of the responsibility for producing capable citizens to the individual, with the state stepping in only to ensure that it got a fair deal, rather than out of a sense of direct and benevolent solidarity with the children of the nation. The bargain it struck was a simple one, impersonal and calculating: for money invested it wanted a taxpayer and a worker. But the idea of two opposing parties to a contract still pervaded this type of thinking. Such a viewpoint differed immensely from the authentic preoccupation with the condition of the people as evinced, for example, by Masterman. He adopted an idea common to progressives of the period—the endowment of motherhood—by which state feeding was seen as a subsidy of the natural work of the mother. He also denied, in common with the Idealists, that individual responsibility could be inculcated by actors external to the individual mind. For Masterman, as for most new liberals, the issue was one of rational development towards universal feeding of children, of the recognition of *qualitative* services by individuals towards the well-being of the community, and of the obligations of the state towards its members.[124]

5. NATIONAL INSURANCE: THE SHARING OF RESPONSIBILITY

It is not the intention within the framework of this study to do justice to the scope and details of the 1911 Insurance Act and its

[122] Lightbody, 'The State and Parental Responsibility', *WR*, vol. 163 (1905), 290.
[123] Lightbody, 'The State and the Children', 438.
[124] C. F. G. Masterman, 'The Feeding of Children', *Speaker*, 2.6.1906.

evolution.[125] Instead, as has been the practice, certain central themes will be examined in relation to the new liberal social welfare thought of the period. It might be interesting at the outset to compare two opinions on national insurance. The first was Massingham's, writing in the *Nation* about Lloyd George's part in the Insurance Bill: 'The Insurance Bill comes of no school; it is pure empiricism; vaguely Socialistic in conception, individualist as to nine-tenths of its machinery and method.'[126] The obvious contradiction between the two parts of the sentence notwithstanding, here is what Lloyd George himself had to say of the scheme: 'Perhaps it is the accumulation of all the thought and teaching that has been going on in the nation in social matters during the last twenty years.'[127] As far as the ground principles rather than the technicalities of the scheme are concerned, Lloyd George was right. In a curious way national insurance, concerning both health and unemployment, though a newcomer to the scene of British social reform and not an established item on socio-political programmes, was a culmination of many aspects of liberal thought on social reform. Though often described as revolutionary, it was a logical continuation of the general trend of ideas and, in fact, no more revolutionary than old-age pensions. But it was a peculiar combination of some of the complex elements that went into liberal social thought.

When the subject of insurance came up in the 1890s it was usually treated by liberals very differently from the prevailing attitude in the following decade. Most reactions were conditioned by attitudes towards the Bismarckian experiment in state insurance; thus the *Speaker* voiced in 1893 the typical liberal opinion when it condemned non-contributory insurance as sapping self-reliance.[128] Robertson was one of the first who applied advanced social doctrines to the subject. In 1891 he envisaged the possibility of provision for old age and sickness by means of what he called 'national insurance' out of general taxation—'the doing of work by every citizen while he has

[125] These have been traced elsewhere. See, e.g. Gilbert, op. cit.

[126] H.W.M., 'The Position of Mr. Lloyd George', *Nation*, 6.1.1912.

[127] D. Lloyd George, *The People's Insurance* (1911), pp. 152–3. See also W. J. Braithwaite, *Lloyd George's Ambulance Wagon*, introduction by Sir Henry Bunbury (ed.) (1957), p. 22.

[128] 'A Test for Socialism', *Speaker*, 1.4.1893.

health and strength being his title to support from the common fund when he is sick or superannuated'.[129] Consequently he dismissed contributory schemes not only because he rejected the fallacy of saving but for a reason that was to remain central to the liberal view—the competition with private insurance companies[130] who, apart from symbolizing the rewards of voluntary effort, simply constituted a very strong vested interest. As has been noted, the *Manchester Guardian* realized in 1905 the crucial principle that if the unemployed were paid from taxes and rates to which they themselves had contributed, this would be a form of mutual insurance.[131] But both that realization and Robertson's suggestion were not really insurance in the narrow sense at all, with its connotation of purposive individual prudence. They attested to a much wider grasp of social responsibility, which was only appreciated later on. As to contributory insurance, Samuel raised doubts about its feasibility as late as 1901 because of the burden it imposed upon the poor, without contemplating any scheme which could alleviate such a burden. He was further disturbed by the lack of discrimination between the deserving and undeserving which unemployment insurance entailed.[132] But the upsurge of interest in social reform in the mid-Edwardian period brought about a change. In 1906 the *Speaker*, referring to the new Compensation Bill for disease, thought it marked the extreme limit which could be attained on the voluntary system: 'The next step must inevitably be the introduction of a universal State insurance system, with contributions exacted in proportion to risk from various trades and compensation paid out of the general fund thus created.'[133]

By 1909 the question of national health and unemployment insurance had come out into the open and liberal views were being crystallized. For technical and financial reasons a compulsory system was deemed necessary, mostly to avoid attracting bad risks only. But despite Lloyd George's visit to Germany in 1908, the opposition to a large degree of state interference in insurance remained. One of the principal

---

[129] Robertson, *Modern Humanists*, p. 272.
[130] Robertson, *The Fallacy of Saving*, p. 143.
[131] Leader, *MG*, 21.11.1905.
[132] Samuel, *Liberalism*, p. 127 n.
[133] 'The New Compensation Bill', *Speaker*, 31.3.1906.

dimensions of ideological dispute was on this level. The *Nation*, for instance, wrote in 1911 that a universal compulsory scheme would possibly raise grave questions of national character and tradition and doubted whether German-type regimentation would work in practice.[134] W. J. Braithwaite, instrumental in engineering health insurance, fought for 'the restoration of some measure of freedom to compulsory insurance' and claimed to have found it in making the friendly societies responsible for payment of their own benefits without state guarantee and control. For him, as for many others, the question of the continued existence of the friendly societies remained one of individual initiative and responsibility. Braithwaite recoiled from the idea of

a real State insurance—simple, uniform, universal... 'Socialism' seems to think that it must be universal and uniform. Must it? What a dull world then it threatens... As, personally, I don't like officialdom and bureaucracies, I am glad to have staved off the evil day for some years at any rate, and as a moderate socialist I think that the State can find much better use for its money elsewhere.[135]

The securing of a free field for voluntary effort and enterprise once again linked up with the liberal interpretation of the national minimum:

It was after all in line with the thinking of the day. We talked then of a 'national minimum', which the State should endeavour to achieve, leaving the rest to private effort.... Let us complete the national minimum, before grasping at a maximum, which may elude us because it is in fact unattainable.[136]

For most new liberals, however, the principle of compulsion was not in itself distasteful. As Chiozza Money put it:

It is not difficult to get the average man who works for his living to see that the compulsion of democratic law is not only a different thing from the economic compulsion to which he must day by day submit or starve, but that by virtue of the compulsion of law he may find mitigation of economic compulsion and even be saved from it.[137]

---

[134] 'Problems of National Insurance', *Nation*, 7.1.1911.
[135] Braithwaite, op. cit., pp. 93–4.
[136] Ibid. 95. This is worth comparing to Rea's attitude in Chapter Four.
[137] C. Money, *Insurance Versus Poverty* (1912), p. 7.

The Government made intensive efforts to persuade the public of the necessity of compulsion. Compulsion was 'a way to get something good which cannot be got without it'. In Idealist terms, a propaganda pamphlet stated: 'Compulsion means simply a larger freedom.'[138] As for unemployment insurance in particular, the schemes would have remained very limited in scope without compulsion.[139] It was, however, symptomatic of the changes that had occurred in the minds of men that the *Nation* could comment in 1911:

> Almost universal assent is given to the three propositions of the Bill— first, that private machinery of self-help is unequal to the full task of making adequate provision for invalidity and unemployment; second- ly, that compulsion may properly be employed to stimulate provision by workers and employers; thirdly, that the public interest in the achievement of these purposes warrants public expenditure on their behalf.[140]

From those points of view, insurance was not the commence- ment but the culmination of a revolution. As liberals themselves perceived, it embodied many of the arch-principles of their social thought.

Hobhouse saw insurance as a further instance of the joint obligation resting on individual and state to provide for the contingencies of life. The peculiar liberal balance of social solidarity and mutual interest was well brought out by him when discussing the role of the employer in unemployment insurance. As Hobhouse remarked: 'We do not wish to revert to the patriarchal view of the relations of employer and employed. We wish the employed to be an independent citizen, and we cannot have it both ways.'[141] On the other hand, the employer did have a certain responsibility towards his workers. But it was not, nor did any liberal expect it to be, one that considered the welfare and interests of the worker as a prime concern. That over-all view was supplied by the state. The state, then, had to manipulate the situation in a manner which Utilitarians would have approved of: to make the protagonists, while pursuing

[138] 'Why the Insurance Act was made compulsory and why it should remain compulsory', leaflet, Liberal Publication Dept., 15.5.1914.
[139] 'Unemployment Insurance', pamphlet, Liberal Publication Dept. (1909).
[140] 'The Burden of Insurance', *Nation*, 20.5.1911
[141] L. T. Hobhouse, 'Workmen's Insurance and Employers' Liability', *Nation*, 4.2.1911.

their own interests, contribute towards the general welfare. But unlike the Utilitarians, new liberals saw the community and the state as directly motivated by ethical values and ends which could only be perceived by the comprehensive outlook of the whole social body. Hence, to return to the question of insurance, Hobhouse suggested giving the employer a direct financial interest in removing the causes of sickness and invalidity, inasmuch as they were under his control. This could be accomplished by making the employer contribute on an actuarial calculation of the cost of his workmen's incapacities to the community. 'So conceived, the employer's contribution would serve the permanent social function of stimulating effort to reduce the costs and losses incident to industrial life.'[142] Though this direct motivation was not established in the Act itself, there was an emphasis on the indirect pecuniary advantage for employers. Side by side with stressing the responsibility of the employer towards his workpeople, new liberals pointed to the vital interest the public and the employers had in maintaining workmen in efficiency.[143] The *Nation* expressed confidence that part, if not all, of the contribution employees and employers were to make would return in the shape of greater industrial productivity. This secondary theme, though removed—as has been seen—from the doctrine of national efficiency, began to carry increasing weight. An important reason for this was no doubt the wider perspective imposed by the burdens of government from 1906 onwards. The question how best to manage the country's economic affairs became for liberals one of balance between an efficient and contented labour force and a willing and energetic employer. Referring to health insurance, the *Nation* suggested once again to turn to the body of wealth truly able to bear taxation as the fund for social progress. National insurance was at present essential but the burdens should not fall heavily either on employers or employees. Ultimately, perhaps, it was only a palliative. The movement of ideas and action appeared to be clearly discernible:

As the pre-eminently social meaning and purpose of Public Health emerge into full consciousness, the purely individual benefits, which at

[142] Ibid.   [143] Money, *Insurance Versus Poverty*, pp. 32–3, 317.

present seem to demand detailed personal contributions, will dwindle in significance, and Public Hygiene will take its place with the protective service of Police as a necessary of life for a civilised community, to be provided out of the reserve fund of wealth at the disposal of the nation.[144]

Social reform was on the way to becoming, as Hobson would have it, social both in its origin and its application.

For the time being, however, contributions were an inevitable feature and had an important educational value in that they brought home a sense of mutual responsibility. Unemployment insurance, for example, reflected the triple aspect of industrial problems, with capital, labour, and society linked together to cope with defects from which each suffered.[145] The idea of insurance hovered somewhere between the notion of co-partnership and the concept of organism. The first was a practical expression of Hobhouse's theories of harmony and joint obligation, 'the alliance of personal and collective responsibility'.[146] In Villiers's words, insurance was the epitome of guarantism—a practical way of dealing with individual grievances of workers by attaining their basic needs through co-operation with the state.[147] The second was connected with what the *Nation* called the growing agreement upon the essentials of national well-being pursued along a number of converging paths. Insurance was thus one of the elements of an interlinked policy. 'The nucleus in our policy of organic reform must be the possession by every family of a money income adequate for all its economic needs.' This was primarily a new conception of social health in which a living wage was not individual right but social security.[148]

The principle of prevention had lifted social reform right out of dealing *ex post facto* with the ailments of the outsiders and failures of society, out of the purely restorative approach. It concerned matters which could potentially affect the welfare of all and especially of the majority of the nation, the working

---

[144] 'The Fund for Social Progress', *Nation*, 28.10.1911.
[145] 'The Policy of Insurance', *Nation*, 22.4.1911.
[146] Hobhouse, 'The Contending Forces', *English Review*, vol. 4 (1909–10), 370. See also 'Problems of National Insurance', *Nation*, 7.1.1911.
[147] Villiers, *Modern Democracy*, pp. 32–3.
[148] 'The Claim for a Share in Life', *Nation*, 28.9.1912.

population,[149] who by their social behaviour had merited the
benefits of full-fledged citizenship. Although, for reasons of cost
and organization, unemployment insurance was as yet restricted to certain professions, there is no doubt that 'The broad
idea of the Social Programme of Liberalism [was] the protection of the mass of the population against the 'risks' of life—
... childhood, sickness, unemployment, invalidity, and old
age.'[150] This, coupled with the notion of an income tailored to
individual needs, amounted to a complete transformation of the
idea of social reform. It was, as the *Nation* had called it, a claim
for a share in life.

The tripartite system of contributions was also a departure of
deeper significance than might seem to be the case. It was not
merely a means of arousing a sense of mutual responsibility but
an immediate financial expression of the solidarity of society.
The financial concept of pooling the risks was second in
importance only to the restoration of socially created value to
the nation. The *Nation* sensed this vaguely in 1909 when it
remarked that unemployment insurance should rank somewhat
higher than a palliative. 'Economically we imagine that its
collective adoption by the nation will have something of the
same equalising effect as it secures to the individual.'[151] Beyond
the economic advantages, Chiozza Money formulated the more
general case: '... the first duty of a civilization is so to pool its
resources and its risks that no man, or set of men, shall be made
to endure the consequences of an irregularity which civilization
cannot prevent.'[152] The reason given for making insurance
contributory, from the workers' side, while old-age pensions
were not, was also connected to a rough sense of fairness in
exchange. Old-age pensions were a distant and often doubtful
benefit, whereas the rewards of insurance were much more
likely to be reaped at an earlier stage.[153] Moreover, pensions
were regarded as a reward for what citizens had already done
for society, whereas insurance was mainly a means to enable
them to perform their role as citizens in the future. And thirdly,

[149] W. H. Dawson, 'Insurance Legislation: The Larger View', *FR*, vol. 89 (1911),
537–9.
[150] 'Problems of National Insurance', *Nation*, 7.1.1911.
[151] 'Insurance and Unemployment', *Nation*, 29.5.1909.
[152] Money, *Insurance Versus Poverty*, p. 312.
[153] See G. P. Gooch, *Hansard*, 5th Ser. V 517–18 (19.5.1909).

old-age pensions were a more comprehensive expression of
social solidarity than insurance, which was functioning within a
circumscribed limit. In addition there was more to insurance
than just 'bringing in the magic of averages to the aid of the
millions',[154] in Churchill's memorable phrase. Social insurance
could never be purely actuarial. The whole essence of a national
insurance scheme was not only in that a few people were helped
by the many but, as another Liberal M.P., A. Sherwell,
remarked, in the inequality of the benefits. Referring to health
insurance he stressed what from the point of view of many
advanced liberals remained a basic defect in the Bill: 'I
respectfully submit that it is one of the tragedies connected with
social reform to-day that it must sometimes, while benefiting the
many, appear to make life harder for the few.' This was due, in
his opinion, to the distinction between a large class of people
who could effectively be helped by such schemes and those—a
smaller class consisting of the most helpless members of the
community—whose lot could only be alleviated. These were
the deposit contributors who for various reasons were not
members of insurance societies. The benefits conferred under
national insurance did not suffice 'for the special needs of the
particular classes' concerned.[155] The participation of the state
in the insurance scheme assured, however, that this was no
mechanical insurance. Thus Masterman, who played a major
role in preparing health insurance, emphasized that one of its
principles was that

those members of the community who to-day, on account of their
increasing age, are debarred from any possibility of insurance...
should find themselves, as far as practicable, by the use of Government
help in no way worse off than the young and healthy members of
society.[156]

In that sense insurance pure and simple was never regarded by
new liberals as a sufficient method of social reform.

Social reform had swung full circle. In establishing a
universal right of welfare, it recognized the claims of specifically
distressed groups, though as Sherwell himself reminded the

---

[154] *Hansard*, 5th Ser. XXVI 509 (25.5.1911).
[155] *Hansard*, 5th Ser. XXX 779–85 (31.10.1911).
[156] Masterman, 'The Case for the Insurance Bill', *Nation*, 9.12.1911.

House: 'Everyone who has studied social questions is alive to the very plausible danger of addressing oneself to an urgent need and forgetting the larger and more permanent need of the rest of the community.'[157] But it was also a question of recognizing the uniqueness of the individual condition. This was notably different from the 'breaking up of the Poor Law' approach of the Webbs. For them, the question of classification was one of categorizing social defects according to their separate causes, rather than regarding the individual as object of a particular application of a general law. Specialization meant for them the breaking up of individuals into their various needs common to all, not the viewing of each individual as a unique whole. Hence on the subject of a legislative minimum wage, liberals insisted that it was not up to the state to fix a minimum itself, but to uphold the principle while leaving the details to be adjusted to individual circumstances by wage boards and tribunals. This was the liberal standpoint both in the case of the anti-sweating legislation of 1909 and the minimum wage for miners in 1912. Even new liberals could not therefore accept the Labour party demand for a standard universal minimum wage of 30s. As P. Alden explained:

You cannot have a universal minimum wage side by side with the application of the Trade Boards Act ... the only method by which we shall ever get a minimum wage in this country ... is by taking an individual trade and suiting yourself to the conditions and needs of that trade in each individual district and locality.[158]

The general ethical principle would only be just when it took into consideration variations in occupations and in the cost of living. Once again, a respect for individuality was retained within the context of forward-looking notions of social reform.

6. THE VALUE OF WELFARE

Transcending the above questions there loomed a central issue which emerged again and again in theoretical discussions and on the practical level: how was the social bond to be interpreted and how was one to judge a 'good society'? Was social welfare to be regarded as need-oriented, and therefore contingent upon

---

[157] *Hansard*, 5th Ser. XXX 784 (31.10.1911).
[158] *Hansard*, 5th Ser. LI 1306–7 (9.4.1913).

the subjective contentment of the individuals who comprised society, or even evaluated by what one might loosely call criteria of social health; or was social welfare to be judged by its tangible, visible, and preferably quantifiable results for the community? The tension between these two different concepts of social justice was not resolved by liberals; indeed, it was aggravated when they came to power. Yet at the same time, as we have seen, most of their arguments—not the least the organism model—were aimed at bridging this gap. The first-mentioned concept of social welfare was the core of the new liberal social philosophy, seeking a fundamentally qualitative enrichment of individual life within a community. But the second point of view was very often the practical test of acceptability by the community which every proposed reform was put to. Once the community had virtually become the arbiter of individuality, individuality had to be consonant with, indeed contribute to, the public good. And, many liberals would claim, this could only be evaluated by the use of notions such as function, achievement, and productivity. Those notions were forced not only upon a world limited in resources and therefore having to establish its priorities in social reform, but upon a world in which competing ideas on social reform had to be assessed. The force of circumstance imposed this viewpoint upon liberalism and, consequently, it was never fully integrated into the liberal way of thinking.

Immediately connected to the question of a 'good' society was the question of how it was to be run. New liberals were of course opposed to defining the social relationship simply as one conditional upon an exact exchange of tangibles and services. The severely contractual approach had been rejected by new liberals when they qualified the doctrine of taxation according to benefit received.[159] It was in fact Webb who best defined the old attitude as 'part of the characteristically Whig conception of the citizen's contribution to the expenses of the social organisation, as a bill paid by a private man for certain specific commodities which he has ordered and purchased for his own use'.[160] This does not mean that new liberals abandoned the idea of social exchange as the basis of social relations. Quite the

[159] See Chapter Four, pp. 136–8.
[160] S. Webb, 'Lord Rosebery's Escape from Houndsditch', *NC*, vol. 50 (1901), 370.

contrary—not only they but Socialists as well would have insisted on this fundamental principle.[161] The objection was, as Sherwell remarked in connection with the deposit contributors to the insurance scheme, to treating individuals 'strictly and solely on a cash basis'.[162] Instead of that came the notion of social function with a twofold theory of reward—as necessary to ensure the adequate motivation and functioning of individuals, and to be distributed in accordance with services, of any variety, rendered to the community and not merely on the basis of results. The intention and effort, rather than the achievement, were to count.[163] Biological, psychological, and ethico-social elements combined to define what was due from the individual to society and from society to the individual. But—and this was of vital importance in the new liberal concept of welfare—full recognition was given to individual inadequacies resulting from social causes. In these cases, too, society reaped what it had sown. Such individuals were impaired by extrinsic forces from making substantial contributions to the social good and should not, therefore, be deprived of benefiting from the fruits of citizenship. All this was admirably expressed by Robertson's ethical maxim of reciprocity 'do as you would be done by' which he too saw as identical to the socialist formula: 'From each according to his abilities, to each according to his needs.'[164] This, then, was a need-oriented concept of welfare, but one which at the same time placed a premium on socially-oriented behaviour of individuals.

The age was, however, also one in which 'efficiency' had a magic ring. And efficiency was measured by concrete results. Even for liberals who perceived the dangerous undertones of

[161] See S. Ball's review of *The Social Problem*, *ER*, vol. 12 (1902), 104, and J. R. MacDonald, who reiterated 'the right of the Service Giver to life, property, and comfort' and denied such rights to the man who gave no service ('The Labour Party and its Policy', *IR*, vol. 8 (1906), 265).

[162] *Hansard*, 5th Ser. XXX 781 (31.10.1911).

[163] The direction of development was that depicted by Hobson: 'Social reform, regarded from the economic and even the moral standpoint, will only be effective in so far as it breaks the direct connection between work and pay. Work should be done by individuals as a pleasurable widening of their powers of self-expression in social service: pay should be the return made by society, not for the work they have done, but to enable them to do more work in the future. This affords the only really moral basis of property, viz. as a social trust.' (Hobson, 'A New Theory of Work', *British Friend*, vol. 13 (1904), 254.)

[164] Robertson, *The Meaning of Liberalism*, pp. 152–3.

this doctrine, it was convenient to demonstrate that their social philosophy could also—as it were, incidentally—score on this account and meet the test of 'business considerations'. Obviously, any ideology in power must entertain a measure of 'business considerations'. To the extent that efficiency meant health, this coincided with aspects of new liberal thought. Gain and utility were, as has been shown, terms adopted by liberals independently of the 'efficiency' doctrine. Hobson considered the living wage to be good business as much as good ethics and this theme was sounded again and again during the period of Liberal reforms. But although actuarial and 'value for money' arguments were heard only on the right wing of liberalism, the sheer ethical argument had to be reinforced by the promise of concrete gains to be achieved from pursuing a course of action. 'A modern State . . . recognising its duty to secure its members against poverty in old age, not as an eleemosynary but as a business proposition'[165] became a typical method of presenting social reform. Alden, for instance, presented state medical treatment for children as an investment which would return useful citizens.[166] The *Nation* said of attempts to determine a minimum wage that they were not, strictly speaking, 'attempts to apply a principle of justice, but a principle of humanity and social expediency'. It simply did not pay the nation to maintain a trade which could not pay a wage of minimum efficiency. This, concluded the weekly, was true economically, politically, and morally.[167] Indeed, contrary to Robertson's attitude, business considerations were not necessarily opposed to the tenets of the liberal ethical tradition—as Hobson's adaptation of a qualitative utilitarianism had shown.[168] But such considerations had to be kept within limits to avoid a collision with ethical maxims. From 1911 onwards, there was a propensity among liberals to overstep such limits, and it was Lloyd George who outdid all others in this respect. He displayed a marked

---

[165] Hobson, 'Old Age Pensions. II. The Responsibility of the State to the Aged Poor', 298. See a similar argument in 'A Legal Minimum Wage', leader, *MG*, 15.12.1908.

[166] *Hansard*, 5th Ser. XXX 811 (31.10.1911).

[167] 'The Policy of the Minimum Wage', *Nation*, 20.4.1912.

[168] Thus Hobson wrote: '[The living wage] must not, however, be understood as the deliberate preference of humanitarian to business principles, but rather as the substitution of a far-sighted view of the public interest for that short-sighted view which prevailed before.' (Hobson, 'A Living Wage', *Commonwealth*, vol. 1 (1896), 129).

tendency to conceive of the affairs of the nation and its members more and more as a going concern. Thus in 1911 he stated that what was necessary for the nation was 'to cultivate in the State a sense of proprietorship over [the nation's] workers. They are the greatest asset of any land.'[169] And in 1914 he wrote: '... we are beginning to apply sound commercial principles to national life and enterprise'. On contributing towards the health and strength of the working classes he commented:

> We are putting more capital into this branch of the national business—putting it in freely and confidently, knowing that it will in time yield an abundant return not only in the increased welfare and happiness of the workers but in larger material gain for the whole nation.[170]

The delicate balance between production and consumption, wealth and welfare, quantity and quality, which the new liberalism had woven into a web could not benefit from such statements. Although 'materialistic' and 'ethical' interpretations of welfare shared a common terminology which obscured the differences between the various implications of wealth, waste, production, and consumption, it is of great significance that the leading new liberal theorists were now themselves shuttling freely back and forth between those interpretations. In the Memorandum on Liberal social policy already mentioned, the signatories resorted to arguments of national efficiency side by side with stating prerequisites for a civilized community. The minimum wage was discussed from the point of view of a burden on capital and commerce; nationalization of railways was commended 'in the words of the Chancellor of the Exchequer "as a business proposition"'.[171] These tendencies had all along existed in new liberal thought; the exigencies of the hour—against a backdrop of almost perpetual political crises—made them very weighty.

Liberals themselves were, however, aware of these tendencies

---

[169] D. Lloyd George, *The Insurance of the People*, Liberal Publication Dept. (1911), p. 6.
[170] D. Lloyd George, introduction to H. A. Walter, *Die neue englische Sozialpolitik* (München und Berlin, 1914), vi.
[171] 'Labour Unrest and Liberal Social Policy', Lloyd George Papers, op. cit., pp. 1–2. See Chapter Four, p. 157.

and continuously warned against them. A 'Radical of '85' wrote in 1908:

... the principle of business is so to balance expenditure and revenue as to leave the largest possible amount of profit; whereas the principle of political government is so to conduct the affairs of the nation as to safeguard the welfare of the inhabitants of the nation, recognising that 'business' values in this respect may be false values, and that a hidden gain may often underlie an apparent monetary loss.[172]

And the *Nation*, which repeatedly stressed that insurance would pay for itself 'not only in abatement of poverty, pain, and degradation, but even in material wealth, market values, hard cash',[173] could also declare unequivocally:

... the State is not going into the business of insurance as it goes into the business of a postal service to make a profit by it or even to pay its way. It is making a large endowment from taxation in order to improve the health and check some of the more easily preventable miseries of the community.[174]

Most liberals would have assented to the view implicit in the organic idea, that a 'business proposition' when applied to social life was a qualitative notion, meaning that what was conducive to national health and welfare was *ipso facto* worthwhile pursuing.

The body of thought new liberals had constructed was manifestly directed at the immediate social problems of the times. It consistently expressed their interest in concrete issues and their need to contribute towards an improved society in the here and now. They never failed to be realistic about their proposals, to recognize the pressures and limitations under which any reform must operate and the conditions it must fulfil, and to point accordingly to the path of action. This no doubt enhanced the viability of their ideas and can explain the major role they played in the reorientation of the Liberal programme.[175] For even if actual legislative achievements did not

[172] 'A Radical of '85', 'Liberalism Without Ideas: A Few Notes', *WR*, vol. 169 (1908), 144.

[173] 'The Burden of Insurance', *Nation*, 20.5.1911.

[174] 'Prevention and Insurance', *Nation*, 22.7.1911. Cf. also Alden, *Democratic England*, p. 214.

[175] As H. V. Emy, *Liberals, Radicals, and Social Politics 1892–1914* (1973), conclusively demonstrates.

embody their most forward notions, they were instrumental in re-establishing a strong connection between a modernized liberal theory and its counterpart in political action. A few general considerations on this subject are now due.

VII

Epilogue

ALTHOUGH in recent years, after a period of eclipse and denial, the importance of political thought and political philosophy has once again been admitted, the case for studying political ideas still seems to require vigorous support. One of the fundamental themes that have shaped the contents of these pages is the conviction that ideas are facts, that they can be treated as empirical phenomena and made the subject of scientific scrutiny, and that political thought is a ubiquitous aspect of political behaviour. Furthermore, granted that human beings not only act but think, that man is not only *homo faber* but *homo sapiens*, political ideas cannot be detached from the study of politics in general. The time has come to bury the fairly common view that the political process should be released from the encumbrances of opinions and emotions ostensibly obscuring it. It has been amply illustrated, and will presently be re-emphasized, that men consciously and intentionally think about politics, that they attach political significance to such activity, and that they believe in the influence of ideas on action.

Further to these assertions, this study gives vent to a dissatisfaction with the standard list of 'Great Men' by means of which political thought is taught and, indeed, encompassed. This self-perpetuating academic tradition has produced a number of distortions from the perspective of the political scientist. It constitutes a 'closed shop' from which new candidates are virtually barred, because it has itself established the criteria of who and what is politically discussable. It has also restricted the domain of political thought to those who exhibit the highest standards of debate and reasoning, to qualitatively 'professional' and expert thinkers, thus continuing the confusion between political philosophy and political thought. And it has led to an over-emphasis on ideas in the abstract—

obviously not the original intention of their wielders—which are then pitted against each other within the framework of central themes, often with purely philosophical or methodological aims in mind.

In contrast, the claim is forwarded here that political thought is to be found at any level of political action, on different levels of sophistication. It is not necessarily identical with the coherent speculation of a number of isolated men regarded as having inherent worth and significant bearing on political life. It is equally profitable to examine the formulation of political values and ends because of their immediate relevance to the functioning of a political system in which they are generated and to some of whose basic problems they are a response. The scope of interest of the scholar, moreover, should range from political philosophy to public opinion. Even if the intention is, as in this study, to concentrate on the *formulation* of politically significant ideas—by definition the work of an intellectual élite—a wide net must be cast to include the articulate elements of the politically conscious intelligentsia. The special merit of the group of thinkers discussed here is in their combination of a high standard of political theorizing with a dedicated, often passionate involvement in 'practical' politics. To focus on political thought as the creation of a group, as a consequence of the interaction of ideas, is at the very least poetic justice for a set of people who came to believe in the social origins of human behaviour. Admittedly, this method cannot apply to periods prior to the spread of the mass media—books and the Press—for sheer lack of documentation. But from the nineteenth century onwards it certainly can be put to use to detect and analyse the history, influence, and political functions of the major political ideas and ideologies.

The critique of liberal thought is often based on the mid-nineteenth century model, though the basic attitudes underlying liberalism are not anchored to a particular point in time. It seems arbitrary to assume that liberalism did not continue to evolve, not the least for the reason that such a broadly based ideology is not dependent for its existence on 'Great Men', be they Mill, Green, or Hobhouse. Indeed, the evidence assembled shows conclusively that liberalism, while undergoing important changes at the turn of the century, was yet clearly discernible as a coherent ideology and that, furthermore, far from being a mere academic exercise in thought, it had widespread social and political influence and was engaged in the affairs of the day.

From a slightly different perspective, this is an analysis of ideological adaptation. Ideology is, after all, action-oriented, geared to the comprehension of a specific political system and, with that as a springboard, to its assessment, critique, and possible transformation. But an ideology, while tailored to a certain measure, tends to be exhibited as the ultimate in fashion, and obstinately clings to that title despite baggy knees and shiny elbows. This is what happened to exponents of mid-Victorian liberalism, who fell into the common error of generalizing one of its particular manifestations. A viable ideology necessitates a constant interplay between the abstract and the concrete to avoid the pitfalls of vanity or insignificance. Its principal components must at any time be detachable from the historical and political scene, but thus freed only to be re-anchored to new sets of facts and events. Late-Victorian liberalism applied this corrective to its mid-century prede-cessor. To survive as an ideology it had to provide workable solutions to the critical socio-political problems of the times, while retaining the articles of faith which could not be altered without depriving the creed of its essentials. It did so by means of a large group of men who brought a liberal viewpoint to apply to the all-pervading social question and by combining this with scientifically and philosophically acceptable modes of thinking. Far from dying with Mill, liberalism transcended the limits he imposed on it and, attaining new levels of intellectual vitality, underwent something of a renaissance.

When assessing the role political thought plays in political practice one has to be exceedingly cautious. Direct influence of a theory on an administrator is not easy to establish, the more so as—and this is definitely the case in Britain—he prefers to describe the process of policy formulation in terms of adjust-ments of claims and interests, in terms of available budget and machinery. The ends to which these are linked appear to be the result of political exigency, and their detailed contents the outcome of expert opinion on departmental level; so that the idea of an *ad hoc*, pragmatic legislative process becomes an unconsciously perpetuated myth, conveniently focusing on legislation and administration to the exclusion of their prime causes, motivation, and ultimate ends. The rise of the welfare state has thus often been described as due to unplanned and unconnected governmental responses to social needs that were pressed upon the state, as it were, out of the blue.[1] Nothing can be further from the truth as far as the period examined is concerned. Legislation does not occur in a vacuum. Legislators and administrators might be unaware of the principles they are upholding while about their job but, in a loose sense, their modes of thinking and acting reflect the movement of thought and prevailing mentality of their times. With open channels of public opinion, and social reformers agitating for the measures they believe in, politicians cannot remain impervious to ideas just as they cannot remain impervious to other major factors in the social climate they dwell in. And whether politicians decide to promote a particular measure for election purposes, or because they are succumbing to blackmail, or because they have a score to settle, they still cannot help being guided by the hard core of existing thought that has accumulated on a certain issue. At the very least, the mental climate of an age defines and

[1] MacDonagh and Roberts (see Chapter One, p. 13 n. 25) state the case for the first half of the nineteenth century. A typical example of this approach that pertains also to the period discussed here is M. Bruce, *The Coming of the Welfare State*, pp. 13–14. Bruce claims that the welfare state has not been the direct outcome of any political or social philosophy, and has been 'no more than the accumulation over many years of remedies to specific problems which in the end have reached such proportions as to create a new conception of governmental responsibility'. But this implies a notion of social philosophy as detached from social problems, surely a one-sided attitude. One can neither unequivocally state that social legislation opened the way to new notions of society and government, as Bruce does, nor the reverse. It seems more profitable to regard the relationship between social theory and practice as parts of one process, in which the one acts upon and reacts to the other. Why, if the problems are practical, must this rule out a social philosophy within whose framework such problems are tackled? Similarly, B. B. Gilbert, *The Evolution of National Insurance*, p. 13, claims that 'the changing view of the nature of distress and poverty that began to affect the minds of reformers and social thinkers in the last quarter of the nineteenth century . . . derived less from a conscious search for a revised philosophy of poverty than from changes in British economic society combined with a growing consciousness among the poor themselves that they had it within their power to alter the conditions under which they lived.' That the conscious search for a new social philosophy played a major part in changing views, this study will have hoped to demonstrate. But, again, the implication that economic changes and the emergence of a consciousness of power could not in themselves both occasion and be spurred on by developments in social philosophy is unwarranted. Where indeed is the social philosophy that has developed entirely independently of the economic and social conditions in which it was formulated? The concept of social philosophy becomes a meaningless abstraction in the hands of Bruce and Gilbert.

constrains the options open to the politician. No Liberal politician could have, in 1906, fought for the extension of the Poor Law and the stigmas attached to it. No Liberal politician could have presented a budget that did not encompass some notion of graduated taxation. The social and political thought of a political system not only delineates the limits of the politically possible but prepares the stage for, refines, analyses, dissects, and often initiates social policy. In fact, Liberal politicians and administrators were on the whole keenly aware of the principles involved in their activities. In the thirty years' span before the First World War social policy, far from being an automated response to political exigencies, was the product of a highly ideological age, when basic ethical values, ground principles of social action, were being moulded out of intense and searching discussions.

The myth that social policy was entirely an unplanned outcome of empirical improvisation, and that the British mind abhors theorizing, is not only belied by the events of the era examined, but was patently alien to the ideas of the new liberal theorists of the time. It is not only that many of the political and policy struggles were battles of ideas, and that far from being piecemeal the mainstream of liberal social reform thought developed a coherent social theory with direct relevance to political and social realities. There was a conscious and deliberate determination among new liberals to prepare a body of social thought that would direct political action. On few subjects, indeed, was there greater unanimity of opinion than on the decisive role of theory in determining welfare legislation and social reconstruction.

The basic confusion underlying these misconceptions is a recurring propensity to equate political thinking or theorizing with the construction of a fixed, immutable, and dogmatic set of principles to which political 'facts' have to be tailored, otherwise 'so much the worse for the facts'. In the words of L. Stephen, 'in politics an idea means a device for saving thought. It enables you to act upon a little formula without taking the trouble to ask whether it be or be not relevant to the particular case.'[2] This heritage, directly traceable to the reaction to the French Revolution, has perpetuated an artificial

[2] L. Stephen, 'The Good Old Cause', *NC*, vol. 51 (1902), 23.

separation of political idea from political activity and could explain most of the continuous hostility and blindness to the role ideas play in social behaviour. It was Jevons who set the tone on this issue by stating that legislation was a matter of practical work, based on experience, not abstractions. In an oft-quoted dictum he declared that each case must be judged on its own merits.[3] By doing so he contributed to the false assumption that theory was necessarily an abstraction and that judging cases on merit ruled out the use of coherent sets of principles. Much of this antagonism had been aroused, of course, by the metaphysical abstractions of political economy.[4] In reacting to that 'science', advanced liberals concurrently contributed much towards a redefinition of the role of theory.

Haldane had already maintained in 1888 that British politics meant much more than administration and that 'the aims of the party which claims to occupy the position of the Liberal party in this country must depend almost entirely upon a theory'.[5] The *Daily Chronicle* when discussing the 'condition of the people' question, wrote in 1892:

There must be at bottom some kind of definite and coherent body of doctrine, from which the various reforms urged are necessary and logical inferences. We know, of course, that it will be said the English people are not logical but practical, and that the party of progress must therefore be practical too, and scout the mere theorist, with his systems and formulas. But ... the older type of Liberalism was strong just because it was based on definite ideas—because its advocates (to use Mr. Morley's words) 'could explain in the large dialect of a definite scheme what were their aims and whither they were going'.[6]

While this was perhaps the voice of 'Fabian liberalism', these views were held by a wide range of liberals. F. V. Fisher considered Jevons's doctrine dangerous and made the important point that 'principle can still be respected without our

[3] W. S. Jevons, *The State in Relation to Labour* (1882), p. 166.

[4] This had been Chamberlain's attitude. ('Favourable Aspects of State Socialism', *North American Review*, vol. 152 (1891), 547). A quaint remark in an obituary on Chamberlain illustrates the preconceptions about liberalism: 'Mr. Chamberlain liked good work better than abstract theories and this alone proves that he was never at heart a Liberal' (M. Woods, 'Mr. Chamberlain', *FR*, vol. 46 (1914), 202).

[5] R. B. Haldane, 'The Liberal Creed', *CR*, vol. 54 (1888), 463. This was entirely compatible with a later statement by Haldane to the effect that politicians must not only be idealists but men of business ('The Eight Hours Question', *CR*, vol. 57 (1890), 250).

[6] *Daily Chronicle*, 29.7.1892.

legislators becoming mere *doctrinaires*.[7] Robertson believed that there would always be a Liberal party standing for the spirit which gave birth to new ideas and programmes, and that the electorate would only respond to a consistent and sequent policy proceeding from established first principles.[8] This was a comment on the new form the opposition to stated principles was now adopting—the reaction to the drawing up of programmes which later developed into the call to 'clean the Liberal slate'. Samuel held that underlying liberal proposals there existed, 'whether the speakers themselves are aware of it or not, a very definite philosophy'.[9] The 'Radical of '85' wanted ideas to become forces and believed 'abstract formulae' important in evaluating policies.[10]

The belief in the importance of ideas, indeed the search for a unifying principle, was of course central to Hobson's approach. All attempts at social reform were condemned to failure, in his opinion, unless guided by larger principles of social justice.[11] As has been noted, he denied that social reform could be guided by induction, by extrapolating from facts: 'The laws or principles needed for the selection, the ordering, and the interpretation of concrete facts of history cannot be got out of these facts themselves, but must be imposed by a process which, at any rate relatively to these facts, is *a priori*.'[12] The demand for order occasioned by mental processes, 'the passion of Wholeness, or Holiness, which is in the blood of man, urges to a new attempt to formulate social order'.[13] In grasping the unity of the social question, man brought to bear upon the concrete problems facing him a universalistic rational social philosophy which paved the way to their solution. Hobson thus obviously maintained that a party without principles was doomed to impotence.[14] One of the weaknesses of the people at large, when

---

[7] F. V. Fisher, 'Social Democracy and Liberty', *WR*, vol. 141 (1894), 647.

[8] Robertson, *The Future of Liberalism*, pp. 4, 11. See also C. F. Millin, 'The New Liberalism', *FR*, vol. 69 (1901), 634.

[9] Samuel, *Liberalism*, p. 7.

[10] 'A Radical of '85', 'Liberalism Without Ideas: A Few Notes', *WR*, vol. 169 (1908), 281–2.

[11] Hobson, 'The Ethics of Industrialism' in S. Coit (ed.), *Ethical Democracy: Essays in Social Dynamics* (1900), p. 88; *The Crisis of Liberalism* (1909), pp. 114–15.

[12] Hobson, *The Social Problem*, pp. 281–2.

[13] Ibid., pp. 2, 3.

[14] Hobson, 'Is the Future with Socialism?', *EW*, 18.3.1899.

reformers tried to persuade them to consider change, was a 'congenital reluctance to do thinking'. This was reinforced by the mistaken conclusion that rapid change could only be dealt with by short-range opportunism.[15] The opening editorial of the *Progressive Review*—of all the intellectual periodicals the closest to the core of new liberal thinkers—queried the diverse enthusiasms for social reform: 'Where is the synthesis, the unity of principle and of policy which shall give solidarity of structure, singleness of aim, economy of force, consistency of action to this medley of multifarious effort?' In calling for the assignment of a new meaning to liberal fundamentals, the editorial recognized that the Liberal party could not continue as a progressive force unless it expressed the new concepts of social philosophy in actual legislation.[16]

Hobhouse was no less emphatic in asserting that ideas were central to social behaviour, in itself a logical concomitant of the crucial role mind played in evolution. Thus he stated:

An ideal is as necessary to the reformer as the established fact is to the conservative... A progressive movement... must have an ideal, and an ethical ideal for the future must be in so far abstract as it is not yet realized and embodied in social institutions.[17]

In a passage which draws out the essence of the issue at hand and which deserves to be quoted at length, Hobhouse wrote:

There are, indeed, those who think that principles are of but little importance in politics, that controversies are decided by the clash of... material interests alone. This would be true only if politics were a whirl of selfish interests in which no social or human progress could be traced. In so far as there is a real advance in public life, in so far as politics are a serious study designed towards the betterment of humanity, there must be principles guiding the actions of statesmen standing above mere self-interest and rooted in something deeper than party. English Liberalism is, we think, coming at length reluctantly to admit the truth of this contention. We do not love principles, as such, in England. We distrust the abstract, and pride ourselves upon holding by hard facts. Yet it is these same hard facts themselves that are at last teaching us to see that men like Cobden and Bright, or,

[15] Hobson, 'A Restatement of Socialist Theory', *Speaker*, 21.10.1905.
[16] [W. Clarke], 'Introductory', *PR*, vol. 1 (1896), 2, 4.
[17] Hobhouse, 'The Ethical Basis of Collectivism' *International Journal of Ethics*, vol. 8 (1898), 139.

again, like Bentham and Mill, who had principles and knew how to apply them, were the real spiritual leaders who moved the masses of social prejudice and political obstruction and made the way plain for reform. The truth is forced upon us that it is precisely the absence of clearly thought-out principles, such as these men understood and applied, that has destroyed the nerve and paralysed the efforts of Liberalism in our own day. The hope for the future of the party of progress must largely depend upon the efforts of thinkers—not thinkers of the study, but thinkers in close contact with the concrete necessities of national life, to restate the fundamental principles of Liberalism in the form which modern circumstances require.[18]

Here are some of the most central themes of the resurgence of liberal thought: the dependence of political action and social progress upon ethical guidelines; the possibility of a core of liberal thought external in source to, and more fundamental in aims than, the Liberal party organization; the concept of a theorist whose ideas are nurtured upon, and directed at, the soil of concrete social phenomena.

The last characteristic was indeed considered by many to be Hobson's outstanding quality. Hobhouse himself wrote that 'Mr. Hobson effects that union of broad principle with concrete fact which is the ideal of all political thinking.'[19] The *Nation*, reviewing Hobson's *The Crisis of Liberalism*, fastened upon Hobson's conception of the thinker as a man with a living and practical function, exercising a deep and lasting influence on the nation.[20] The fact that Hobson has dominated the pages of this study is due to his being by far the most original and penetrating of the new liberal theorists at the turn of the century, one who deserves far greater credit as an outstanding social thinker with a much larger amount of influence than is generally realized.[21] Though his contribution to liberal thought equals, if it does not surpass, that of Hobhouse, he has been underestimated as a social and political philosopher by later generations. That this was not always the case in his time can be seen in the appreciation accorded him by many of his contemporaries. The

[18] Hobhouse, 'England, A Nation', leader, *MG*, 17.12.1904.
[19] Hobhouse, 'Towards a Social Philosophy', *MG*, 2.12.1904.
[20] 'The Re-Statement of Liberalism', *Nation*, 8.1.1910.
[21] A major reason for the overlooking of Hobson's work appears to be the boycott the British academic establishment imposed on him because of his economic theories. See *Confessions of an Economic Heretic* (1938), pp. 30–2, 83–4.

article just quoted mentioned the need for 'an apostolic succession of thinking men who will constantly re-state political principles in terms of the living needs of each generation'. Current liberalism, it believed, was suffering no more from the lack of a Gladstone than of a Mill. Only a few of Hobson's ideas were absorbed into Liberal party programmes. But, as the *Nation* put it, he more than any other man was filling Mill's role in a spirit worthy of the latter: 'More recent years have seen the beginnings of a reconstruction to which Mr Hobson's writings have contributed perhaps more than any single intellectual cause.'[22] Or, as a social philosopher and sociologist acknowledged:

He ... has done more than any other thinker to bring the treatment of economics into close and living relation to the facts of social life ... He is ... more nearly a *social* economist than any other recognised writer; he is also more intelligible, and much more interesting.[23]

Still, it must not be forgotten that the new liberalism was the product of a generation, rather than the creation of outstanding individuals. Its durability and viability as political thought was in its integration in the life-experiences of many of those who combined social involvement and communal activity with intellectual creativity.

On the historical level of interest, this book attempts to probe the changes in liberal mentality prior to the unparalleled activity of the Liberal party in social legislation—a subject which had been a negligible part of the Liberal programme. The concentration on social reform thought is not just a singling out of one aspect of the liberal mentality; it is the nucleus of and the key to the transformation liberalism underwent at the turn of the century. Of central significance was the emergence of the concept of community in liberal thought, not as an appendage forced on it by circumstances, but as a logical development of liberal fundamentals when confronted with the changing needs

---

[22] 'The Re-Statement of Liberalism', *Nation*, 8.1.1910. See also 'The Overplus of Wealth', *Nation*, 29.5.1909 (Review of Hobson's *The Industrial System*).

[23] E. J. Urwick, 'A Social Economist', *Nation*, 5.8.1911. Even a hostile reviewer wrote of Hobson's *The Industrial System*: 'We observe that some attempt has been made to represent Mr. Hobson in the light of the philosopher of the modern Liberal party ... Regarded in that light the book must be highly commended.' ('Industry and Employment', *Edinburgh Review*, vol. 211 (1910), 18.)

of a society. The answers to the perennial question about the causes of collapse of the Liberal party cannot relate to the quality of the ideology available to it. Liberalism was by 1906 intellectually better equipped than any other ideological force to handle the pressing social problems that had at last secured the political limelight.

Seen from this angle, this study also points in the direction of a reassessment of the role of socialism and, more specifically of the Labour party, as the ideological basis of welfare thought and legislation in Britain. It was the new liberalism which essentially provided the successful and viable intellectual solutions to the problems of the day. As a general rule it would be quite incorrect to talk of liberalism in connection with any blatant borrowing of ideas other than the free exchange that exists in any open society. To a large degree the progressive forces developed a similar approach to social questions, nourished by the liberal, rational, ethical, and positivist traditions. To the extent that advanced liberalism differed from the views of organized Socialism, the first usually supplied the remedy which came to answer a concrete and immediately satisfiable need.[24] Liberal influences among many Socialist leaders and intellectuals seem to have been stronger than the reverse,[25] and if liberals adopted ideas which originated outside the liberal mainstream, they were assimilated and transformed with the aim of making them compatible with liberal fundamentals. Once again the under-estimation of liberalism appears to be the result of equating it with the Liberal party, of an aversion to considering ideology outside the aegis of party, and of a fixation with the mid-century liberalism of the utilitarians and the early Mill. Condemning liberalism by relating it to its earlier prototype was a crude method of anti-liberal propaganda used by its opponents at the turn of the century, but later transformed into a myth not refuted by scholarship.

Of major importance to the success of the transformed liberal

[24] As an official liberal pamphlet put it, at the same time testifying to the role of ideas in politics: 'The great thing in politics is to get principles recognized and embodied in laws . . . that is the service that Liberalism has rendered to Labour.' (*What Has the Liberal Government Done for Labour?*, Liberal Publication Dept. (1908).)

[25] See K. O. Morgan, *Keir Hardie, Radical and Socialist* (1975), and R. Barker, 'Socialism and Progressivism in the Political Thought of Ramsay MacDonald', in A. J. A. Morris (ed.), *Edwardian Radicalism 1900–1914* (1974).

ideology was its adept combination of two factors together with liberal tenets. Liberal social reform was the meeting-ground, if not the fusion, of a science and an ethics. As a science it had one root in the utilitarian tradition, humanized by Ruskin, in that it aspired to discover the way of creating the greatest number of happy beings. The second root was in the growing systematic and methodical nature of research into social phenomena, the reliable use of field study and statistics which in the able hands of Booth, Rowntree, and others had changed men's knowledge about their society. The third and not the least important root was in the realization of the significance of biology[26] to the understanding of the human condition. This extended the scope of the study of society as well as assimilating liberal thought into the most important scientific trends of the time. It contributed to liberal social reform a general framework, unifying laws and guiding principles, which reinforced the validity and gave added weight to accepted liberal maxims. Biological theory bridged the gap between science and ethics in that it appeared to confirm empirically progress towards collectivism and co-operation, and the existence of a social entity whose welfare had to be the yardstick of human activity.

On the other hand, the ethical element in liberalism gained new significance not only through scientific 'confirmation', as it were, but through the re-evaluation of the relationship between individual and society. It is no coincidence that positivism and the Ethical Movement were vital nourishers of the new liberalism. Many of the new ideas on society and social reform were formulated in such frameworks, notably the South Place Ethical Society[27] and the Rainbow Circle. The latter was probably a central breeding ground of advanced liberal social thought. Its aim was

to provide a rational and comprehensive view of political and social progress, leading up to a consistent body of political and economic doctrine which could be ultimately formulated in a programme of action, and in that form provide a rallying point for social reformers . . . It is proposed to deal with: (1) the reasons why the old Philosophic Radicalism and the Manchester School of Economics can

[26] And, to a much lesser degree, psychology, though its implications for social policy were as yet miniscule.

[27] Among whose members were Robertson and Hobson.

no longer furnish a ground of action in the political sphere; (2) the transition from this school of thought to the so-called 'New Radicalism' or Collectivist politics of to-day; (3) the bases, ethical, economic and political, of the newer politics, together with the practical applications and inferences arising therefrom in the actual problems before us at the present time.[28]

The membership of this group—which met regularly from 1894 until 1932—shows how well equipped it was to serve, as it no doubt did, as the ideological core of advanced social, and especially liberal social, thought.[29]

Compared to its nineteenth-century antecedent, liberalism before 1914 had changed vastly, but the connection with its past was recognizable. It had come to stress social rather than political reform not only because so many of its political aims had been achieved but because liberals now appreciated that man as social being was the basic concept of political thought. Liberalism was still concerned with the optimal expression and development of the individual, but this was attainable by reflecting the scientific and ethical truth that man could only realize himself in a community, rather than through a human organization tending towards theoretical anarchy. Old Individualist notions were finally discarded in favour of a fusion of individualism and socialism. A new trust emerged in social action via the state—not as necessary evil but as the just and right way of attaining human ends. Personality was considered in varying degrees to be social and had to be expressed as such both in individual conduct and in social institutions. But this realization also pointed the way to a higher qualitative individuality which now seemed to be in reach of ever-wider sections of the population. The improvement of the individual as social individual could be furthered by the cultivation of the specific in each member of society, inasmuch as this was

[28] Samuel Papers, A/10.
[29] Among its members were Hobson, W. Clarke, J. A. M. Macdonald, J. R. MacDonald, G. F. Millin, Samuel, R. Rea, C. P. Trevelyan, P. Alden, G. P. Gooch. Robertson, G. Wallas. Among the occasional members were Haldane, Hammond, Hirst, and E. R. Pease. Discussions were held, e.g., on papers by Samuel on the New Liberalism (1895), Hobson on Individual and State property (1896), the Unemployed (1898), and Collectivism (1908), J. R. MacDonald on the Organisation of Industry (1905), and Robertson on the origins of Socialism (1907). See Rainbow Circle Minutes, British Library of Political and Economic Science, London.

compatible with the good, health, and welfare of the community.

Many liberal values were preserved in modified form. Competition, incentives, and motivation—characteristics of a capitalist society—were considered integral parts of human behaviour but were adapted so as not to impair the welfare of others. Equality of opportunity was extended in conjunction with agreed standards of minima necessary to dignified human life. Gradualism and practicability remained the criteria of political action. Participation and variation were given scientific validity. Terms such as 'unearned increment' and 'the masses versus the classes' were drawn from the liberal tradition and employed as mechanisms which ensured a smooth blending between that heritage and the universalistic orientation towards society that biology and Idealism were reinforcing.

On the other hand, new ideas concerning the network of rights and duties were formulated. Organicism and interconnectedness, the partial fusion of the social and the individual to the benefit of both, reciprocity as an ethical interpretation of mutual responsibility—these were the central themes of the new liberalism. The age-old problems of social life, the tensions between individual and social claims, were of course not resolved at a stroke. But an important step towards their elucidation had been taken by liberals when they realized that individual liberty had to share a place with social welfare as a final human good. The only rational liberty was that conducive to the welfare of all; the only true welfare was the one that acknowledged individual liberty as its indispensable ingredient. Here was the crucial balance at the heart of the new liberalism. The omnipresent ethical element in liberalism was channelled in the direction of a modified concept of social justice. Universal welfare was combined with the recognition of individual needs. And social justice was seen to be in the *interest* of the community.

The ethical factor in social reform became an essential concomitant of what might otherwise have been relegated to the sphere of material improvements in the conditions of living. This was the special achievement of liberal thought: while harnessed to the solution of immediate and concrete problems of an industrial society, it yet transcended the mere issues of economic redistribution by insisting on a change in human social behaviour, in ethical motivation. Pervading liberalism was the awareness of the need for constant action of an optimistic and rational spirituality upon a world which at best was only dimly conscious of ultimate ethical values, values which inevitably eroded under the pressures of political activity dependent upon quantifiable and visible results. The dissemination of ideas became itself part and parcel of liberal social reform, which was directed towards an improvement of the minds of men no less than towards a provision for their bodies. The ideal of a free and self-realizing human will was retained, only adding to its self-consciousness an awareness of its social components. The new liberalism appeared, in Hobson's apt summary,

as a fuller appreciation and realisation of individual liberty contained in the provision of equal opportunities for self-development. But to this individual standpoint must be joined a just apprehension of the social, viz., the insistence that these claims or rights of self-development be adjusted to the sovereignty of social welfare.[30]

On the eve of a cataclysmic world war liberalism had designed a fitting climax to the rational faith in human perfectibility. The twentieth century, host to and victim of ideologies of a very different nature, presented as wholesome successors to a decaying liberalism, is perhaps inadequately equipped to assess the value of its heritage.

[30] Hobson, *The Crisis of Liberalism*, xii.

Select Bibliography

1. UNPUBLISHED SOURCES

A. Private Papers only collections quoted from have been mentioned
In the Bodleian Library, Oxford
 Asquith Papers
In the British Library
 H. Gladstone Papers
In the House of Lords Record Office
 Samuel Papers
In the Beaverbrook Library
 Lloyd George Papers
    B. Official Papers
In the Public Record Office, London
 Cabinet Papers, 1880–1914, Cabinet 37
    C. Newspaper Archives
The Index of Contributors,
Manchester Guardian Office, Manchester

2. PUBLISHED SOURCES

A. Primary works until 1914
a. *Hansard's Parliamentary Debates, 3rd, 4th, and 5th Series*
b. *Newspapers, Periodicals, Yearbooks*
 Albany Review
 Commonwealth
 Contemporary Review
 Daily Chronicle
 Daily News
 Economic Journal
 Economic Review
 Eighty Club Yearbooks 1887–1914
 English Review
 Ethical World
 Eugenics Review
 Fortnightly Review
 Independent Review
 International Journal of Ethics
 Liberal Magazine

Liberal Yearbooks (Liberal Publication Department)
Manchester Guardian
Monthly Review
Nation
National Liberal Club. Political Economy Circle (afterwards Political
and Economic Circle). *Transactions* (1891–1914).
National Liberal Federation. Annual Proceedings 1886–1914
New Liberal Review
New Quarterly
New Review
Nineteenth Century
Progressive Review
Sociological Papers (1905–7)
Sociological Review
South Place Magazine
South Place Monthly List
Speaker
The Times
Tribune
Westminster Gazette
Westminster Review
World's Work

c. Books, Speeches, Pamphlets

Alden, P., *Democratic England.* With an Introduction by Charles F. G.
Masterman (New York, 1912).
——— *The Unemployed. A National Question* (London, 1905).
Asquith, H. H., *Speeches 1892–1908.* Selected and Reprinted from *The
Times* (London, 1908).
——— *The Government and its Work.* Speech on 19.6.1908 (London,
Liberal Publication Dept., 1908).
——— *The Mission of Liberalism.* Speech on 19.7.1901 (London, Liberal
Publication Dept., 1901).
——— *The Three Capital Issues.* Speech on 10.12.1909 (London, 1910).
Barnett, Revd. S. A. and Mrs, *Practicable Socialism. Essays on Social
Reform* (London, 1888; 2nd ed., revised and enlarged, 1894).
——— (Canon) and Mrs., *Towards Social Reform* (London, 1909).
Bateson, W., *Biological Fact and the Structure of Society* (Oxford, 1912).
Belloc, H., *The Servile State* (London, 1912).
Beveridge, W. H., *Unemployment. A Problem of Industry* (London, 1909).
Blease, W. L., *A Short History of English Liberalism* (London, 1913).
Bliss, W. D. P. (ed.), *The Encyclopedia of Social Reform* (New York,
1897).

Bliss, W. D. P. and Binder, R. M. (eds.), *The New Encyclopedia of Social Reform* (New York and London, 1908).
Booth, C., *Life and Labour of the People in London* (London and New York, 1902).
Booth, W., *In Darkest England and the Way Out* (London, 1890).
Bosanquet, B. (ed.), *Aspects of the Social Problem* (London, 1895).
—— *The Philosophical Theory of the State* (London, 1899; 3rd ed., 1920).
—— *The Social Criterion: or, How to Judge of Proposed Social Reforms* (Edinburgh and London, 1907).
Bradlaugh, C., *The Radical Programme* (London, 1885).
Bray, R. A., *The Town Child* (London, 1907).
Burns, J., *The Liberal Government and the Condition of the People*. Speech at Bradford, 11.11.1912 (London, Liberal Publication Dept., 1912).
Burrows, H., and Hobson, J. A. (eds.), *William Clarke. A Collection of his Writings* (London, 1908).
Campbell-Bannerman, H., *Liberal Policy and Liberal Principles*. Speech on 8.3.1899 (London, Liberal Publication Dept., 1899).
—— *Speeches*. Selected and Reprinted from *The Times* (London, 1908).
Chamberlain, J., *The Radical Platform* (Edinburgh, 1885).
Churchill, W., *For Liberalism and Free Trade* (Dundee, 1908).
Churchill, W. S., *Liberalism and the Social Problem* (London, 1909).
Churchill, W., *The People's Rights* (London, 1910).
Coit, S. (ed.), *Ethical Democracy: Essays in Social Dynamics* (London, 1900).
Dicey, A. V., *Lectures on the Relation between Law and Public Opinion in England* (London, 1905).
Dickinson, G. L., *Justice and Liberty* (London, 1907).
Dyer, H., *Christianity and the Social Problem* (Glasgow, 1890).
—— *The Evolution of Industry* (London, 1895).
—— *The Foundations of Social Politics* (Glasgow, 1889).
Eighty Club, Members of the, *The Liberal View* (London, 1904).
Fabian Essays (with a New Introduction by Asa Briggs (London, 1962)).
Ferri, E., *Socialism and Positive Science Darwin—Spencer—Marx* (London, 1906).
Gardner, L. (ed.), *Converging Views of Social Reform* (London, 1913).
Gaston, E. P. (ed.), *British Supplement to the new Encyclopedia of Social Reform* (London and New York, 1908).
George, D. Lloyd, *Better Times. Speeches* (London, 1910).
—— *The Insurance of the People* (London, 1911).
—— *The People's Budget* (London, 1909).
—— *The People's Insurance* (London, 1911).
—— *The State and the People* (London, 1913).

George, H., *Progress and Poverty* (London, 1881).

Gibbon, I. G., *Unemployment Insurance*. With a Preface by Professor L. T. Hobhouse (London, 1911).

Gore, C. (ed.), *Property, Its Duties and Rights* (London, 1913).

Graham, W., *The Social Problem: In Its Economical, Moral, and Political Aspects* (London, 1886).

Gray, B. Kirkman, *Philanthropy and the State, or Social Politics* (London, 1908).

Green, T. H., *Lectures on the Principles of Political Obligation* (London, 1941).

—— *Liberal Legislation and Freedom of Contract* (Oxford, 1881).

—— *Prolegomena to Ethics* (Oxford, 1924 edn.).

Hammond, J. L. (ed.), *Towards a Social Policy, or Suggestions for Constructive Reform* (London, [1905]).

Hand, J. E. (ed.), *Good Citizenship* (London, 1899).

—— *Science in Public Affairs* (London, 1906).

Hobhouse, L. T., *Democracy and Reaction* (London, 1904).

—— *Development and Purpose* (London, 1913).

—— *Liberalism* (London, 1911; reprinted in Galaxy Books, New York, 1964).

—— *Mind in Evolution* (London, 1901).

—— *Social Evolution and Political Theory* (Columbia U.P., New York, 1911).

—— *Sociology and Philosophy. A Centenary Collection of Essays and Articles* (London, 1966).

Hobhouse, L. T., *The Labour Movement* (London, 1893).

—— *The Metaphysical Theory of the State* (London, 1918).

Hobson, J. A., *A Modern Outlook* (London, 1910).

—— *Imperialism: a Study* (London, 1902; revised ed. 1938).

—— *John Ruskin Social Reformer* (London, 1898).

—— *Problems of Poverty* (London, 1891).

—— *The Crisis of Liberalism: New Issues of Democracy* (London, 1909).

—— *The Evolution of Modern Capitalism* (London, 1894; 4th ed., London, 1926).

—— *The Industrial System. An Inquiry into Earned and Unearned Income* (London, 1909).

—— *The Problem of the Unemployed* (London, 1896).

—— *The Science of Wealth* (London, 1911).

—— *The Social Problem* (London, 1901).

—— *Traffic in Treason* (London, 1914).

—— *Work and Wealth* (New York, 1914).

Hunt, Revd. W. (ed.), *Preachers from the Pew* (London, n.d. [1906]).

Huxley, T. H., *Evolution and Ethics* (London, 1893).

—— *Social Diseases and Worse Remedies* (London, 1891).

Jevons, W. S., *The State in Relation to Labour* (London, 1882).
Jones, H., *The Working Faith of the Social Reformer and other Essays* (London, 1910).
Kidd, B., *Principles of Western Civilisation* (London, 1902).
—— *Social Evolution* (London, 1894).
Kirkup, T., *A History of Socialism* (3rd ed., London, 1906).
—— *An Inquiry into Socialism* (London, 1887).
Loch, C. S., *Charity and Social Life* (London, 1910).
MacDonald, J. R., *Socialism and Government*, 2 vols. (London, 1909).
—— *Socialism and Society* (London, 1905).
Mackay, T. (ed.), *A Plea for Liberty* (London, 1891).
—— *Methods of Social Reform. Essays Critical and Constructive* (London, 1896).
Mackenzie, J. S., *An Introduction to Social Philosophy* (Glasgow, 1890).
Macnamara, T. J., *The Great Insurance Act. A Year's Experience* (London, 1913).
Masterman, C. F. G., *In Peril of Change* (London, 1905).
—— *The Condition of England* (London, 1909).
[—— (ed.)], *The Heart of the Empire* (London, 1901).
—— *Youth and Liberalism* (Young Liberal Pamphlets, 16.2.1911).
—— and Hodgson, W. B., *To Colonise England. A Plea for Policy* (London, 1907).
Mill, J. S., *On Liberty* (London, 1910).
—— *Principles of Political Economy*, ed. by D. Winch (Penguin Books, Harmondsworth, 1970).
—— *Utilitarianism* (London, 1910 edn.).
[Millin, G. F.] *The Social Horizon* (London, 1892).
Money, L. G. Chiozza, *A Nation Insured. The National Insurance Bill Explained* (London, 1911).
—— *Insurance Versus Poverty.* With an Introduction by the Rt. Hon. D. Lloyd George, M.P. (London, 1912).
—— *Riches and Poverty* (London, 1905).
—— *The Nation's Wealth. Will it Endure?* (London, 1914).
Morley, J., *The Liberal Programme* (London, 1894).
National Liberal Club. Collection of Election Addresses and Leaflets.
Parker, P. L. (ed.), *Character and Life* (London, 1912).
100 Points in Liberal Policy and of the Liberal Record (London, Liberal Publication Dept., 1909).
Prescott, C. W. B., *Young Liberalism* (Young Liberal Pamphlets, 28.2.1912).
Rae, J., *Contemporary Socialism* (London, 1884).
Rea, R., *Social Reform versus Socialism* (London, 1912).
Rees, J. A., *Our Aims and Objects* (Young Liberal Pamphlets, September 1903).

Reid, A. (ed.), *The New Liberal Programme*. Contributed by Representatives of the Liberal Party (London, 1886).
—— (ed.), *Why I am a Liberal* (London, n.d. [1885]).
Ritchie, D. G., *Darwinism and Politics* (London, 1889).
—— *Darwin and Hegel* (London, 1893).
—— *Natural Rights* (London, 1894).
—— *Philosophical Studies*, edited with a Memoir by R. Latta (London, 1905).
—— *Studies in Political and Social Ethics* (London, 1902).
—— *The Moral Function of the State* (London, 1887).
—— *The Principles of State Interference* (London, n.d. [1891]).
Robbins, A. F., *Practical Politics or the Liberalism of To-day* (London, 1888).
Robertson, J. M., *Modern Humanists* (London, 1891).
—— *The Eight Hours Question* (London, 1893).
—— *The Fallacy of Saving* (London, 1892).
—— *The Future of Liberalism* (Bradford, n.d. [1895]).
—— *The Great Budget* (London, Liberal Publication Department, 1910).
—— *The Meaning of Liberalism* (London, 1912).
—— *The Mission of Liberalism* (Young Liberal Pamphlets, 20.1. 1908).
Rosebery, Lord, *Municipal and Social Reform* (London, 21.3.1894).
Rowntree, B. Seebohm, *Poverty: A Study of Town Life* (London and New York, 1901).
Rowntree, J. and Sherwell, A., *The Temperance Problem and Social Reform* (London, 1899: revised ed. 1900).
Samuel, H., *Liberalism. An Attempt to State the Principles and Proposals of Contemporary Liberalism in England*. With an Introduction by the Rt. Hon. H. H. Asquith, K.C., M.P. (London, 1902).
—— *Village Reform. Cottages and the Land* (London, n.d. [1899]).
Sidgwick, H., *The Elements of Politics* (3rd ed., London, 1908; 1st ed., 1891).
Six Oxford Men, *Essays in Liberalism* (London, 1897).
Spencer, H., *The Man Versus the State* (edited with an Introduction by D. Macrae, Penguin Books, Harmondsworth, 1969). First published 1884.
—— *The Study of Sociology* (London, 1907 edn.).
Spender, J. A., *The State and Pensions in Old Age*. With an Introduction by Arthur H. D. Acland, M.P. (London, 1892).
The Industrial Unrest and the Living Wage. With an Introduction by the Rev. William Temple, M.A. Converging Views of Social Reform, No. 2 (London, 1914).
Toynbee, A., *Lectures on the Industrial Revolution of the Eighteenth Century in England* (London, 1884).

Unemployment Insurance, Liberal Publication Department, (London, 1909).

Villiers, B. [F. J. Shaw], *Modern Democracy. A Study in Tendencies* (London, 1912).

—— *The Opportunity of Liberalism* (London, 1904).

—— *The Socialist Movement in England* (London, 1908).

Wallas, G., *Men and Ideas* (London, 1940).

Walter, H. A., *Die neuere englische Sozialpolitik. Mit einem Geleitwort des englischen Schatzkanzlers D. Lloyd George* (München und Berlin, 1914).

Waxweiler, E. (ed.), *The Policy of Social Reform in England* (Brussels, 1913).

Wells, H. G., *The New Machiavelli* (London, 1911; Penguin Books, Harmondsworth, 1966).

What Has the Liberal Government Done for Labour? Liberal Publication Department (London, 1908).

Why the Insurance Act was made compulsory and why it should remain compulsory, Liberal Publication Department (London, 1914).

Woods, R. A., *English Social Movements* (London, 1892).

d. Articles

Adkins, W. R. D., 'Liberalism and the Land', *CR*, vol. 103 (1913), 457–72.

Allen, G., 'Individualism and Socialism', *CR*, vol. 55 (1889), 730–41.

Allen, J. E., 'Liberalism and Local Veto', *IR*, vol. 11 (1906), 338–44.

Annand, J., 'The Demoralisation of Liberalism', *NR*, vol. 13 (1895), 248–56.

Anon., 'A Plea for a Programme', *IR*, vol. 1 (1903), 1–27.

—— 'Liberalism Philosophically Considered', *WR*, vol. 132 (1889), 337–47.

—— 'On Which Side Art Thou?', *WR*, vol. 152 (1899), 369–82.

—— 'Parties and Principles', *Monthly Review*, vol. 1 (1900), 25–34.

—— 'The Government and its Opportunities', *IR*, vol. 8 (1906), 2–13.

—— 'The Reform of Taxation', *IR*, vol. 3 (1904), 1–25.

Armsden, J., 'First Principles of Social Reform', *WR*, vol. 169 (1908), 639–46.

Atherley-Jones, L. A., 'Liberalism and Social Reform: A Warning', *NR*, vol. 9 (1893), 629–35.

—— 'Liberal Prospects: Mr. Chamberlain's Proposals', *New Liberal Review*, vol. 6 (1903–4), 486–504.

—— 'The New Liberalism', *NC*, vol. 26 (1889), 186–93.

—— 'The Story of the Labour Party', *NC*, vol. 60 (1906), 576–86.

Ball, S., 'A Plea for Liberty: A Criticism', *ER*, vol. I (1891), 327–47.

Ball, S., 'Individualism and Socialism', *ER*, vol. 8 (1898), 229–35.
—— 'Socialism and Individualism: A Challenge and an Eirenicon', *ER*, vol. 7 (1897), 490–520.
Barnett, S. A., 'Charity Up-to-Date', *CR*, vol. 101 (1912), 225–31.
—— 'Distress in East London', *NC*, vol. 20 (1886), 678–92.
—— 'Our Present Discontents', *NC*, vol. 73 (1913), 328–37.
—— 'Public Feeding of Children', *IR*, vol. 6 (1905), 154–62.
—— 'Sensationalism in Social Reform', *NC*, vol. 19 (1886), 280–90.
—— 'Social Reform', *IR*, vol. I (1903–4), 28–38.
—— 'The Unemployed', *FR*, vol. 54 (1893), 741–9.
Barrow, F. H., 'Free Meals for Underfed Children: A Means to an End', *Monthly Review*, vol. 19 (1905), 1–16.
Benson, G. V., 'The Social Problem', *WR*, vol. 128 (1887), 610–19.
Beveridge, W. H., 'Labour Exchanges and the Unemployed', *Economic Journal*, vol. 17 (1907), 66–81.
—— 'The Problem of the Unemployed', *Sociological Papers* (1906), 323–31.
Brabrook, E., 'Old Age Pensions. I. The Dangers of the Non-Contributory Principle', *SR*, vol. I (1908), 291–4.
Bradlaugh, C., 'The Individualist Ideal: A Reply. II—Politics', *NR*, vol. 4 (1891), 109–18.
Bray, R. A., 'Science and the Social Problem', *Commonwealth*, vol. 8 (1903), 121–3.
Burns, J., 'The Labour Question—The Unemployed', *NC*, vol. 32 (1892), 845–63.
Buxton, C. R., 'A Vision of England', *IR*, vol. 7 (1905), 149–57.
Caird, M., 'The Survival of the Fittest', *SPM*, vol. 4 (1899), 97–101; 113–17.
Chamberlain, J., 'Favorable Aspects of State Socialism', *North American Review*, vol. 152 (1891), 534–48.
—— 'The Labour Question', *NC*, vol. 32 (1892), 677–710.
Champion, H. H., 'The Labour "Platform" at the Next Election', *NC*, vol. 30 (1891), 1036–42.
[Clarke, W.] 'Introductory', *PR*, vol. I (1896), 1–9.
Clarke, W., 'The Influence of Socialism on English Politics', *Political Science Quarterly*, vol. 3 (1888), 549–71.
—— 'The Limits of Collectivism', *CR*, vol. 63 (1893), 24–43.
Clay, A., 'Free Meals for Underfed Children. A Means to an End—A Reply', *Monthly Review*, vol. 20 (1905), 94–104.
Columbine, W. B., 'Social Problems', *WR*, vol. 151 (1899), 375–80.
Cook, E. T., 'Ruskin and the New Liberalism', *New Liberal Review*, vol. I (1901), 18–25.
Cox, H., 'The Budget of 1909', *NC*, vol. 65 (1909), 909–24.
—— 'The Eight Hours Question', *NC*, vol. 26 (1889), 21–34.

Cox, H., 'The Taxation of Land Values', *NC*, vol. 65 (1909), 191–205.
C[rossfield], H., 'The Ethical Movement and the New Liberalism', *SPM*, vol. 7 (1902), 181–5.
Darnton-Fraser, H. J., 'A Programme of Real Social Reform', *WR*, vol. 177 (1912), 117–25; 237–44.
Davis, R. G., 'Individualism and Socialism, and Liberty', *WR*, vol. 178 (1912), 144–51.
—— 'New Tendencies in Political Thinking', *WR*, vol. 173 (1910), 505–10.
—— 'The Evolutionary Trend of British Political Parties', *WR*, vol. 157 (1902), 514–18.
Dawson, W. H., 'Insurance Legislation: The Larger View', *FR*, vol. 89 (1911), 534–47.
Dell, R. E., 'Cleaning the Slate', *Monthly Review*, vol. 7 (1902), 58–69.
Dicey, E., 'The Plea of a Mal-Content Liberal', *FR*, vol. 38 (1885), 463–77.
Didden, R., 'Individualism or Collectivism? Which Way Does Evolution Point?', *WR*, vol. 149 (1898), 655–66.
Dilke, C. W., 'A Radical Programme', *NR*, vol. 3 (1890), 1–14; 157–67; 250–6; 404–13.
—— 'John Stuart Mill 1869–1873', *Cosmopolis*, vol. 5 (1897), 629–41.
Dolman, F., 'Political Economy and Social Reform: A Protest', *WR*, vol. 133 (1890), 634–42.
Dyer, H., 'The Future of Politics', *WR*, vol. 145 (1896), 1–13.
Ellis, H., 'Individualism and Socialism', *CR*, vol. 101 (1912), 519–28.
Fabian Society, The, 'To Your Tents, Oh Israel!', *FR*, vol. 54 (1893), 569–89.
Fairfax Cholmeley, H. C., 'To Replace the Old Order', *IR*, vol. 4 (1904), 335–48.
Farrar, F. W. (Archdeacon), 'Social Problems and Remedies', *FR*, vol. 43 (1888), 350–63.
Fisher, F. V., 'Social Democracy and Liberty', *WR*, vol. 141 (1894), 643–51.
Fremantle, W. H., 'Individualists and Socialists', *NC*, vol. 41 (1897), 311–24.
Gardiner, A. G., 'The Social Policy of the Government', *CR*, vol. 101 (1912), 380–90.
Godard, J. G., 'The Liberal Débâcle', *WR*, vol. 158 (1902), 597–620.
Gray, M. I., 'The Present Crisis in Social Reform', *ER*, vol. 23 (1913), 301–9.
Greenwood, F., 'The Revolt of Labour', *NR*, vol. 4 (1891), 41–51.
Hake, A. E., 'The Coming Individualism' in *National Liberal Club. Political and Economic Circle*, Transactions, vol. 3 (London, 1901), 1–14.

Haldane, R. B., 'Social Problems' in *Eighty Club Yearbook* (1892).

—— 'The Eight Hours Question', *CR*, vol. 57 (1890), 240–55.

—— 'The Liberal Creed', *CR*, vol. 54 (1888), 461–74.

—— 'The Liberal Party and its Prospects', *CR*, vol. 53 (1888), 145–60.

—— 'The New Liberalism', *PR*, vol. I (1896), 133–43.

Hammond, J. L., 'The Opportunity of the Next Government', *IR*, vol. 5 (1905), 141–9.

Hardie, J. Keir and MacDonald, J. R., 'The Liberal Collapse. The Independent Labour Party's Programme', *NC*, vol. 45 (1899), 20–38.

Harrison, F., 'The Condition of England', *SR*, vol. 2 (1909), 396–400.

Hirst, F. W., 'Individualism and Socialism', *ER*, vol. 8 (1898), 225–9.

Hoare, A., 'Liberalism in the Twentieth Century', *World's Work*, vol. I (1902–3), 85–8.

Hobhouse, L. T., 'The Contending Forces', *English Review*, vol. 4 (1909–10), 359–71.

—— 'The Ethical Basis of Collectivism', *International Journal of Ethics*, vol. 8 (1898), 137–56.

—— 'The Prospects of Liberalism', *CR*, vol. 93 (1908), 349–58.

Hobson, J. A., 'A Living Wage', *Commonwealth*, vol. I (1896), 128–9.

—— 'A New Theory of Work', *British Friend*, vol. 13 (1904), 253–4.

—— 'A Possible Programme for a Liberal Party', *SPM*, vol. 6 (1901), 91.

—— 'Charity as an Instrument of Social Reform', *SPM*, vol. 14 (1909), 161–3.

—— 'Considering the Poor', *SPM*, vol. 14 (1909), 100–2.

—— 'Eugenics as an Art of Social Progress', *SPM*, vol. 14 (1909), 168–70.

—— 'Herbert Spencer', *SPM*, vol. 9 (1904), 49–55.

—— 'Mr. Kidd's "Social Evolution"', *American Journal of Sociology*, vol. I (1895), 299–312.

—— 'Old-Age Pensions. II. The Responsibility of the State to the Aged Poor', *SR*, vol. I (1908), 295–9.

—— 'Political Ethics of Socialism', *SPM*, vol. 13 (1908), 128–31.

—— 'Ruskin and Democracy', *CR*, vol. 81 (1902), 103–12.

—— 'State Interference', *SPM*, vol. 13 (1908), 78–9.

—— 'Syndicalism', *South Place Monthly List* (July, September, October 1912).

—— 'The Approaching Abandonment of Free Trade', *FR*, vol. 71 (1902), 434–44.

—— 'The Economics of the Temperance Movement', *Commonwealth*, vol. I (1896), 209–11.

—— 'The Ethics of the Licensing Bill', *SPM*, vol. 13 (1908), 171–4.

Hobson, J. A., 'The Extension of Liberalism', *English Review*, vol. 3 (1909), 673–86.
—— 'The General Election of 1910', *SR*, vol. 3 (1910), 105–17.
—— 'The Industrial Situation and the Principle of a Minimum Wage', *South Place Monthly List* (April, May 1912).
—— 'The Influence of Henry George in England', *FR*, vol. 62 (1897), 835–44.
—— 'The New Aristocracy of Mr. Wells', *CR*, vol. 89 (1906), 487–97.
—— 'The Population Question. Pt. II', *Commonwealth*, vol. 2 (1897), 170–2.
—— 'The Re-Statement of Democracy', *CR*, vol. 81 (1902), 262–72.
—— 'The Significance of the Budget', *English Review*, vol. 2 (1909), 794–805.
—— 'The Taxation of Monopolies', *IR*, vol. 9 (1906), 20–33.
—— 'The World We Make', *SPM*, vol. 12 (1907), 82–3.
Holland, H. S. 'Socialism and Society', *Commonwealth*, vol. 11 (1906), 89–92.
—— 'The Church of God and Social Work', *ER*, vol. 5 (1895), 1–18.
—— 'The Right to Work', *Commonwealth*, vol. 14 (1909), 65–7.
Holms, J. D., 'Is There "A New Liberalism"?', *WR*, vol. 134 (1890), 237–50.
Huxley, T. H., 'Administrative Nihilism', *FR*, vol. 10 (1871), 525–43.
Kidd, B., 'Social Evolution', *NC*, vol. 37 (1895), 226–40.
Latham, E., 'A Negative Ideal', *ER*, vol. 22 (1912), 415–21.
Liberal-Conservative, A, 'Mr. Morley and the New Radicalism', *NR*, vol. 1 (1889), 612–18.
Lightbody, W. M., 'Socialism and Social Reform', *WR*, vol. 167 (1907), 289–94.
—— 'The State and Parental Responsibility', *WR*, vol. 163 (1905), 288–93.
—— 'The State and the Children', *ER*, vol. 17 (1907), 435–9.
Lilly, W. S., 'Illiberal Liberalism', *FR*, vol. 58 (1895), 641–61.
Low, S., 'Darwinism and Politics', *FR*, vol. 86 (1909), 519–33.
MacDonagh, O., 'The Nineteenth-Century Revolution in Government: A Reappraisal', *Historical Journal*, vol. 1 (1958), 52–67.
Macdonald, J. A. Murray, 'The Problem of the Unemployed', *NR*, vol. 9 (1893), 561–77.
MacDonald, J. R., 'Sweating—Its Cause and Cure', *IR*, vol. 2 (1904), 72–85.
—— 'The Labour Party and Its Policy', *IR*, vol. 8 (1906), 261–9.
Mackay, T., 'Politics and the Poor Law', *FR*, vol. 57 (1895), 408–22.
Macnamara, T. J., 'In Corpore Sano', *CR*, vol. 87 (1905), 238–48.
—— 'The Great Insurance Act', *CR*, vol. 102 (1912), 153–64.

Massingham, H. W., 'Essays in Liberalism', *Commonwealth*, vol. 2 (1897), 162–3.
—— 'Liberalism—New Style?', *NR*, vol. 7 (1892), 454–65.
—— 'Wanted, A New Charter', *NR*, vol. 4 (1891), 255–66.
—— 'What Mr. Gladstone Ought to Do. III', *FR*, vol. 53 (1893), 271–5.
Masterman, C. F. G., 'Causes and Cures of Poverty', *Albany Review*, vol. 2 (1907–8), 531–47.
—— 'Homes for the People. The Present Position in London', *Commonwealth*, vol. 6 (1901), 156–8.
—— 'Liberalism and Labour', *NC*, vol. 60 (1906), 706–18.
—— 'Politics in Transition', *NC*, vol. 63 (1908), 1–17.
—— 'The Next Step', *Commonwealth*, vol. 6 (1901), 29–31.
—— 'The Outlook for Social Reform', *IR*, vol. 7 (1905), 132–48.
—— 'The Problem of the Unemployed', *IR*, vol. 4 (1904–5), 553–71.
—— 'The Unemployed', *CR*, vol. 89 (1906), 106–20.
—— 'The Unemployed. A Hopeful Outlook', *Commonwealth*, vol. 10 (1905), 361–4.
—— 'Towards a Civilisation', *IR*, vol. 2 (1904), 497–517.
McCleary, G. F., 'The State as Over-Parent', *Albany Review*, vol. 2 (1907), 46–59.
Mill, J. S., 'Chapters on Socialism', *FR*, vol. 25 (1879), 217–37; 513–30.
Millin, G. F., 'The New Liberalism', *FR*, vol. 69 (1901), 634–42.
Money, L. G. Chiozza, 'Liberalism, Socialism, and the Master of Elibank', *IR*, vol. 11 (1906), 9–14.
—— 'Taxation and Social Reform', *Commonwealth*, vol. 11 (1906), 276–8.
Morley, J., 'Liberalism and Social Reforms', in *Eighty Club Yearbook* (1889).
Moulton, J. Fletcher, 'Old-Age Pensions', *FR*, vol. 51 (1892), 463–77.
Muirhead, J. H., 'Liberty—Equality—Fraternity', *SR*, vol. 3 (1910), 197–204.
Paley, G. A., 'Biology and Politics', *New Quarterly*, vol. 1 (1907), 121–34.
Pigou, A. C., 'The Principle of the Minimum Wage', *NC*, vol. 73 (1913), 644–58.
Radical of '85, A, 'Liberalism Without Ideas: A Few Notes', *WR*, vol. 169 (1908), 137–50.
Rae, J., 'State-Socialism', *CR*, vol. 54 (1888), 224–45; 378–92.
—— 'State Socialism and Popular Right', *CR*, vol. 58 (1890), 876–90.
—— 'State Socialism and Social Reform', *CR*, vol. 58 (1890), 435–54.
Rashdall, H., 'The Rights of the Individual. III', *ER*, vol. 6 (1896), 317–33.

Ritchie, D. G., 'Social Evolution', *International Journal of Ethics*, vol. 6 (1896), 165–81.

Robertson, J. M., 'Ethics and Politics', *SPM*, vol. 8 (1902), 42–5.

—— 'The Ethics of Taxation', *SPM*, vol. 14 (1909), 164–6.

—— 'The Right to Work', *SPM*, vol. 14 (1909), 52–3.

Rogers, J. Guinness, 'Is the Liberal Party in Collapse?', *NC*, vol. 43 (1898), 135–53.

—— 'The Middle Class and the New Liberalism', *NC*, vol. 26 (1889), 710–20.

Rosenbaum, S., 'The Budget and Social Revolution', *NC*, vol. 66 (1909), 158–67.

Russell, G. W. E., 'The New Liberalism: A Response', *NC*, vol. 26 (1889), 492–9.

Samuel, H., 'The Independent Labour Party', *PR*, vol. 1 (1896), 255–9.

—— 'The Village of the Future', *IR*, vol. 3 (1904), 391–404.

Seton-Karr, H., 'The Radical Party and Social Reform', *NC*, vol. 68 (1910), 1119–33.

Shaw, G. B., 'What Mr. Gladstone Ought to Do. IV', *FR*, vol. 53 (1893), 276–80.

Socialist Radical, A, 'Mr. Morley and the New Radicalism', *NR*, vol. 1 (1889), 604–11.

Spender, H., 'The Government and Old-Age Pensions', *CR*, vol. 93 (1908), 94–107.

Spender, J. A., 'Why I am a Liberal', *New Liberal Review*, vol. 4 (1902–3), 470–86.

Stephen, L., 'The Good Old Cause', *NC*, vol. 51 (1902), 11–23.

Sturge, M. Carta, 'Kidd's "Social Evolution"', *Commonwealth*, vol. 1 (1896), 231–3.

Thomasson, F., 'Political Principles', *WR*, vol. 155 (1901), 366–9.

Touchstone, 'Will the Liberals Repent?', *WR*, vol. 151 (1899), 606–14.

Wallace, R., 'The New Liberalism', *PR*, vol. 1 (1896), 143–7.

Webb, S., 'Lord Rosebery's Escape from Houndsditch', *NC*, vol. 50 (1901), 366–86.

—— 'Modern Social Movements', *The Cambridge Modern History of the World*, XII (Cambridge, 1910).

—— 'The Difficulties of Individualism', *Economic Journal*, vol. 1 (1891), 360–81.

—— 'The Policy of the National Minimum', *IR*, vol. 3 (1904), 161–78.

—— 'What Mr. Gladstone Ought to Do. V', *FR*, vol. 53 (1893), 281–7.

Whittaker, T. P., 'A Minimum Wage for Home Workers', *NC*, vol. 64 (1908), 507–24.

B. *Autobiography and Biography*

Asquith, Earl of Oxford and, *Memories and Reflections* (London, 1928).
Asquith, M., *The Autobiography of Margot Asquith* (Penguin Books, 1936).
Atherley-Jones, L. A., *Looking Back* (London, 1925).
Ball, O. H., *Sidney Ball. Memories and Impressions of 'An Ideal Don'* (Oxford, 1923).
Beveridge, Lord (W. H.), *Power and Influence* (London, 1953).
Bowle, J., *Viscount Samuel. A Biography* (London, 1957).
Braithwaite, W. J., *Lloyd George's Ambulance Wagon*. Edited, with an Introduction by Sir Henry N. Bunbury, K.C.B. and with a commentary by Richard Titmuss (London, 1957).
Churchill, R. S., *Winston S. Churchill. Vol. II Young Statesman 1901–1914* (London, 1967).
Churchill, W. S., *Great Contemporaries* (London, 1937), reprinted 1965.
de Bunsen, V., *Charles Roden Buxton. A Memoir* (London, 1948).
Gwynn, S., and Tuckwell, G., *The Life of the Right Hon. Sir Charles Dilke*, 2 vols. (London, 1917).
Haldane, R. B., *Autobiography* (London, 1929).
Hammond, J. L., *C. P. Scott of the Manchester Guardian* (London, 1934).
Hirst, F. W., *In the Golden Days* (London, 1947).
Hobson, J. A., *Confessions of an Economic Heretic* (London, 1938).
—— and Ginsberg, M., *L. T. Hobhouse* (London, 1931).
Jenkins, R., *Asquith* (London, 1967).
—— *Sir Charles Dilke. A Victorian Tragedy* (London, 1968).
Keynes, J. M., *Essays in Biography* (London, 1951).
Masterman, L., *C. F. G. Masterman. A Biography* (London, 1939).
Mill, J. S., *Autobiography* (Oxford U.P., 1924).
Milner, A., *Arnold Toynbee. A Reminiscence* (London, 1895).
Muirhead, J. H., *Reflections by a Journeyman in Philosophy* (London, 1942).
Owen, F., *Tempestuous Journey. Lloyd George, his Life and Times* (London, 1954).
Samuel, Viscount (H.), *Memoirs* (London, 1945).
Spender, J. A., and Asquith, C., *The Life of Lord Oxford and Asquith*, 2 vols. (London, 1932).
Webb, B., *My Apprenticeship* (London, n.d. [1926]).
—— *Our Partnership* (London, 1948).

C. *Secondary*

a. Books and Monographs

Abrams, P., *The Origins of British Sociology 1834–1914* (University of Chicago Press, 1968).

Annan, N. G., *Leslie Stephen: His Thought and Character in Relation to his Time* (Harvard U.P., 1952).

Annan, N., *The Curious Strength of Positivism in English Political Thought* (L. T. Hobhouse Memorial Trust Lecture No. 28, London, 1959).

Anschutz, R., *The Philosophy of J. S. Mill* (Oxford, 1953).

Ausubel, H., *In Hard Times. Reformers Among the Late Victorians* (New York, 1960).

Barker, E., *Political Thought in England 1848 to 1914* (London, 1963).

Beales, H. L., *The Making of Social Policy* (L. T. Hobhouse Memorial Trust Lecture No. 15, London, 1946).

Beer, S. H., *Modern British Politics* (London, 1969).

Bowle, J., *Politics and Opinion in the 19th Century* (London, 1954).

Brailsford, H. N., *The Life-Work of J.A. Hobson* (L. T. Hobhouse Memorial Trust Lecture No. 17, London, 1948).

Briggs, A., *Social Thought and Social Action. A Study of the Work of Seebohm Rowntree 1871–1954* (London, 1961).

Brinton, C., *English Political Thought in the 19th Century* (Harper Torchbooks, New York, 1962).

Brown, K. D. (ed.), *Essays in Anti-Labour History* (London, 1974).

Bruce, M., *The Coming of the Welfare State* (4th ed., London, 1968).

Bullock, A., and Shock, M. (eds.), *The Liberal Tradition* (Oxford, 1956).

Burrow, J. W., *Evolution and Society. A Study in Victorian Social Theory* (Cambridge U.P., 1966).

Carter, H., *The Social Theories of L. T. Hobhouse* (University of North Carolina Press, 1927).

Checkland, S. G., *The Rise of Industrial Society in England 1815–1885* (London, 1964).

Cheyney, E. P., *Modern English Reform. From Individualism to Socialism* (University of Pennsylvania Press, 1931. Reprinted in Perpetua Books, New York, 1962).

Clarke, P. F., *Lancashire and the New Liberalism* (Cambridge U.P., 1971).

Cole, G. D. H., *British Working Class Politics 1832–1914* (London, 1946).

Cole, M. (ed.), *The Webbs and their Work* (London, 1949).

Cox, C. B. and Dyson, A. E. (eds.), *The Twentieth Century Mind. I. 1900–1918* (Oxford U.P., 1972).

de Ruggiero, G., *The History of European Liberalism* (Boston, 1959).

de Schweinitz, K., *England's Road to Social Security* (University of Pennsylvania Press, 1943. Reprinted in Perpetua Books, New York, 1961).

Douglas, R., *The History of the Liberal Party 1895–1970* (London, 1971).

Emy, H. V., *Liberals, Radicals, and Social Politics 1892–1914* (Cambridge U.P., 1973).

Ensor, R. C. K., *England 1870–1914* (Oxford, 1936).

Fletcher, R., *Auguste Comte and the Making of Sociology* (Auguste Comte Memorial Trust Lecture 7, London, 1966).

Ford, P. and G., *A Breviate of Parliamentary Papers, 1900–1916: The Foundation of the Welfare State* (London, 1957).

Fyfe, H., *The British Liberal Party* (London, 1928).

Gilbert, B. B., *The Evolution of National Insurance in Great Britain. The Origins of the Welfare State* (London, 1966).

Ginsberg, M., *Evolution and Progress* (London, 1961).

—— (ed.), *Law and Opinion in England in the 20th Century* (London, 1959).

—— *Reason and Unreason in Society* (London, 1947).

Girvetz, H. K., *From Wealth to Welfare: The Evolution of Liberalism* (Stanford, 1950).

Gulley, E. E., *Joseph Chamberlain and English Social Politics* (New York, Columbia University, 1926).

Halévy, E., *A History of the English People in the Nineteenth Century*, vols. 5, 6 (London, 1961).

—— *The Growth of Philosophic Radicalism* (London, 1972).

Hamburger, J., *Intellectuals in Politics: John Stuart Mill and the Philosophical Radicals* (Yale U.P., 1965).

Hamer, D. A., *John Morley. Liberal Intellectual in Politics* (Oxford, 1968).

Harris, J., *Unemployment and Politics. A Study in English Social Policy 1886–1914* (Oxford, 1972).

Harrison, R., *Before the Socialists. Studies in Labour and Politics 1861–1881* (London, 1965).

Hay, J. R., *The Origins of the Liberal Welfare Reforms 1906–1914* (London, 1975).

Hayes, C. H., *British Social Politics* (Boston, 1913).

Hearnshaw, F. J. C. (ed.), *Edwardian England 1901–1910* (London, 1933).

—— *Social and Political Ideas of the Victorian Age* (London, 1933).

Himmelfarb, G., *Victorian Minds* (New York, 1970).

Hughes, H. S., *Consciousness and Society: The Reorientation of European Social Thought 1890–1930* (Paladin Books, Frogmore, 1974).

Hutchison, T. W., *A Review of Economic Doctrines 1870–1929* (Oxford, 1953).

Huxley, T. H. and Huxley, J., *Evolution and Ethics 1893–1943* (London, 1947).

Hynes, S., *The Edwardian Turn of Mind* (Princeton, 1968).

Ideas and Beliefs of the Victorians (London, 1949).

Inglis, K. S., *Churches and the Working Class in Victorian England* (London, 1963).

Jones, G. Stedman, *Outcast London* (Oxford, 1971).

Jones, P. d'A., *The Christian Socialist Revival 1877–1914. Religion, Class, and Social Conscience in Late-Victorian England* (Princeton, 1968).
Langshaw, H., *Socialism: and the Historic Function of Liberalism* (London, 1925).
Laski, H. J., *The Decline of Liberalism* (L. T. Hobhouse Memorial Trust Lecture No. 10, Oxford U.P., 1940).
—— *The Rise of European Liberalism* (London, 1936).
Lynd, H. M., *England in the Eighteen-Eighties. Toward a Social Basis for Freedom* (New York, 1945).
Maccoby, S., *English Radicalism 1886–1914* (London, 1953).
—— *English Radicalism: The End?* (London, 1961).
Mallet, B., *British Budgets 1887–1913* (London, 1913).
Matthew, H. C. G., *The Liberal Imperialists: The Ideas and Politics of a Post-Gladstonian Élite* (Oxford U.P., 1973).
Marshall, T. H., *Class, Citizenship, and Social Development* (Anchor Books, New York, 1965).
—— *Social Policy* (London, 2nd edn. 1967).
Masterman, C. F. G., *The New Liberalism* (London, 1920).
McBriar, A. M., *Fabian Socialism and English Politics 1884–1918* (Cambridge U.P., 1966).
McCallum, R. B., *The Liberal Party from Earl Grey to Asquith* (London, 1963).
McDowell, R. B., *British Conservatism 1832–1914* (London, 1959).
McKibbin, R., *The Evolution of the Labour Party 1910–1924* (Oxford U.P., 1974).
Milne, A. J. M., *The Social Philosophy of English Idealism* (London, 1962).
Morgan, K. O., *Keir Hardie, Radical and Socialist* (London, 1975).
—— *The Age of Lloyd George* (London, 1971).
Morris, A. J. A. (ed.), *Edwardian Radicalism 1900–1914* (London, 1974).
Nemmers, E. E., *Hobson and Underconsumption* (Amsterdam, 1956).
Nowell-Smith, S. (ed.), *Edwardian England 1901–1914* (Oxford U.P., 1964).
Pease, E. R., *The History of the Fabian Society* (London, 3rd ed., 1963).
Peel, J. D. Y., *Herbert Spencer. The Evolution of a Sociologist* (New York, 1971).
Pelling, H., *Popular Politics and Society in Late-Victorian Britain* (London, 1968).
—— *The Origins of the Labour Party* (Oxford, 1965).
Perkin, H., *The Origins of Modern English Society 1780–1880* (London, 1972).
Pipkin, C. W., *Social Politics and Modern Democracies*, vol. I (New York, 1931).
—— *The Idea of Social Justice. A Study of Legislation and Administration*

and the Labour Movement in England and France between 1900 and 1926 (New York, 1927).

Plamenatz, J. P., *Consent, Freedom and Political Obligation* (2nd ed., Oxford U.P., 1968).

Poirier, P. P., *The Advent of the Labour Party* (London, 1958).

Porter, B., *Critics of Empire* (London, 1968).

Quillian, W. F., *The Moral Theory of Evolutionary Naturalism* (New Haven, 1945).

Ratcliffe, S. K., *The Story of South Place* (London, 1955).

Richter, M., *The Politics of Conscience: T. H. Green and his Age* (London, 1964).

Ryan, A., *J. S. Mill* (London, 1974).

Sabine, G. H., *A History of Political Theory* (London, 1951).

Schultz, H. J., *English Liberalism and the State. Individualism or Collectivism?* (Lexington, Mass., 1972).

Searle, G. R., *The Quest for National Efficiency* (Oxford, 1971).

Semmel, B., *Imperialism and Social Reform* (London, 1960).

Simon, W. M., *European Positivism in the Nineteenth Century* (Cornell U.P., 1963).

Slesser, H., *A History of the Liberal Party* (London, n.d. [1944]).

Smith, P., *Disraelian Conservatism and Social Reform* (London, 1967).

Somervell, D. C., *English Thought in the Nineteenth Century* (London, 1929).

Spiller, G., *The Ethical Movement in Great Britain* (London, 1934).

Stokes, E., *The English Utilitarians and India* (Oxford, 1959).

Thompson, P., *Socialists, Liberals, and Labour. The Struggle for London 1885–1914* (London, 1967).

Thomson, D., *England in the Nineteenth Century 1815–1914* (Penguin Books, Harmondsworth, 1950).

Ulam, A. B., *Philosophical Foundations of English Socialism* (Harvard U.P., 1951).

Vincent, J., *The Formation of the Liberal Party, 1857–1868* (London, 1966).

Wagner, D. O., *The Church of England and Social Reform Since 1854* (New York, 1930).

Watson, G., *The English Ideology: Studies in the Language of Victorian Politics* (London, 1973).

Wiener, M. J., *Between Two Worlds. The Political Thought of Graham Wallas* (Oxford, 1971).

Wilson, T., *The Downfall of the Liberal Party 1914–1935* (London, 1968).

b. Articles

Barnes, H. E., 'Benjamin Kidd and the "Super-Rational" Basis of

Social and Political Processes', *American Journal of Sociology*, vol. 27 (1922), 581–7.

—— 'Some Typical Contributions of English Sociology to Political Theory. Pt. II. Leonard T. Hobhouse and the Neo-Liberal Theory of the State', *American Journal of Sociology*, vol. 27 (1922), 442–85.

Brebner, J. B., 'Laissez-Faire and State Intervention in 19th Century Britain', *Journal of Economic History*, supplement VIII (1948), 59–73.

Briggs, A., 'Liberal Economics', *The Listener*, 14.6.1956, 798–800.

—— 'The Welfare State in Historical Perspective', *European Journal of Sociology*, II (1961), 221–58.

Burn, W. L., 'The New Liberalism', *The Listener*, 7.6.1956, 758–9.

Clarke, P. F., 'The Progressive Movement in England', *Transactions of the Royal Historical Society*, 5th Series, vol. 24 (1974), 159–81.

Freeden, M., 'J. A. Hobson as a New Liberal Theorist: Some Aspects of his Social Thought until 1914', *Journal of the History of Ideas*, vol. 34 (1973), 421–43.

Glaser, J. F., 'English Nonconformity and the Decline of Liberalism', *American Historical Review*, vol. LXIII (1957–8), 352–63.

Halliday, R. J., 'Social Darwinism: A Definition', *Victorian Studies*, vol. 14 (1971), 389–405.

Hart, J., 'Nineteenth-Century Social Reform: A Tory Interpretation of History', *Past and Present*, 31 (1965), 39–61.

Herrick, F. H., 'British Liberalism and the Idea of Social Justice', *American Journal of Economics and Sociology*, IV (1944), 67–79.

Hoover, K. R., 'Liberalism and the Idealist Philosophy of Thomas Hill Green', *Western Political Quarterly*, vol. 26 (1973), 550–65.

Inglis, K. S., 'English Nonconformity and Social Reform, 1880–1900', *Past and Present*, 13 (1958), 73–88.

Keynes, J. M., 'The End of Laissez-faire (1926)', in *Essays in Persuasion* (London, 1933).

McGregor, O. R., 'Social Research and Social Policy in the Nineteenth Century', *British Journal of Sociology*, vol. 8 (1957), 146–58.

Nicholls, D., 'Positive Liberty, 1880–1914', *American Political Science Review*, vol. LVI (1962), 114–28.

Roach, J., 'Liberalism and the Victorian Intelligentsia', *Cambridge Historical Journal*, vol. 13 (1957), 58–81.

Rodman, J., 'What is Living and What is Dead in the Political Philosophy of T. H. Green', *Western Political Quarterly*, vol. 26 (1973), 566–86.

Rogers, J. A., 'Darwinism and Social Darwinism', *Journal of the History of Ideas*, vol. 32 (1972), 265–80.

Simon, W. M., 'Herbert Spencer and the "Social Organism"', *Journal of the History of Ideas*, vol. 21 (1960), 294–9.

Weiler, P., 'The New Liberalism of L. T. Hobhouse', *Victorian Studies*,
  vol. 16 (1972), 141–61.
Young, R. M., 'Malthus and the Evolutionists: The Common
  Context of Biological and Social Theory', *Past and Present*, 43
  (1969), 109–41.

3. UNPUBLISHED THESES

Brown, J., 'Ideas Concerning Social Policy and their Influence on
  Legislation in Britain, 1902–1911' (Ph.D., London, 1964).
Clark, L. A., 'The Liberal Party and Collectivism, 1886–1906'
  (Cambridge M.Litt., 1957).
Lee, A. J., 'The Social and Economic Thought of J. A. Hobson'
  (Ph.D., London, 1970).

INDEX

INDEX

287

Morley, J., 43 n., 250
motivation, 61, 134, 137, 156, 161, 165, 202, 217, 234, 240, 258
Moulton, J. F., 204
Muirhead, J. H., 40 n.
municipalization, 36, 37, 52, 63

Nation, 38, 50, 131, 133, 137, 138, 139, 143, 155, 156, 157, 158, 162, 163, 168, 175 n., 184, 188, 189, 191, 192, 203, 205, 214, 215, 224, 227, 230, 232, 233, 234, 235, 236, 241, 243, 253, 254
National Liberal Club, 4, 168
nationalization, 37 n., 45, 146, 149, 150, 196, 221, 222, 242
Natural Rights, 216
new liberalism, viii, 5, 39, 49, 58, 59, 70, 73, 76, 77, 81, 125, 126, 138, 145, 146, 149, 153, 157, 167, 182, 188, 196, 204, 207, 208, 209, 211, 215, 221, 223, 227, 228, 230, 237, 243, 250, 254, 255
  aims of, 40, 74, 85, 132, 167, 170–1, 236
  and New Liberalism, vii, 144 n., 160, 195, 197–8, 213, 244
  characteristics of, viii, 3, 6, 42, 46, 65, 74– 5, 80, 89, 91–2, 115, 117, 120, 122, 128–9, 139, 145, 148, 151, 152–3, 158, 161, 164, 168–9, 174–5, 184, 195, 198, 199–200, 201, 206, 210, 214, 216, 219, 222, 224, 232, 234, 239, 240, 241, 242, 249, 256–9
  continuity of, 22, 24, 44, 52, 74, 127
  contrasted with old liberalism, 33, 41, 57– 8, 79, 96, 159, 204–5, 212, 220, 228–9, 247
  critique of, 133, 202 n., 246–7, 255
  origins of, 8–9, 11–20, 51, 56
Nonconformism, 15–16, 197

old-age pensions, 135, 142, 146, 147, 196, 197, 200–6, 210, 215, 216, 222, 224, 230, 236–7
organicism, 5, 30, 59, 61, 94–9, 102, 106, 108, 110, 112, 113, 114, 126, 127, 136, 144, 149, 158, 168, 175, 176, 184, 199, 200, 203, 223, 227, 228, 235, 239, 243, 258
  social, 84, 94–9, 102–5, 110, 112, 113, 114, 115, 125, 176, 177, 184, 216, 218, 221

Paley, G. A., 88, 188, 194 n.
participation, 113, 135, 183, 223, 224, 258
pauperism, 174, 175 n., 200, 201, 205, 206, 213, 226
Pease, E. R., 257 n.
Peel, R., 49
personality, 45, 57, 64, 66, 67, 68, 69, 109, 112, 177, 180, 223
  social, 46, 70, 220, 257
philanthropy, 118
Phillimore, J. S., 62 n.
Philosophical Radicals, *see* Utilitarians
Pigou, A. C., 179
Plamenatz, J. P., 57
political economy, 9, 12, 19, 20, 21, 23, 30, 93, 100, 101, 250
political philosophy, 162, 245–6, 248 n.
political thought, vii, 1, 6, 7, 9, 116, 245–50, 254, 257
politics, 3, 28, 79, 93, 114, 162, 175, 187, 245–6, 248–50, 252, 255 n., 257, 259
poor, *see* poverty
Poor Law, 119, 160, 200, 202, 203, 205, 206, 207, 208, 214, 218, 238, 249
population question, 77, 88, 186–7, 194, 211
positivism, 7, 8, 9, 21, 78, 91, 96, 97, 115, 255, 256
Positivists, 3, 4 n., 7, 27, 74
poverty, 4, 41 n., 92, 118, 123, 126, 129, 131, 133, 139, 140–1, 142, 153, 166, 174, 175 n., 184, 187, 188, 201, 202, 203, 204, 205, 206, 208, 212, 231, 241, 243, 248 n.
Practicable Socialism, 38
programmes, 37, 39, 124, 145–9, 159, 196, 197, 198 n., 236, 243, 251, 254, 256
progress, 48, 55, 66, 69, 73, 75, 78, 81, 83, 86, 91, 92, 93, 95, 96, 101, 112, 119 n., 127, 132, 144, 151, 156, 157, 162, 167, 168, 170, 171, 174, 178, 183, 186, 188, 189, 190, 194, 218, 219, 234, 252, 256
Progressive Review, 252, 257 n.
property, 20, 23, 24, 30, 43, 44, 63, 142, 215
  individual, 23, 25 n., 45–6, 61, 134, 136, 141, 145, 203, 204, 217, 220, 221, 240 n.
  social, 20, 42, 44, 45–6, 115, 134, 137, 142, 220, 221
psychology, 9, 10, 13, 20, 105, 107, 112, 156, 164, 165, 186, 217, 240, 256 n.